Over the Edge

BOOKS BY LEO BOGART

Over the Edge

HOW THE PURSUIT OF YOUTH
BY MARKETERS AND THE MEDIA
HAS CHANGED AMERICAN CULTURE

Leo Bogart

CHICAGO   IVAN R. DEE   2005

Library of Congress Cataloging-in-Publication Data:
Bogart, Leo.
  Over the edge : how the pursuit of youth by marketers and the media has changed American culture / Leo Bogart.
       p. cm.
  Includes bibliographical references and index.
  ISBN 1-56663-633-7 (alk. paper)
  1. Mass media—Social aspects—United States. 2. Mass media and youth—United States. 3. Mass media and culture—United States. 4. Popular culture—United States. 5. Young consumers—United States. 6. Target marketing—United States. I. Title.
  HN90.M3B64 2005
  302.23'0835'0973—dc22
                        2004056102

Acknowledgments

This book owes its inception to Ivan Dee, who urged me to expand on a casual statement I made in a footnote in my earlier book, *Finding Out*. He has skillfully nudged me along through the editorial process. My wife, Agnes Bogart, provided both encouragement and expert commentary on the manuscript. I also received comments on portions of the book from Oscar Brand, Henry Geller, Melvin Goldberg, Richard Heffner, and Arthur Pober. I am grateful to all of them for sharing their experience and knowledge with me. I greatly appreciate the cooperation of the many informants who took the time to talk with me about their work and their feelings about it. Writing a book is a learning process for the author, and I consider this one to be part of my continuing education.

Contents

Preface

This book deals with the enduring question of how words and images become an autonomous force that reshapes the very culture in which they originate and which has shaped them. American culture in the early years of the twenty-first century is a complex of discordant strains. It reflects the realities of a society that has undergone an unprecedented transformation in where and how people live, in their relations with one another, and in the ideas they value. It is a profoundly materialistic society, suffused with exhortations to buy and consume, based on an economy that has shifted from producing physical objects to providing services centered on intangible knowledge and ideas.

The mass media of communication present an anomaly. Both their advertising and nonadvertising content are strong motivators of consumer demand to enhance life's material aspects. Yet the media also exert powerful and incessant pressure in the nonmaterial realm. They infuse new and unanticipated elements into the established patterns of people's thinking and behavior.

In observing the rapidly changing phenomena of the American media system, what we see at a given moment becomes obsolete as quickly as the words are put on paper (or keyed into the computer). The accumulated evidence is quickly buried under new facts.

Books are offered as a more permanent record, in contrast to the evanescence of periodical publications. Yet books that deal with any aspect of present-day life are bound to be out of date by the time they reach the reader. References to current events and personalities quickly lose their relevance and meaning. Therefore any author who seeks to describe the workings of contemporary institutions must treat them cautiously—as the transient phenomena they really are. If I necessarily refer to what is true as I write in 2004, I trust the reader to distinguish the specific facts from the larger points I hope to register.

This is a story about unintended consequences. My argument is that the comportment and values of Americans have been deeply affected by the perceived commercial interests of the popular entertainment industry, which provides them with powerful images and models of behavior. To a large degree, these images are contrived to appeal to only a particular part—the youthful part—of the population rather than to "everyone." This focus first arose in response to the unprecedented jump in births after World War II and the consequent impact of the resulting "baby boomers" on the economy and the culture. Although the birthrate bulge has long since receded, it remains fixed in the minds of America's marketers.

The producers of films, musical recordings, and video games have a direct stake in satisfying young people, who are disproportionately represented among their audiences. The producers of television programming are spurred by advertisers and their agencies to go after the same age group.

Movies and television, by far the main wellsprings of popular culture, vie with each other to attract young audiences. In doing so, they have cultivated a tolerance for interpersonal conduct that departs strongly from the society's former norms. This has prompted a strong reaction from traditionalists, with political repercussions. The consequent attempts by the entertainment industry to regulate itself by labeling content have been self-defeating.

The initial premise that drives this whole process is, I argue, flawed. That premise, originating in the population surge after World War II, is that America's youth must be the media's main target. Flawed also is the belief that warning audiences about media content will stanch the flow of what they are being warned against.

I deal first with those aspects of media content that arouse most criticism: the changes in how Americans act toward one another, and the way the media have interacted with a number of other social forces to modify the norms of behavior. I show examples of media content that transgress the usual boundaries of civility and taste. My purpose is not to pass judgment on them but to illustrate why they arouse strong conservative reactions.

The changes in contemporary mores must be seen in historical perspective, but those changes induced by the media can in large measure be traced to the pursuit of youthful audiences. I offer evidence that contradicts many advertisers' belief that young people are of disproportionate value for them. I show that the pursuit of youth is reflected in the messages that media carry. I maintain that the ongoing effort to control that content is counterproductive

My concentration throughout this book is on the two audiovisual entertainment media that have the greatest impact on the American psyche—motion pictures, which create the most vivid imagery and arouse the most stirring fantasy, and television, which occupies a much more significant part of the public's time and requires a major share of attention. In 2004, American television was a $50 billion business. This gives it an overwhelming influence and makes it the appropriate medium to consider at the outset. (By comparison, Americans spent $10.7 billion at movie box offices and another $25.8 billion buying and renting video disks and cassettes.[1])

I touch on the subjects of video games and popular music, but these important media play less powerful roles in the national culture. I also give short shrift to that formidable medium, the internet, which is still being used chiefly for individual rather than mass communication.

The hold that popular entertainment has on American time, values, and behavior reflects the enormous amount of money invested in it and earned from it. It also reflects the amazing creative resources mobilized by this investment. In writing this book I interviewed dozens of people involved with one aspect or another of the communications business and transcribed (in shorthand) what they had to say. I quote them with the anonymity they were promised in return for their candor. Several dozen others responded by e-mail to questions I posed.

In dwelling on the media's questionable assumptions and on some of their disturbing consequences, I hope the reader will not lose sight of my respect and admiration for the talented people who produce what we see and hear in the dense media environment that surrounds us. I just think they can do better.

L. B.

New York City and Amagansett
November 2004

Over the Edge

1

The exceptional enters the mainstream

Artistic expression and commercial needs. A poet, whether starving in a garret or enjoying the comforts of a tenured professorship, composes what the spirit dictates and abilities permit. A court poet may be required to compose a paean of praise for the ruler on a ceremonial occasion, but the general rule is that creative expression must well from the heart. In our commercial culture this rule has not altogether lost its appeal, but it is commonly subordinated to worldly demands. Curiously, a recurring theme in self-examining Hollywood films (like *Barton Fink*) is the conflict between a novice scriptwriter's innocent pursuit of his muse and the voracious demands of the studio system to which he has sold his soul. (It is always a male scriptwriter who faces this dilemma. Female actresses never seem to confront this spiritual conflict.)

An independent force always at work is the desire of the people who create films, programs, games, and recordings to express their own beliefs and feelings. But those private impulses must almost always be subordinated to the financial goals of the enterprises that use their skills. A studio may indulge a star director's desire to produce an "art" film that is destined to lose money, just as a book publisher may allow a prizewinning poet's volume of verse to creep onto the list. This is done with the same steely realism with which a department store introduces a "loss leader" to attract customers who may go on to buy more expensive merchandise.

In the jargon of the industry, media executives speak of "monetizing" what they produce. In a media system geared to produce profits rather than excellence, market forces—or predictions about market forces—determine what is worth doing and what is not. Media content is modified to conform to the best assessment of the size and characteristics of its consumers.

The preoccupation with youth has become more intense in recent years as the mass media have seized upon young people as their primary target. This is true for music and video games as well as in film and its television offspring. These last two media are intertwined, in their ownership, their production facilities, and their talent pool. But their pursuit of young audiences has come about for different reasons.

Media and society. We are addicted to the media but sometimes worry about what they say to us and especially to our children. Apart from sleep and work, the mass media occupy more of America's time than any other activity. (I should not say "apart from work" because radio and television are a presence in many workplaces, and the use of the internet for work purposes often shifts into its use for personal reasons.) All this has happened since the beginnings of broadcasting in the 1920s. Before then, reading had been a main source of diversion, and film and musical recordings had entered the scene, but all these occupied less time than conversation, play, and avocational pursuits. As a shorter work week afforded more leisure, the time available for media continued to expand.[1]

Television news and public affairs programming have had great political consequences through their influence on public opinion, electoral choices, and legislative agendas. But the content and presentation style of television news and talk shows have been modified to fit the model of entertaining viewers rather than informing them, just as the character of professional sports has been altered to accommodate the needs of broadcasters' scheduling and advertising requirements. A large proportion of news programming is in fact devoted to talk about the personalities of show business.

Whatever its political influence, television is overwhelmingly devoted to entertainment, and most of that entertainment is fictional in character: either the original dramas of daytime serials and evening police series or the airing of feature films. Fantasy is at the core of even such formats as quiz and game shows or "reality" programs, which place carefully selected "everyday" people into abnormal situations. Americans devote a substantial part of their waking hours swathed in a cocoon of make-believe.[2]

The model for TV's fictional fantasy is to be found in Hollywood, where a high proportion of network and syndicated programming is produced. Motion pictures, with their enormous budgets, their brilliantly publicized stars, and their relative freedom from advertising pressures, have led the way for changes in the subjects and styles that television presents.

Films in the theater retain a unique importance because they are seen in the dark without commercial interruptions, because they are taken seriously in reviews and news reports, and because their stars, familiarized through promotion, are idolized for their fame, wealth, and good looks (though seldom for their talent). Films that generate interest (or "excitement," in the industry's parlance) in the weekend after they are released become "events" that may outweigh real news happenings in the public's attention and discussion. Yet theater showings represent a minor part of the public's total exposure to feature films; they are surpassed by showings on television and on videocassettes and DVDs.

What are the consequences of this massive immersion of the public psyche in the realm of the unreal? Is it "escapism" from the ugly and intractable realities of the news of an increasingly and unavoidably interconnected world? Is it a mechanism for coping with those realities by permitting a release of the anxieties and hostilities they evoke? Or is it simply a way of passing the time, of avoiding the boredom of workaday existence? All these forces are at play with different force for different content and different audiences.

People take refuge in entertainment when they are beset by unpleasant realities at times of stress like the Great Depression and World War II. (Movie attendance rose from 3.1 billion in 1940 to 4.3 billion in 1943. In the first half of 2002, movie attendance was a fifth higher than in the preceding year, before the terrorist attacks of 9/11, 2001). During the 2003 war with Iraq, film comedies did well at the box office while war-related films did poorly.

More and more media content departs from the rules that once governed popular entertainment. Because people are so deeply engaged with this content, it affects and alters the way they behave and relate to one another in the world away from the theater and the home entertainment center. While the vivid pictorial character of audiovisual media now fills the public's dreams, the barriers of self-control (or self-censorship) were initially breached in print. Deeper cultural forces are at work than those introduced by the media of the twentieth century or their more recent electronic successors. But it is those nineteenth-century inventions, films and musical recordings, that have done most to change the rules of the media game.

What television has changed. From childhood on, all human beings have private thoughts, emotions, and activities they do not show to others, not even to those closest to them. Private behavior has always been distinct from the public sphere in which, with varying degrees of guardedness, we present ourselves to society.

The very frequency of human contact forces people to set up invisible walls to protect their private selves, as astute social commentators like Sigmund Freud and Georg Simmel observed a century ago in describing the effects of urbanization. Television, from its start, reduced the amount of time formerly spent interacting face-to-face with family and friends and thus accelerated this tendency toward impersonality in human relationships.

Television has had other important effects on the national psyche, apart from the way people relate to one another in more or less public situations. Its endless succession of commercial messages has homogenized and heightened aspirations to consume, and transformed what were once seen as extravagant luxuries into familiar everyday commodities. The bombardment of viewers with images of plenty has built their awareness of what is beyond their reach. Comparing oneself to more fortunate others may create as much bitterness and anxiety as real deprivation of the necessities of life. Television, with its gorgeous models and performers, has raised the public's consciousness of physical beauty at the same time that poor diet and growing obesity have removed many people farther and farther from that ideal appearance. Most important, television has altered perceptions of the social norms, the accepted ways of dealing with our fellows.

Beyond the edge. As a more permissive outlook infused the culture, it was fortified by increasingly powerful commercial interests.

The people who shape the content of mass entertainment constantly use the term "edgy" to describe what they think attracts audiences to their products. The adjective probably derives from the expression "cutting edge," used as a synonym for "innovative" and "fresh." But as currently used it signifies a defiance of convention, an ability to shock, an aggressive rejection of traditional proprieties. These allusions apply especially to the use of language and to the display of intimate behavior.

I asked an ad agency media director who uses the term to define "edgy." His answer: "Controversial, dealing with violence, sex, homosexuality, subjects that used to be forbidden. Stuff that's not appropriate for a family medium."

Violence is rarely called "edgy"; sex is. Yet fictional violence and sex cannot easily be separated. Both have been used as devices that appeal to a part of the public that producers consider of the greatest commercial value.

A feature of Hollywood films from their beginnings has been mortal combat—fights to the death between cowboys and Indians, cops and robbers, humans and malevolent invaders from outer space. These battles have in the past been stylized and orchestrated, always leaving the audience with the comfortable knowledge that the dead will nonchalantly arise to shower and dress after the cameras are packed away. Impersonal and antiseptic killing has now been largely replaced with bloody and often gruesome imagery, matched by furious grimaces in the accompanying drama. It may be done in the black-humored spirit of *Grand Guignol*, as in *The Texas Chain Saw Massacre*; more often it is presented in all seriousness, as in Sam Peckinpah's *Straw Dogs*.

Film violence escalated as digitization opened up a whole new set of special effects that permitted unprecedented depictions of mutilation and of awful natural events (earthquakes, volcano eruptions, floods, plagues) or barbaric forces terrorizing humanity. "When we created weather, fire, and smoke," says Jeff Gaeta, a Time Warner executive, "we wanted it to move not realistically but impressionistically."[3] This transformation of plausible reality into fantasy has been demonstrated in such blockbuster films as *Star Wars*, *The Matrix*, *The Lord of the Rings* trilogy, and countless other Hollywood spectacles in which violence is visualized on a gigantic scale.

It is easy to identify examples of content that most of the American public might consider "over the edge" by viewing the brutal "coming attractions" trailers in any movie theater. Graphic violence is only a part of what many people may find objectionable. Other examples may be found on websites and internet chat groups where pedophiles make contact with children; in the steamy and convoluted couplings portrayed on daytime television; in the blatherings of radio "shock jocks." The political obscenity of rabid talk-show hosts is matched by the studied vulgarities of personalities like the radio star Howard Stern, who in spite of fines and other attempts at censure have thrived on the notoriety produced by their freedom from inhibitions of language.

I interrupt my writing to see a freshly released film,[4] prompted by a highly favorable newspaper review. The film depicts thugs spraying bullets wantonly at revelers in a jammed night club, their killing and burning in a car doused with gasoline, a conventional car chase through crowded streets, with a police car overturned and countless other vehicles smashed in the process. The hero-detective, who has three divorces behind him and several children who are mentioned but otherwise apparently entirely absent from his thoughts, is asked by his buddy, "When did you last get laid?" and is soon thereafter shown in bed with the wife of another member of the L.A.P.D. His buddy, meanwhile, finds a casual female acquaintance, whose name he can't recall, awaiting him nude in a conveniently placed hot tub; naturally he dives right in. Throughout, the dialogue is laced with vulgarity, including the sardonic witticism, "Fuck you very much!" All of this is totally extraneous to the plot, such as it is. The film is rated PG-13 by the Motion Picture Association of America, meaning that parental guidance is advised for those under the age of thirteen. Within the theater a number of children probably ten to twelve periodically run up and down the aisle.

Another recent release said to be especially popular with young moviegoers was Quentin Tarantino's film *Kill Bill: Vol. 1.* It depicts a woman knifed before her young daughter, a pregnant woman beaten and shot on her wedding day, the decapitation of another woman, a man's tongue pulled out, and limbs being sliced off. It makes free use of the foul language with which the director liberally enlivens his own private conversation.[5]

Television has not lagged far behind in such imagery. Dan Rattiner, a Long Island newspaper editor, sat down to watch TV one October evening in 1993 and recorded what he saw:

On CNN, a high school boy is paralyzed after lying down on the double yellow line in the middle of a highway, as he had seen done in the Walt Disney movie *The Program.*

On Showtime, Anthony Perkins in *Psycho IV*, finds the fully dressed skeleton of his dead mother.

On Cinemax, a Bruce Willis film shows a policeman asking the driver of a parked car if anything is wrong. "'As a matter of fact there is, officer. . . . There are too many bullets in this gun.' He whips out a pistol and fires two shots at the officer. Camera cuts to officer. We see a bloody hole appear in his cheek, another between his eyes."

On the movie channel, a fully clothed man is told by a woman to walk out on a diving board and jump. He does, into an empty swimming pool. "He is lying on his stomach in a small pool of water at the bottom of the pool, which begins to turn pink. The woman is still smiling."

On the Fox Channel, a replay of a moment in a football game in which a player has just dislocated his hip. "'Just like that, the end of a playing career,' the announcer says."

On HBO, a *cinéma vérité* program shows a seven-year-old girl with schoolbooks in one hand and a needle and syringe in the other, walking past a sign saying, "This is a drug-free zone."

On Bravo, "a severed hand moves slowly across the screen."

On MTV, Beavis and Butthead put a dog into a washing machine and turn it on.[6]

Critics and observers of television cite many other examples of content that defies old conventions of propriety. In a Fox comedy, "Action," four-letter words, used profusely, are bleeped out but can easily be lip-read. In one scene a hooker puts her hand down the pants of a film star; in another a father tells his young daughter about the size of his penis. Bill Carter and Lawrie Mifflin describe other TV episodes: a teenager masturbating into a pie; a talk show host vomiting; "a character sipping from a beverage made of excrement"; two actors urinating in the direction of the Statue of Liberty; animated characters representing children "spewing torrents of foul language"; "a comedian stopping women of all ages in the street and asking them if they will have sex with him."[7]

The Jerry Springer Show on MTV features an episode in which a man tells a woman's boyfriend that he was sleeping with her; the two then have a fistfight. A single episode of Comedy Central's "South Park" in 2001 carries 162 occurrences of the word "shit."

In one episode of a popular series, "Friends," a husband assures his wife that his pornographic interest centers on "just normal American girl-on-girl action."[8] And on a prime-time episode of Fox's "Fastland," an undercover female detective joins her main suspect and her lesbian lover in a hot tub—all three topless and kissing passionately.

Masturbation, impotence, and adolescents' sex with adult teachers were themes of the WB Network's "Dawson's Creek," a teenage favorite. In one episode, girls mocked a football player's impotence.

In 2002–2003 prime time, on ABC's show "MDs," a physician's vibrating pager is given a nonmedical application. Incest jokes were central in CBS's "Bram and Alice." On a CBS docudrama, high school students enjoy oral sex in school.[9]

Some of the linguistic lapses on television may be inadvertent rather than scripted, though since few shows are broadcast live there is ample opportunity to edit them. When an actor, Glenn Farrell, said "shit" during a preliminary to the 2003 Golden Globe awards ceremony, this was a spontaneous utterance, but on ABC's "NYPD Blue" the word "bullshit" was written into the script, and approved.

From Westerns to quiz shows to sitcoms to mysteries, television programming genres have shifted from season to season.

In 2004 "reality television," using "ordinary" people rather than professional actors, was rapidly displacing scripted dramas and commentaries on the major networks, which were losing ground to cable, especially among younger viewers.[10] Reality shows are cheaper to produce than fully scripted dramas; they also lend themselves readily to "product placement," which provides a constant reminder of who the sponsors are. Programs like "The Apprentice," "Survivor," "American Idol," "The Bachelorette," and "Joe Millionaire" attracted huge audiences in contrast to television's usual program fare. (In the last-mentioned show, women vied for the attentions of a handsome young man who had falsely been described as rich. In one episode of this program, when a couple went into the woods, subtitles ["aah," "slurp," and "gulp"] were added to leave no doubt as to what was going on.)[11]

On NBC's "Fear Factor," contestants were given the task of eating a horse's rectum.[12] On the Fox Channel's "Keen Eddie," a prostitute was employed to have sex with a horse. "The Sunday Night Sex Show" suggested that a washing machine during the spin cycle is an interesting place to have sex.

The way had been shown by programming on pay cable. HBO's "Cathouse," premiered in December 2002, used hidden cameras to show the patrons and service providers in a Las Vegas brothel. The highly popular HBO drama series "The Sopranos" featured foul language, sexual episodes, and violence.

In another popular and heavily promoted HBO series, "Sex and the City," "Samantha recounts a mildly traumatic sexual experience she had with 'Mr. Cocky,' a man she just met whom she describes as particularly well endowed. 'I'm telling you, Carrie,' Samantha says, 'It was like a wall of flesh coming at me.' Carrie responds sarcastically, 'There is nothing really scarier than a really big one coming at yah.' Samantha continues, 'I didn't even want to get my mouth near it. I was afraid I'd get lockjaw.'" Carrie quells her anxieties: "It's a penis, not Mount Everest."[13] Another episode proposed that a three-way encounter would make a good birthday present.[14]

The barriers have also been lowered in advertising, which traditionally was least inclined to be adventuresome in tinkering with the mores. The networks once drew the line on the products they permitted to be advertised, excluding Scott Tissue and Ex-Lax. But advertisers themselves were wary of overstepping the bounds. They have always shied away from placing their messages in contexts that might arouse consumer hostility, such as controversial television programs. Advertising income of $800,000 fled in the mid-1990s from an episode of the police show "Law and Order" that dealt with the bombing of an abortion clinic. Such squeamishness is still felt by some big advertisers, but there are now many others willing to rush in.

The changed outlook applies to the content of advertising as well as the programming environment. In years past, both liquor and cigarette magazine advertisements posed models provocatively, suggesting that indulgence led to sexual conquest. We have come a long way from that.

The scripts of television commercials are often routinely infused with sexuality. In 2003, Miller Lite beer advertising featured buxom, scantily clad women wrestling in wet concrete. (The campaign was considered unsuccessful and was curtailed.)

As the top TV buyer for a large agency group notes, "The commercials have been pushing the envelope." He cites Budweiser commercials featured women mud-wrestling—"All T & A."

Although advertising's purpose is to persuade rather than to gain attention for its own sake, the 2004 Super Bowl carried commercials (each costing $2.4 million for thirty seconds) that showed a horse breaking wind and a dog biting at men's private parts. An ad for Cialis, an impotence pill, cleverly warned men to consult a physician if their erection lasted more than four hours.

Michael Watrous, president of a "corporate- and brand-identity consulting company," explains why stars of porno-graphic films are used as models in television commercials: "It's the rebelliousness factor, a nonconformist attitude. By being involved with porn stars, it brings an edge."[15] According to Come Chantrel, an artist management agency, "For the 20-year-old kid, porn stars have kind of replaced what models used to represent." Steve Hirsch, co–chief executive of Vivid Entertainment, observes that "the adult-entertainment industry has become very mainstream."[16]

New York Times advertising columnist Stuart Elliott comments on the baring of body parts in ads: "Bodily functions from pass-ing gas and urination to vomiting and defecation are depicted and alluded to in advertising for shoes, automobiles, software, games—even food. Earthy catchphrases or sayings with double meanings are repeated constantly. . . . Some ads flaunt signs of [sexual] arousal, others are festooned with phallic symbols while still others present simulations of sexual intercourse."

A commercial for Kohler bathroom fixtures shows a man sit-ting on the toilet reading a magazine. In a TV commercial for an online computer store, a high school marching band is attacked by a pack of wolves as a man laughs and says, "That's good stuff!" In a commercial for Qwest long-distance service, a priest beats a heavily bandaged hospital patient whose monitor is beeping. A commercial for SmartBeep beeper service shows a woman fart-ing in a car, oblivious to a couple in the back seat.[17]

The musical scene, even more adventurous, has been em-broiled in contention over aggressive content. In 1985 the singer Ozzy Osbourne was unsuccessfully sued by the parents of a teenage suicide who allegedly had been influenced by the song

"Suicide Solution." Other songs have attracted attention not for their hidden recommendations but for their language and imagery. W.A.S.P.'s "Animal": "I start to howl, I'm in heat / I moan and growl and the hunt drives me crazy / I fuck like a beast"; and The Mentor's "Bend up and smell my anal vapor / Your face is my toilet paper."

In 2000, Eminem's "Kill You": "Put your hands down bitch, I ain't going' shoot you / I'm a pull you to this bullet and put it through you / Shut up slut, you're causin' too much chaos / Just bend over and take it like a slut, OK Ma?"

The pop star Prince (whose records are distributed by a former Time Warner subsidary) has shown his poetic skills in the lyrics of his songs: "I sincerely want to fuck the taste out of your mouth" ("Let's Pretend We're Married," 1982). "I knew a girl named Nikki . . . I met her in a hotel lobby; she was masturbating with a magazine" ("Darling Nikki," 1985).

In 1990 the Supreme Court overturned a Florida judge's ban on 2 Live Crew's "Me So Horny": "Put your lips on my dick, and suck my asshole too / I'm a freak in heat, a dog without warning / . . . Fuckie suckie. Me fuckie suckie." In 1992, Ice-T withdrew a number from his album: "I'm 'bout to bust some shots off / I'm 'bout to dust some cops off / Cop killer! / It's better you than me."

A video game, "Extreme WTC Jumper," pokes fun at the victims of the World Trade Center attack. Another, "Sniper's Revenge," follows up on a series of random shooting attacks in the Washington area; still another is based on the 2002 Columbine High School student killings in Littleton, Colorado.[18] "Kaboom: The Suicide Bomber Game" offers a victory to the player who kills or wounds the most victims.

By offering the foregoing illustrations of "edginess" I do not mean to pass moralistic judgment on them nor to suggest that they now represent a fair sampling of media content. But they serve as useful examples of how rapidly that content has been transformed, away from the boundaries of what used to be permissible.

A network executive: "The line is constantly moving, and it's not just about TV, it's about society. There's clearly more tolerance with respect to an edgier sensibility. . . . We're just one aspect of the social culture." Pointing to the fact that the average household can receive eighty-eight TV channels, compared to thirty-three in 1990, he says, "You probably aren't going to watch the channels that are going to be more likely to offend you."[19]

That is true, but if channels are available, someone will watch them.

How media producers view media content. Rap lyrics may be spontaneous expressions of the performers' own customary speech patterns and personal beliefs. But these expressions are disseminated by a complex set of business organizations whose concern with content is limited to its ability to generate revenues.

A television executive proclaims, "Television is better than it's ever been." Not all his colleagues agree, though many consider the changes in what is aired to be mere manifestations of what has been happening in "the real world," and insist that the public regards them with complacency.

Doug Herzog, president of Fox Entertainment: "This is all happening because society is evolving and changing. But the bottom line is, people seem to be buying it." When he was at Comedy Central, he reports, the word "fuck" was accidentally left unbleeped from an episode of "South Park," and "we didn't get one call."[20]

Donny Deutsch, an ad agency head: "Slang, bathroom humor, jokes about sex are all part of life. Using them says to consumers, 'We understand you, we speak your language, we live in the same world as you.'"[21]

Media content, so goes the argument, simply reflects consumer demand. Janet Borelli, MTV's vice president of standards: "If we didn't show homosexual relationships, our viewers would complain."[22]

Entertainers may say that vulgarity is essential to achieve the catharsis that the audience expects from them. A stand-up comedian, interviewed on television, explains that "four-letter words let the audience get rid of their anger!" and points out that they have been an essential part of the comedy routine since the days of Lenny Bruce, who was imprisoned for his public use of obscenities and posthumously pardoned as a symbolic testament to society's changed outlook.

But in contrast to such defenses, many television and film executives reveal a widespread discontent with what they view as the excesses of an unbridled rush across traditional boundary lines.

A former film industry mover and shaker: "I'm convinced that the media present a clear and present danger to us."

Cyma Zarghami, Nickelodeon's vice president and general manager: "It's more violence for violence's sake than I've ever seen."[23]

A writer-producer, speaking indignantly about a program he had recently seen: "'Off-Center' focused on a large dump in a toilet, and the camera kept returning to it."

A top agency media executive: "The content is there to attract the viewers. Hollywood is looking to press the envelope. It's their answer to more aggressive TV [on cable]. They're constantly getting criticized because they produce boring programs. They put in that language to attract viewers, to press all the buttons."

A high-level TV industry executive: "I don't know how they get away with that shit. Where's the standards? If you look at the automobile commercials on the air, they're all about speeding. We wouldn't have allowed them to broadcast those, but now nobody turns down a commercial. There's a lot more license, no sexual taboos."

A nonpay cable network executive: "On an interview on ABC the other night, [the singer] Michael Jackson spelled out F-U-C-K and nobody complained. People know that if they call the FCC [the Federal Communications Commission] to complain they would be written off as a crank. There's more freedom of expression now. We have totally lost our standards of what's appropriate in mixed company or in the home. Anything goes if you put in a disclaimer. Since we've seen absolutely everything, there's no reason to do so. If they're naked or having sex, no one gives a damn. On one show we had a former nun who was a go-go dancer. We want both our cake and our pie. If I say, 'Let's just develop the best show we can,' that won't go. Shows are carefully tailored to meet the demographics." Demographic, an adjective commonly used as a noun in marketing circles, refers to the audience characteristics that advertisers, agencies, and producers carefully mull over.

A network watchdog on standards: "In the dramas, I don't know how some of the language gets there. I *angst* about it. It's a responsibility. I worry about what it's doing to society. We've become desensitized. Look at reality television. 'Joe Millionaire.' What does it say about us and our society? We have been dumbed down. It's just amazing!"

If media executives are themselves awed by the excesses of the system in which they perform essential functions, their reactions are muted compared with those of professional defenders of public morality.

Since advances in printing technology and literacy in the mid-nineteenth century, the corrupting influence of the media has been a subject of public debate. In the last half of the twentieth century, as the spread of cable television and the VCR brought quantum changes in media content, evangelical voices were raised in an ever more shrill crescendo, demanding censorship of vulgar imagery and language. At the same time film and televised violence became increasingly salient subjects of discussion by parent groups and of research by social scientists. These kinds of pressures inevitably led to congressional hearings, threats of government-imposed restrictions, and defensive gestures by media industry associations promising self-restraint.

I shall return to the subject of how media content is shaped and controlled, but we must first consider the reasons for the great changes that I have so far only roughly sketched.

2

The mutability of mores

What is acceptable?   Why should anyone take offense at the kinds of expressions I have just categorized as mass
entertainment horror stories? The principal objections commonly raised to them are that they corrupt children and threaten
the decorum essential in a society that requires its members to
trust in the good intentions of strangers.

Are these valid criticisms? Not according to postmodernist
doctrine, which holds that all values and points of view are
grounded in the perspective of particular groups and societies.
Thus such concepts as objectivity and truth are rejected. Differ-
ing faiths—in the literal truth of the Burning Bush, the resur-
rection of Christ, or the revelation of the Koran to Mohammed
by the angel Gabriel—deserve respect and are not susceptible to
empirical disproof. Why shouldn't similar tolerance be shown to
the casual use of weaponry, sexual athleticism, or the compulsive
use of profanity in conversation?

The values we live by are neither indelible nor immutable. Human societies, with all that they have in common, show enormous variations. We look with horror upon the vicious manifestations of tribalism in contemporary Africa—the lopping off of limbs in Sierra Leone, the killings and rapes in Congo and Rwanda—forgetting that these ancient practices were the seedbed of the slave trade and provided the rationale for nineteenth-century European colonialism. Yet what Westerners see as barbarism in the murderous rampages of Pakistanis and Indians or of Javanese in Timor and Irian Jaya seems insignificant in scale compared to the massive slaughter perpetrated under Nazi and Communist regimes that maintained the outward guise of adhering to "Western civilization."

That civilization has gone through periods of sadism and ferocity as well as of prim Puritanism in which burning suspected witches was considered necessary to safeguard morality. Memory of the Inquisition's *auto-da-fé* arouses revulsion today, though this was practiced as a safeguard of righteousness and public order.

In times past the Western public has delighted in watching innocents eaten by wild beasts and gladiators fighting to the death in the Colosseum; it has assembled to cheer at public executions, to thrill at the immolation of yowling cats, and to jeer at cartloads of aristocrats headed for the guillotine. In the United States it has gathered in lynch mobs waving the dismembered body parts of victims and in hordes of rioters gleefully looting and torching their own neighborhoods.

Just as the acceptance of violence has flourished and ebbed at different times, standards of personal propriety and of interpersonal conduct have undergone cycles of constriction and permissiveness. After the traumas of the barbarian invasions, the bacchanals of the Romans succumbed to Christian piety. The heavily swathed saints of medieval painting gave way to the glorification of the nude human body in Michelangelo's sculpture and in the paintings of Rubens. A few centuries later, fig leaves were placed over Renaissance and Roman genitalia or their existence was discreetly denied, as in the watercolors of William Blake. The asceticism of Cromwell's Protectorate was replaced by the licentiousness of the Restoration. The outer prudery of the Victorians gave way to Edwardian cancans and to the abandon of the flapper era after the First World War.

As we look around the world today, we can see that different societies show different degrees of tolerance for violent or aggressive behavior. Even within the relatively homogeneous societies of Europe, similar variations have occurred at different times. The ferocity of the Vikings contrasts starkly with the low crime rate of contemporary Scandinavia. The equanimity of life as idealized in middle-class middle America must be seen against a historical background: the turf wars of rival urban gangs, the feuds of Hatfields and McCoys, the frenzy of mobs gone out of control.

The acceptance of violence and sexual display in everyday life has followed the same cycle as fashions in dress and in the arts. The same rule applies to what today's mass media say and how they say it.

The forces propelling change. The content of mass media always and necessarily reflects how people live and the values they hold. Conversely, media affect those living patterns and values. And what media communicate cannot be separated from the way they are organized and operate as institutions.

A number of interacting forces have come together to alter the media system: they are (1) technological, (2) legal, (3) social, and (4) commercial.

Technology creates and transforms the forms of communication. Media compete with each other for the public's time. As new media arrive or are transformed by inventions, other media respond by introducing changes of their own. The phonograph destroyed the player-piano industry. Radio shook musical recording. Television, quickly establishing a grip on the nation's leisure time, gobbled advertising and forced great newspapers and magazines out of business. The competition from television sharply reduced film theater attendance and encouraged the film industry to go to color (while TV was still black and white), to widen the screen format, to introduce stereo sound and experiment with three-dimensional projection. Most important, however, television forced the movies to tackle controversial themes that had long been taboo and to test the limits of permissible language and plot situations. Thus changes in the mechanics of mass communication are translated into the nature of what they communicate.

The spread of cable as the dominant avenue for receiving television, the creation of dozens of new cable networks offering specialized subject matter or appealing to particular groups of people, the spread of satellite dishes—all have expanded the spectrum of viewer choice and fractionated the viewing audience. (In 2004, 69 percent of households had cable; another 11 percent, without cable, subscribed to satellite services.[1])

The increase in the typical number of TV sets in a household made viewing more of an individual experience rather than a shared one. The remote-control device made it less likely that a viewer would stay with a particular program from beginning to end. Channel switching, a reduction in the length of commercials, and the slow but steady increase in the amount of air time dedicated to commercials and "promos" (promotional announcements for the network's other shows) all made the viewing experience more disjointed, less intense. Viewers could watch several programs at once on split screens. The videocassette recorder and, more recently, personal digital video recording devices like TiVo enable viewers to store programs for later viewing, bypassing commercials and skimming past unwanted elements.

These developments, arising from new technology, altered the economics of television advertising and therefore its messages. Pay cable, supported by viewer subscriptions, was freed of advertisers' influence over programming, and quickly differentiated itself by offering content that the broadcast networks would never accept and from which most advertiser-supported cable networks would also shy away. Television was becoming interactive, allowing viewers to watch sports events from different angles. Video games introduced a new element of interactivity that intensified players' engagement with the fantasies they spin.

The internet broadened the possibilities of constant instantaneous contact not only with intimate family and friends but with distant and unknown individuals and with websites that reflected every aspect of human knowledge and experience.

In the music business, recording shifted from vinyl to cassettes and next to CDs, which required the release of songs in packaged bundles rather than as single items. This raised the stakes in production, fattened marketing budgets, and concentrated sales within an ever more limited range of heavily promoted releases. The shift accompanied a similar concentration in the musical offerings of radio stations specialized in their listener appeal but owned and homogenized by an ever smaller number of corporations.

The downloading of music without charge on the internet was rapidly changing the economics of the music business, forcing CD prices lower and perhaps strengthening the herd instinct to concentrate on the most popular numbers.

The loosening of constraints. As technology transformed the means and soon the substance of media communication, the legal framework for media operations became steadily less constrictive. A series of court rulings, starting with the removal of the ban on James Joyce's *Ulysses* in 1933, led to the virtual elimination of restrictions on the printed word, except where public safety was endangered. The *Village Voice* first printed "fuck" in 1962 and the *Berkeley Barb* in 1965.[2] These two pioneers of the youth-oriented underground or alternative press in big cities had counterparts on a national scale in *Playboy* and its raunchier competitors *Penthouse* and *Hustler.* These magazines did not share the same leftist political slant as the local weeklies, but they went much further in satisfying prurient interests.

Broadcasters licensed by the FCC had long been bound to operate in the "public interest, convenience, and necessity" and required to adhere to the "fairness doctrine" in presenting controversial subjects. These requirements were wiped away during the Reagan administration as part of its crusade against government regulation. Congress took some halfhearted measures to ensure programming for children. The Telecommunications Act of 1996 hastened the process of concentration in media ownership, long under way, and thus reinforced the centrality of short-term profit-making in the management of media enterprises. Federally mandated changes in the relations between television networks and stations and between the networks and program producers forced changes in the scheduling and control of prime-time programming.

But even more important than government-imposed changes in media companies' organization and operation were vast changes in American society itself.

Social change. Once upon a time, on a leafy street in a residential neighborhood of a pleasant American city, lived a happy, comfortably off family. Each morning, after Mom had prepared a hearty breakfast, Dad read the morning newspaper and headed off to the nearby streetcar stop for his trip to work downtown. Mom walked the kids to school, then came back to do the household chores while listening to her favorite radio soap operas. After lunch she read the newspaper, which Dad had thoughtfully left behind for her. If she had the time she could also check the recipes in the *Woman's Home Companion*. In the afternoon, Mom might watch more soap operas on television. Sometimes a friend or neighbor dropped in to pass the time, and once a week there was a bridge game. Before long it was time to pick up the children and get them to do their homework while she began preparing dinner. Dad's martini was ready when he arrived home and settled in to finish the morning paper. (He had already bought the afternoon paper and read it on the journey back home.) After the dinner dishes were done, the whole family could settle down to watch the "Jack Benny Show" or the "Texaco Hour," starring Ed Wynn. It was an era of clean, wholesome living!

Even if the myth of the 1950s ever conformed to reality for a part of the population, it still survives as an idealized model of connubial happiness. Undoubtedly some people still think they live this way, but if they do, they are strange survivors in a country that is now dramatically different.

The years since the end of World War II have seen a huge expansion in population, the arrival of millions of predominantly non-European immigrants—legal and illegal, and the concentration of the population into great metropolitan areas. The urbanization of blacks and the accompanying movement of whites out of central cities made suburban living the predominant mode of

American life. Remoteness from live big-city diversions made people rely more on prepackaged media entertainment that was accessible anywhere. Downtown movie theaters closed, reducing street traffic into restaurants and retail stores, and thus accelerating the abandonment of the city centers. At the same time a new type of multiplex cinema flourished at suburban malls.

Meanwhile the American economy was growing, its structure shifting from manufacturing goods to providing services. It was increasingly interdependent with the economies of other countries with lower living standards. The assembly-line worker in Dearborn, Michigan, perhaps the archetype of the American labor force in the 1920s, was replaced by the man in the grey flannel suit working in a high-rise central city building. But that man, in turn, was now often replaced by a woman in a suburban office park.

As women entered the workforce they changed their relationship to men and to their children. The educational gap between the sexes was eliminated and then reversed. Better-educated women asserted a new independence, married later, and postponed motherhood. In families with two wage earners, both spouses were under increased time and emotional pressure, juggling work and household chores. The life experience of women who worked became less differentiated from that of men. With fewer women living sheltered lives, their speech patterns and emotional lives became less inhibited.

With the invention of the contraceptive pill the emancipation of women advanced into a new freedom of sexual experience and expression. The casual sex that came in its wake may have discouraged the development of deep emotional attachments between men and women.[3] As extramarital unions grew in number, the rate of divorce doubled. In impoverished urban neighborhoods with high unemployment and welfare rates, single-parent families became common, often including several generations. The result was that symptoms of social pathology multiplied, in some part fueled by drug abuse. In a recent thirty-five-year period, the rate of aggravated assault in the United States rose almost eightfold.[4]

The composition of American households changed dramatically. The proportion consisting of married couples with children fell from 45 percent in 1972 to 24 percent in 2000.[5] Single mothers and homosexual couples became more prevalent. Births to unwed mothers rose from 5 percent in 1960 to 33 percent in 2000, and one-third of all children were being reared in single-parent households.[6] Two-thirds of all black children (compared to one-third at the time of the 1965 hackle-raising Moynihan Report on the weakness of the black family) lived in single-parent households.[7]

All the well-known social changes I have just listed helped redefine the standards of conduct that the American public considers acceptable. This is seen in a more tolerant attitude toward sex and what was formerly considered sexual deviancy, and also in more informal dress at work, more casual address and displays of intimacy with strangers, more complacency with respect to coarse language. These trends are not confined to the United States; they are visible in other Western societies. And they are reflected in the media's representation of contemporary reality. But we must look back into history to grasp the fact that standards of behavior are far from constant.

Civility. Henry VIII's table manners would not have pleased Emily Post. She would have considered them "uncivilized." The European notion of civility evolved as part of the changing structure of class relationships after the feudal era, according to the social historian Norbert Elias. As medieval warriors were transformed into courtiers of a centralized national monarchy, violence became the monopoly of the king and his court. Formerly unrestrained emotions could no longer be displayed.[8] As social relations become more complex, there was more need for self-control and for foresight in determining how an individual's own actions might influence his relations with others.

In a society where even kings and queens ate meals without benefit of spoons and forks, there was no

> invisible wall of affects which seems now to rise between one human body and another, repelling and separating, the wall which is often perceptible today at the mere approach of something that has been in contact with the mouth or hands of someone else, and which manifests itself as embarrassment at the mere sight of many bodily functions of others and often at their mere mention, or as a feeling of shame when one's own functions are exposed to the gaze of others.[9]

The distinction between the manners of the cultivated nobility and the boorish conduct of peasants had a parallel in the contrast between the controlled behavior of adults and the instinctual expressions of children. In fact, Elias contends, the very concept of *civilité* is derived from an instructional treatise for boys, written by Desiderius Erasmus in 1530 and widely reprinted and translated. Erasmus decries the commonplace behavior of people urinating or defecating in public.[10] "There should be no snot in the nostrils. . . . A peasant wipes his nose on his cap and coat, a sausage maker on his arm and elbow. It does not show much more propriety to use one's hand and then wipe it on one's clothing."[11] (I have observed such behavior among Sicilian peasants.[12])

In his instructions, Elias observes, Erasmus was not telling the *boys* how they ought to behave, but how *adults* ought to behave. At that time,

> boys lived very early in the same social sphere as adults. And adults did not impose upon themselves either in action or in words the same restraint with regard to the sexual life as later. . . . The idea of strictly concealing these drives in secrecy and intimacy was largely alien to adults themselves. All this made the distance between the behavioral and emotional standards of adults and children smaller from the outset.[13]

Children were familiar with the existence of brothels. Adults spoke about sex freely in front of them. Only in the nineteenth century, as the gap between children and adults widened, did sexual behavior begin to invoke modesty, concealment, embarrassment, and shame while a "thick wall of secrecy" was built around the adolescent.

In medieval Europe, bodily functions aroused none of the concern that led a Renaissance writer to insist that "You should not poke your teeth with your knife, as some do." Erasmus warned that moving back and forth in one's chair suggests that one is breaking wind.[14] He points out that "a well-bred person should always avoid exposing without necessity the parts to which nature has attached modesty. If necessity compels this, it should be done with decency and reserve, even if no witness is present." He cautions that farts should be replaced with coughs, to "hide the explosive sound."

Another writer, Giovanni Della Casa, in *Galateo* (1609), observes that "It does not befit a modest, honorable man to prepare to relieve nature in the presence of other people, nor to do up his clothes afterwards in their presence." The sight of naked bodies began to arouse shame only in the sixteenth century. La Salle

(1729) urges, "When you need to pass water, you should always withdraw to some unfrequented place. And it is proper (even for children) to perform other natural functions where you cannot be seen." Elias cites these instructions to demonstrate that, even as late as the eighteenth century, Europeans were commonly doing what the writers considered improper.

The sense of shame, in Elias's view, reflects a "defenselessness against the superiority of others." It is "not merely a conflict of the individual with prevalent social opinion; the individual's behavior has brought him into conflict with the part of himself that represents this social opinion. . . . He fears the loss of the love or respect of others, to which he attaches or has attached value."[15]

The high visibility in today's mass media of behavior that, in the past, aroused sentiments of "shame and embarrassment" has progressively attenuated the shock of what formerly would have been perceived as transgression. It is against this background that we must assess the generational changes in behavior that appear to have accelerated in the last fifty years.

Bad habits. In the American context, John Burnham, another cultural historian, views "sexual misbehavior" and swearing as components of a "constellation" of "bad habits" that also encompasses drinking, smoking, taking drugs, and gambling.[16] Popular culture, disseminated by the mass media, creates the impression that such activities are widespread and thus give them an aura of normality.

These "minor vices" (as Burnham terms them) were prevalent in the "underworld" inhabited by the urban immigrant "lower orders" of American society during the nineteenth century. They migrated upward through the "respectable" classes as a result of intellectual rebelliousness and commercial greed (for example, in the marketing of alcoholic beverages).

Burnham considers swearing "an act of aggression, even beyond the bounds of personal insult."[17] It was associated with the
speech of slaves and others of a lower social order and tested "the
boundaries of deviance." Blasphemy and vulgarisms were equally
inappropriate for the nineteenth-century middle class.

Sexual laxity, Burnham observes, increased as immigration
and industrialization spurred the growth of cities, with their innumerable sensual temptations. The spread of venereal disease
brought out a new concern with moral purity, a rejection of the
"double standard" for men and women, and an idealization of
sexual fulfillment within marriage. The great wars of the twentieth century made the casual use of profanity commonplace
among men. Four-letter words quickly lost their power to shock.
The army's distribution of contraceptives in World War II made
millions take extramarital sex for granted while the invention of
penicillin dampened fears of venereal disease.[18]

In the mid-1960s the exercise of sexual freedom became a
major element in popular culture and in the lyrics of popular
music. The era of defiance was under way. The world had
changed, and young people were leading the way.

Defying the mores.   To what extent is the rejection
of social constraints a perennial stage of human development
rather than a peculiar feature of present-day America? In primi-
tive societies where every life is lived under the close scrutiny of
an extended kin, adolescence is marked by certain commonly
accepted and endured rites of passage into adulthood. Rebellion
against parental values and strictures is simply inconceivable. But
ours is a complex social order, marked by a host of relationships
of varying degrees of affinity and emotional charge. Innumerable personal and impersonal influences beyond those of the immediate family help form every individual. It is therefore only

natural to question and challenge the imposition of parental authority over ideas and behavior as well as over the conduct of life. This estrangement, which seems to have accelerated in the course of the nineteenth century, reached new force as America's complacency and comfort were wrenchingly disturbed.

Discontinuities accumulated in the outlook of different generations as a higher proportion of adolescents entered college, living away from home sooner than in the past. This was especially marked in the age group born after the return of military veterans from World War II. The new families established during these years produced an exceptionally large crop of children for which society's institutions were ill-prepared.

When these children approached adulthood in the 1960s, their rebelliousness was symbolized by a revival of the long hair of early nineteenth-century French poets and the beards worn by seventeenth-century Spanish grandees and late Victorian British gentlemen. But it was also expressed more forcefully when university offices were occupied and trashed. The use of strong obscenities was vigorously defended by the 1965 "Free Speech" movement on the Berkeley campus. The uninhibited use of four-letter words became a form of political protest. It was dramatized by the contempt the "Chicago Seven" showed for court procedures at their trial for provoking the riots that accompanied the 1968 Democratic convention (which probably won Richard Nixon the presidency).

Would such displays of ideological rebellion have occurred if there had been no Vietnam War as the focal point for the anger of those potentially subject to the military draft? Undoubtedly, as demonstrated by the no less militant displays by French and other European students during the same period. Rejecting established institutions and conventions of behavior was an inevitable expression of anger by those who had gone to overcrowded schools and had been reared with the threat of nuclear war always on the horizon. The civil rights movement and the emergence of a self-conscious struggle for women's rights became part of the same massive confrontation with an established social system that preached and practiced constraint on emotion, language, and expressions of intimacy.

It may be that everywhere in every time it is only human to question and even reject parental authority and values. But this does not necessarily entail a rejection of all the established social order's values. The leftist political currents of the 1930s were not marked by vast changes in the moral or dress codes of an emerging generation. In the 1960s, however, the calls to "kill your parents" and to "never trust anyone over thirty" were inseparable from the attacks on the personalities and institutions of the Establishment. The pies thrust in the faces of liberal politicians did not merely demonstrate rage against "the System," with all of its inequities and other faults; they marked a defiance of one's elders and their right to discipline and rear their offspring to repeat their own meaningless and banal existences.

The generation gap.   In 1946, Roberto Rossellini's great film *Open City* portrayed Italian Resistance fighters in the last days of the German occupation of Rome in World War II. In one particularly harrowing scene set in the headquarters of the Nazi Gestapo, officers are amusing themselves while, in the adjacent room, the hero is being tortured and uttering heartrending screams. I went back to see this memorable film recently in the auditorium of New York's Museum of Modern Art, which was packed with a youthful crowd. When the film reached the moment of torture, and the hero's cries sounded, a large part of the audience was convulsed with laughter. Their exposure to the patently phony violence of Hollywood's movies and television shows had desensitized them to the reality that they lived in a world where pain and suffering were genuine and terrible. Between them and me, a veteran of that war, there was a sharp abyss in sensibility—the Generation Gap made audible.

A distinguished analyst of social trends, the National Opinion Research Center's Tom Smith, defines the generation gap as the difference between those 18–24 and those 65-plus at any given point in time. Examining 153 trends, Smith finds this gap narrowing over the three decades from 1970 to 2000.[19] In 1973 the opinions of young and old on sexually explicit materials differed by 51 points, more than on any other topic. In 1997 this was still the number one difference, but it had fallen to 41 points. The gap in opinions about actual sexual behavior fell from 32 to 22 points. In fact, between 1973 and 1997 the young became less permissive in their attitudes on sexual matters. That does not mean, however, that the difference in outlook has disappeared.

Smith reports that while young adults socialize more than their elders, they are "consistently the most negative age group" in evaluating their own happiness and their satisfaction in being the age they are. They are more "disconnected from society" and have become more cynical about people and human nature and more distrustful of institutions.

"The young are generally more supportive of modern or egalitarian gender roles than older age groups . . . but older age groups have moved toward the modern perspective even more than the young have and thus closed the generation gap."

On balance, says Smith, they "have moved in a liberal direction, but their political leanings "have shown some notable zigzags. . . . The young were generally the most for civil liberties in 1973 and 1997, but were mostly towards the middle in 1985. Their net change from 1973 to 1997 was typically quite small except for views on homosexuals."

Opinions are not the only indicators of change. Since the end of World War II, young people have experienced a sharply higher incidence of psychosocial problems: "criminal activities, suicidal behavior, alcohol and drug abuse, depression and eating disorder."[20] Today half of high school students in "Middletown" (Muncie, Indiana, the subject of a landmark community study during the Great Depression) say, "I am usually happy."[21] (The implication is that the other half is not.) They show more trust in parents than in friends.[22]

In a survey of 274 directors of university counseling centers in 2001, over 80 percent reported an increase over the preceding five years in the number of students with severe psychic disorders.[23] As a concrete example, between 1989 and 2001 the percentage of Kansas State University students treated for depression doubled; so did the percentage of suicidal students.

The problems start well before college. Murderous rampages against teachers and fellow students by disturbed adolescents invariably attract media attention, as in the highly publicized shootings at Columbine High School. Such cases arouse interest in the troubles of teenagers but not much, apparently, in their easy access to weapons. A nationwide study of twelve thousand junior and senior high school students found that 38 percent of blacks, 36 percent of Hispanics, and 22 percent of non-Hispanic whites said they had carried or used a weapon or had been involved in a weapon-related incident within the past year.[24]

Coarse words and expressions appear to have gained currency. Three-fourths of high school students say they often hear cursing in the hallways and cafeteria at school.[25] Much of this occurs out of adult earshot, and most parents of teenagers are either unaware of it or prefer to ignore it.[26] Nearly two of three parents say their child never uses "bad language."[27] But three of five agree that "I would never have dared to say to my parents some of the things that my child says to me." Over a third say the child never listens to music with bad language, but half say it happens sometimes, and 12 percent say it happens constantly. In the process of growing up, not only musical recordings but all the media are powerful agents of acculturation.

Changing personal conduct. To what extent are the generational changes consciously reflected in the way people act toward one another? Most Americans do not feel that standards of interpersonal conduct have changed. (People's perceptions of changes are really reflections of their present outlook rather than accurate reports of how the present contrasts with the past.)

People tend to generalize about public behavior from what they see in their own circles, but these circles differ in their prevailing customs. Younger people are less inclined than older ones to think that Americans used to treat each other with more respect and courtesy in the past.[28]

The proportion who often see people who use "bad or rude language out loud in public" is lower among those over 65 (38 percent) than among the young (51 percent).[29] But those over 65 are much more bothered by this (68 percent) than those under 30 (37 percent). Among those under 30, over half admit to using such language themselves, compared to a fifth of those over 65.[30]

It is evident from these figures that young people use language more freely and are much less inclined to take offense when someone else does. In short, for many of them such language has become an acceptable norm. The way they address each other is linked to the media that show them how to behave.

There are no past benchmarks against which to judge such reports, but that does not make them any less significant. A national survey of high school students in 2002 found that 28 percent of the girls smoke cigarettes, 45 percent drink alcohol, 26 percent binge drink, and 20 percent use marijuana.

The generation gap is most striking in the realm of sexual practices and attitudes. The media did not bring about the revolution in sexual activity, but they have certainly forced a reassessment of what adolescents consider to be the norms of behavior.

Over three people in five agree that premarital sex is "not at all" or "only sometimes" wrong.[31] This percentage is more than four of five for young people 18–29, but is only two of five among those in their seventies. The proportion who hold a permissive attitude rose between 1969 and 1973 but has hardly changed since the early 1980s. Since the 1970s the proportion of eighteen-year-olds with a permissive view has remained virtually unchanged.[32]

These attitudes reflect what happens in real life. Half of high school students say they have engaged in sexual intercourse.[33] Nearly a fourth (23 percent) of teenagers say they have learned "a lot" from movies and television about birth control, and 40 percent say they have used them to get ideas for conversation with their sexual partners.[34] Teenagers also use the media to learn romantic techniques.[35] Those who watch a lot of television begin sexual activity early.[36]

The generation gap may be diminishing as those set in their ways die off, but on the subject of sex a mighty difference persists.

The decline of civility.   Is the generation gap evident in a change in the consideration or courtesy that people show one another? Abbott Ferriss, a sociologist, examined a number of social indicator trends and detected a slight decline in civility over a thirty-year period.[37] But civility may be defined in a variety of ways. Another sociologist, Corey Keyes, points to evidence of charity and helpfulness and concludes that "while it may be true that people are less engaged in civic activities, the implication that the level of social civility is also low may be unwarranted."[38]

Age groups do not differ in the proportions who say that people are basically treating each other with enough respect and courtesy.[39] But, looking back retrospectively, young people are less inclined to accept the myth of "the good old days." Fewer of them think that Americans used to treat one another more courteously in the past.[40]

In the twenty-first century, generational differences in outlook and conduct may be less marked than they were a quarter-century earlier, but they remain substantial. While everyone's youthful beliefs and activities are modified as time goes by, certain critical values and habits are apt to persist in any individual. People growing up at a time when racial tolerance is the norm are unlikely to become bigots when they grow older. Similarly, those reared in an environment that encourages early sexual experimentation will be less shocked when they encounter it in their children and grandchildren. What young people think and do today therefore becomes a good, if imperfect, predictor of what they will think and do in maturity.

Intimacy and false intimacy. The burka that swathes women in certain traditional Muslim cultures is not merely an indicator of female subjugation; it confirms a familial intimacy that must be shielded from the outer world. Western notions of "modesty" in feminine attire were gradually attenuated in the nineteenth century, as painters felt free to depict the nude figure and as women's clothing became progressively more revealing. The cumbersome, baggy, two-piece bathing suits worn at the turn of the century were cut shorter and shorter, progressing through the daring one-piece suits of the 1930s to the bikinis of the 1950s. As these successively more provocative costumes were commonly depicted in newspaper advertisements and then in films and television, the sight of ever more scantily clad bodies, female and male, became steadily more familiar, though full-frontal nudity continued to be deemed unacceptable for "family audiences," presumably consisting of children and virginal old maids.

Exposure of the naked body, like sexual acts and the excretory functions, is still generally considered to be a private matter. Similarly, the use of profanity and coarse expletives within the family, or among close friends or drinking buddies, has long been deemed acceptable if contained within an intimate and private sphere, but not when used with strangers (except in the course of vigorous disputes) or in public.

The vulgar language of films, TV drama, and late-night comedy shows raised the threshold of acceptance for such language in everyday use. (One indication of this was George W. Bush's casual use of the word "asshole" [recorded by an open microphone] to describe a highly respected *New York Times* political reporter, Adam Clymer, to his running mate, Dick Cheney, and—like a number of his predecessors—his liberal use of even more flavorful profanity in conversation with subordinates.)

A network television vice president offers a familiar explanation of TV's changed approach to language:

There's been a coarsening of the society. You can say "prick" on [a police series] if it's artistically relevant and gets the younger audience and everybody else is doing it. There's no list of words we can't use. A lot of this comes from shock radio. Howard Stern, in the guise of satire, says things that a lot of his audience believe but don't say. Five hours a day, five days a week. It desensitizes the listeners. That's been one of the main reasons why the rules have changed. Network TV ends up following the lead of the culture.

The unrestrained use of coarse language is an expression of false intimacy, since it sweeps strangers into the same sphere of uninhibited speech that customarily is limited to family members, close friends, or work associates. Casual sex, facilitated by improved contraception technology, similarly reflects the expansion of what were once thought of as private relationships among individual adults.

Another evidence of false intimacy is in the way people talk to one another. Television personalities, a daily presence in every home, acquire an aura of personal familiarity that instantly places them in a spuriously close relation to their viewers. A new model for social behavior can be found in the cozy informality with which television stars routinely engage each other, the casual false chumminess of talk show hosts addressing guests they have never met before. Public embraces, once rare to see among unrelated members of the same sex, have become a standard form of greeting.

Only a few years ago, the use of first names was generally limited to relatives, friends, and co-workers. Today they are employed automatically by strangers. Even so, only 5 percent of the public prefer to be called by their first names in unsolicited phone calls from sales or customer service people; 28 percent prefer last names and 62 percent don't care. The indifference of the majority has encouraged telemarketers.[41]

Paradoxically, the expansion of false intimacy accompanies the appearance of a fresh concern about personal privacy, already demonstrated before telemarketing, spam, and computerized data bases brought realistic concerns about the sanctity of personal information.

The rise of false intimacy is not a purely American phenomenon. Of course the pattern of formality has always varied from country to country. In England, for example, writes Brian Knox-Peebles, the last publisher of *Punch*:

> Among my generation, the use of indiscriminate, sexually orientated coarse language in mixed company is almost unheard of. The use of Christian names varies a bit. A junior employee would be unlikely to address his CEO in this manner, for instance; equally, tradespeople or manual workers such as plumbers would be unlikely to do so with those using their services, at least till they know them well. My kids (now well into their thirties), however, say that among their age group there are few such inhibitions, though they would not address their parents or the parents of their friends in this manner unless they knew them very well.
>
> If you ever read even a mainstream magazine for 11–14 girls, there is NOTHING about the human body that would be strange to them after reading a couple of issues. . . . I think my eight-year-old grandson and daughter knew as much as I did at eighteen. . . . This may be a part of what we are talking about too.

Wolfgang Donsbach, a German professor of communication, writes that

> Decades ago, in the middle and upper classes the "Du" [the intimate form of address] was rare and by all means had to be

introduced formally (by the person with the higher social status, or women toward men offering it). In the lower classes the
"Du" was often accepted informally as the way to interact,
sometimes with a mixture of "Du" and "Herr Suchandsuch,"
which indicated some insecurity about the proper way.

Today, and starting from the late sixties and seventies even
among middle- and upper-class youth, the "Du" is the standard
form. You come to a party and without getting formally introduced to a person and without talking explicitly about the right
way of addressing each other, people say "Du" to each other.
This happens even among the middle-age generation (to
which, unproperly, I count myself).

Coarse language is another observation which probably applies to both countries. There are several words of sexual language that are almost accepted in any regular and even public
conversation. "Geil" (horny) is used for almost every (at least
younger) person to express excitement, and even commercials
use it ("Geiz ist geil"—being miserly is . . .). There are other
examples where the boundaries of socially acceptable language
have been extended on and on over the last few years.

Claude-Jean Bertrand, a French professor of journalism,
reports:

As regards language, yes, more "vulgar" words and phrases. I've
not noticed an increased use of "tu" or first names (although
when I was at school, unless you were close friends, you would
normally call each other by your last name, which my boys
would not think of doing). What I have noticed and what I dis-
approve of is the habit of kissing. Everybody cheek-kisses
everybody on meeting and on taking leave. And some kiss
three, four, five times.

Carlos Soria, a Spanish philosopher, comments that the changes I have observed in the United States are also apparent in Spain and in a good part of Latin America.

> Young people, when you ask their names, answer by their first names only. Any Spanish store clerk uses the [intimate] "tu" with any customer who comes in the door, regardless of his age. The supposition is that this youthful form of treating both young and older people facilitates the transaction, and the empathy in the relationship arouses a bit of vanity in an older person who feels younger because he's addressed like this.
>
> In the bosom of the family there's also been an intense democratization of relationships, including grandparents. In Medellín, Colombia, a recent newspaper article commented that the [traditional honorific] terms "Don" and "Doña" have fallen into disuse.

Soria suggests that the use of "tu" is generally seen as youthful while the use of [the formal] "usted" evokes the sense of an old, protocol-bound establishment. He also notes that mobile phones have created an easy, convenient, and simplified egalitarianism.

Very likely the changes I have just described reflect the working of deep forces that emerge from the changing structure of work and the breakdown of traditional social-class hierarchies within the workplace as corporate bureaucracies replace family-owned and -run businesses. But they also surely have been stimulated by the practices of the entertainment business, most pervasively on television. These practices are shaped by commercial interests and pressures, the fourth and perhaps the most important of the forces that have altered the media system. We must now look more closely at how TV practices have been modified to attract the young people whose values are reshaping society.

3

The pursuit of youth

Media habits of the young.   If, as we have seen in Chapter Two, the habits and beliefs of young people differ from those of their parents, this should be reflected in their consumption of media, and it is. This is a good reason for media producers to single them out for special attention, which is evident in the substance of what the producers communicate.

Young people differ from older ones in myriad ways that everyone instinctively understands. Their physical, intellectual, and emotional development is changing rapidly. They are making their way into the responsibilities of mature adulthood. And among themselves they differ widely according to their individual origins and circumstances.

They spend much of their free time socializing and courting. They are active patrons of bars and nightclubs, but not of restaurants, which are more expensive.[1] They are more likely than average to play a musical instrument.[2]

In contrast, they spend less time in solitary activities like reading.[3] Even though many of those 18–24 are attending college, they read books only two-thirds as often as the average adult.[4] They are less engaged with the world around them (in spite of the political activism of a minority). Political apathy among young people has its counterpart (or perhaps its origins) in declining levels of exposure to newspapers, newsmagazines, and television news.[5] (It is unclear whether their below-average attention to the news is responsible for their low voting turnout and discourages other forms of political participation.[6])

In the past, young people began to read newspapers regularly when they settled into jobs, marriage, home ownership, and the responsibilities of family and civic life. But as is well known, both by newspaper people and by advertisers, movement into the mainstream of daily readership has become progressively less of a sure thing. Most young people remain newspaper readers, but they have abandoned the kind of regularity with which their parents perused the home-delivered paper.[7] They are, however, avid readers of free newspapers, of the alternative weekly press, with its heavy emphasis on popular entertainment and its often iconoclastic political outlook.

Unlike newspapers, magazines have largely abandoned the search for a mass audience to concentrate on narrowly defined publics. Some, like *Rolling Stone, Teen People, Marie Claire,* and *Seventeen,* are specifically aimed at the younger age group.[8]

Young people's magazine-reading preferences have their counterparts in their response to different types of films and television programs. With radio, too, there is a sharp distinction between their above-average time spent listening to music-driven FM and their far below-average listening to AM (predominantly talk).[9]

Because they spend so much time out of the home, young adults are below average in their television viewing time. People 18–34 account for 37 percent of the adult population, but they make up only 24 percent of the adult audience for the average network television program.[10] Precisely because young adults view television less than older ones, advertisers are especially eager to find programs that can reach them. Naturally, a further separation of this age group by sex, marital status, and so on reveals strong distinctions in the viewing patterns.

Cable programming reaches far more special-interest audiences than the broadcast networks do. Cable networks have been set up to reach highly specific segments of the mass audience, and the same has happened in over-the-air broadcasting as well.

Jordan Levin, the thirty-five-year-old president of WB Entertainment, says, "The demographic bulge was coming, and we saw it and created a business plan to target it." The WB network, according to the *New York Times*'s James Rutenberg, has targeted young women 18–34. He says:

> Marketers will pay a premium to reach Generation Y, who are thought to be too distracted by video games, e-mail, and other entertainment choices to watch as much television as their over-35 brethren. So WB created a world where young women with bare midriffs and pretty faces fight monsters, bewitch thieves, or fall in love with attractive young men in music-videolike montages.[11]

An agency executive approves. "Being associated with the programs on WB, and the other advertisers there, helps position you as younger."[12]

Although cable programming has captured a majority of prime-time viewing hours, the largest television audiences still go to the broadcast networks. An advertiser can reach more young people on a youth-oriented network show than with a schedule on MTV or the Comedy Channel—but the broadcast show will draw in more older viewers as well, raising its total price to the advertiser. The networks have steadily tinkered with their programming formulas to appeal to the young adult viewers with whom advertisers are obsessed. The first years of the new millennium saw the rise of the already mentioned "reality shows." Most of these productions, featuring attractive, nubile young people contesting for each other's attention, centered on highly contrived mating rituals, offered with a dollop of sex. They were particularly successful in reaching young adults.

The viewing of certain television channels shows strong differentiation by age.[13] Young viewers strongly gravitate to certain channels whose programming is oriented to them: VH1, MTV, Comedy Central. They shy away from the cable news networks, the Weather Channel, and movie channels (A&E, AMC, Bravo).

They are 22 percent of the viewers of talk shows and documentaries but only 14 percent of the viewers of news. They make up 20 percent of the viewers for drama, evening and daytime, but only 12 percent of the audience for audience participation and quiz shows.

Mothers of young children are heavily concentrated in the 18–34 age group, so it is not surprising that they make up 42 percent of the adult audience for children's programming in the daytime and 45 percent in the evening. Young viewers are drawn to situation comedies and science-fiction shows. Variety shows and adventure shows draw them at slightly above-average levels.[14]

Contrary to what is commonly assumed, sports (23 percent) attract them at close to the average rate.[15] Those 18–24 view the cable sports network ESPN about the same amount as everyone else, but their sports interests are different from the norm. They have above-average interest in basketball, below-average interest in major league baseball and professional golf, average interest in both college and NFL football and in professional tennis.

They watch feature films on television at about the average rate (23 percent). This is noteworthy, because the 18–24 group is almost twice as well represented as the average among the people who have attended four or more theater movies in the past three months, and among those who usually see new films within the first two weeks after they open. Evidently it is not so much a passion for movies per se but an urge to participate in what's fresh and new that provides the main motivating force for theater filmgoing.

Television and its advertisers. The movies depend on young theatergoers. Television—except for public broadcasting and pay or subscription TV—is supported by advertising. It is programmed to help marketers achieve their goal—selling products by delivering persuasive messages to potential customers. Advertisers and the agencies that counsel them and prepare commercials have their own notions of what constitutes an appropriate environment for their messages and what kind of audience they want to reach. To understand what they are looking for and how this is reflected in what viewers see and hear, we must first understand how advertising decisions are made.

Anyone who has something to sell understands instinctively that some people are more likely to be prospects than others. The likelihood of their buying depends on their purchasing power, the item's potential usefulness for them, and the personal characteristics that may make the item more or less attractive. To take the obvious examples, older people buy more denture adhesives than younger ones. Poor people are infrequent purchasers of luxury goods. Women and men consume different products

and generally have somewhat different responsibilities for purchasing the products they use in common. (When almost all
women were stay-at-home housewives, marketers referred to
them as "homemakers" and considered them the primary "purchasing agents" for their families.)

Such commonsense definitions are as familiar to vendors in a
tropical street market as they have been for over a century on
Madison Avenue. Advertisers for beauty products put their ads in
different lists of magazines than those selling razor blades or automobiles. Marketers of grocery products ran ads on newspapers'
food pages; tire manufacturers ran theirs on the sports pages. Such
decisions required no special information or marketing genius.

Broadcasting complicated the picture. Its audiences were
huge and relatively undifferentiated compared to the obvious and
clear-cut differences between, say, the readers of *Vogue* and those
of *Popular Mechanics*. Consumer surveys provided information
about the characteristics of a product's customers and those of
the radio and television programs they watched. Different times
of day yielded not merely audiences of different total size but
varying proportions of men, women, and children.

During the long reign of three television networks that absorbed 90 percent of the total viewing time, minute variations in
audience profiles were trumpeted to advertisers. When dozens of
channels, many with specialized content and appeal, became
available to the average cable household, the size of the total audience for a channel became less important to advertisers than
the number of viewers who conformed to their targeted speci-
fications. Still, at least one television executive seems to question
the notion of targeting altogether:

I have seen over the years the attempt to be specific as to
whom we want to reach, and I have seen us just try to develop

the best shows, which is what works best. We are certainly mindful of whom the show is going to reach. When a show is successful it has a huge audience, and that includes the people advertisers want.

Many of the people who invent and produce programs may share this viewpoint, but it defies both theory and practice in advertising, which seeks to pinpoint messages only to the people who might be persuaded to buy. Not all potential customers are easy to categorize. Baby food is bought by the mothers of babies, who are found only within a certain age group (albeit one that is steadily expanding at both ends of the scale). But hay-fever sufferers are scattered throughout the population, making it difficult for makers of allergy remedies to single them out through clever media selection.

Intelligent research on the market for anything that is advertised usually reveals a complex pattern, in which individual motivations and tastes are hard to reduce to a few catchall categories. Looking at characteristics like race, place of residence, marital status, and family size in combination yields insights into consumption that go far beyond the significance of the same attributes taken one at a time. While such information is incorporated into consumer surveys, it is not conveniently accessible through the research services that provide the universally used data on television's audience.

In past years, advertising planners and buyers typically looked at the incomes of viewing households and at the gender of viewers, when such information was available. This practice was complicated by the fact that until 1987 the A. C. Nielsen Company, now the monopolistic provider of audience figures, based its ratings on meter readings that recorded what stations the sets in a sample of households (in their parlance, "homes") were tuned to.

The numbers on individual viewing came from a separate sample in which residents were asked to fill in "diaries" of their viewing. The two sets of numbers then had to be laboriously reconciled. (Nielsen first moved from household to individual ratings because of pressure from ABC, then a relatively new network with a youthful viewer profile.) For its national viewing reports, Nielsen has switched to a "people meter," asking viewers in its sample to push buttons to indicate who is watching. At the time of the change, baby boomers were just becoming adults.

Viewers typically had five choices in 1970, but in 2004 more than ninety. Since viewers began to use the remote control device to switch channels, some watching several programs simultaneously, it became more challenging than ever to produce reliable estimates.

Media research consultant Erwin Ephron tells us: "Demo-targeting [that is, devising a media schedule based on the audience's demographic attributes] is a mess. It's a TV concept which has taken over the media world, and it's a big waste of money. For most brands, false positives (nonusers who are in the target demo) and false negatives (users who are not in the target demo) exceed the number of users within the target demo." In other words, the misses outnumber the hits.

In radio's "Golden Age" in the 1930s, advertisers sponsored whole programs and sought to identify their brands with the shows' star personalities. Although vestiges of such exclusive sponsorship can still occasionally be found, the rising costs of broadcast time forced advertisers to disperse their messages among a number of programs. What they lost in identity was compensated for by a capacity to place their messages before a wider range of viewers than those for the continuing episodes of a particular show. Networks responded with "scatter plans" that spread messages among an array of different kinds of programs.

The sale of television time for the next broadcast season became an annual spring auction. The cost per thousand viewers became the primary criterion for buying commercial positions.

Marketing practice requires that a product's purchasers be identified in terms of standard personal characteristics defined through consumer surveys. When advertisers and agencies plan their schedules, often under extreme time pressures, the actual complexity of consumption habits and viewing choices is commonly reduced to simply matching product use with a handful of the audience attributes for a given program. Age has become especially salient among these attributes.

The life cycle.   When we place people into bins, we inevitably oversimplify. When we classify them by age, for instance, as children or adults, we shortcut many of their most distinguishing features.

The influences that shape any individual are varied and continuous. An infant enters the world in a state of utter dependence on its mother or those who substitute for her. As children grow and become aware of the presence and identity of others, they develop trust and begin to model their own behavior after the others. Once beyond the nursery stage, children show increasing interest in age-mates and others outside the immediate family circle; they enter the institutional world of formal schooling. And from the very start they are, in American society, enveloped in the audiovisual world of television, radio, and recordings, filled with ideas, imagery, and rhythms that go far beyond what they experience directly.

Human beings are consumers from the moment they are born. They begin to clamor for what they want long before they have the means to acquire anything on their own. Even a baby's consumption is shaped by individual affinities and tastes as well as by the choices made for the child by elders and by the exhortations of advertising.

The physical, emotional, intellectual, and social stages of child development are commonly defined by the years of schooling. Adults speak casually of "children" but understand well that a third-grader is distinctly different from a sixth-grader in appearance, capacities, and interests. In puberty, age differences become more pronounced and often arouse parents' anxiety as their adolescent offspring struggle to find an autonomous identity.

Teenagers are no more an undifferentiated mass than grade-schoolers. The recreational and social patterns of ninth-graders are vastly different from those of twelfth-graders. At every age level such variations may seem like minor determinants of character and outlook compared to those of gender, ethnicity, social class, and living environment.

Just as there is no clear line of demarcation between childhood and adolescence, so there is no absolute divide between adolescence and young adulthood. Marketers periodically rediscover the vast potential of the "child market" or the "teen market," assembling data on the vast purchasing power accrued from parental allowances and part-time employment and happily dispensed on sweets, entertainment, sporting goods, games, soft drinks, and trendy clothing.[16]

What an individual likes to eat or wear or watch on TV is not merely a composite of what her classmates or her family eat, wear, or watch; it is the expression of an idiosyncratic self that emerges differently in a drug-infested urban housing complex than in a suburban town whose diversions center on the closest shopping mall.

I have spelled out these truisms to emphasize the contrast between the extremely complex set of forces that help define a person as consumer and citizen and the sharp delineations of standard statistical breakdowns that categorize people by age, sex, race, and income.

The complexity extends well beyond childhood and adolescence, as some young people leave home for college or work while others remain at home with their parents. Throughout the first two decades or so of adulthood (if that is defined by the legal voting age of eighteen), people may be living alone or in every possible combination with others. Where and how (or if) they fit into the workforce, the nature of their work opportunities and aspirations, their earning power—all these determine their consumption of goods, services, and media content, no less than their domestic arrangements. The diminishing majority who form families and rear children are still faced with the challenges of adapting to a changing economy, an expanding population, and miraculous, often disturbing new technology that makes their life experience different from that of their own parents at the same age.

People in their thirties and forties are commonly thought of as being in a life-stage of acquisition, living up to or beyond their means, incurring the expense of rearing children and attending to aged parents. Beyond that, to the age of retirement, empty-nesters can savor more leisure and disposable income, allowing them to indulge new consumption interests. For a decade or so after retirement, with only slightly diminished vigor and income but with their belongings still in place, some can take life easy, travel, and move to gated communities in warmer climates while others settle into long-running poverty and dependence.

Highly intelligent and sophisticated professionals supervise the appraisal and selection of media in the large agency groups that dominate advertising in America and around the world.[17] They are well aware that people cannot be described in simple terms and pigeonholed with others of their ilk. They invariably protest that a good media plan for television, as for any other medium or media combination, must begin by carefully examining who a product's buyers are and continue by establishing an appropriate fit with the audiences for available "vehicles"[18] or programs.

An important media executive insists that her agency does not make media plans by formula:

> Targets are set scientifically. You look at what constitutes the brand's market. The target should be set by the agency account group and the client in consultation with the media people. It's all about marketing, after all. You've got to ask what is the competitive situation, how is the brand positioned, where do you want it to go.

Despite this protestation, most of the same agency's media plans are oriented to youth. Marketers widely share that orientation. It has had profound effects on television and thus on American culture.

Defining generations. The changes in generational outlooks that I have described in Chapter Two are at the root of the changes in what the media say and show. That is because media managements have increasingly sought to satisfy the tastes of young people whom they consider to be the most important part of the public.

To write of the generation gap, as I did in the previous chapter, presupposes that it makes sense to speak of generations. The word defies any precise definition.

The 1920s were identified with the "Lost Generation" whose lives had been disrupted by the First World War. The rebellious youth of the depression 1930s found expression in a variety of contesting radical political organizations. The jitterbugging hep-cats of the early forties were "cool," "spaced out," obsessed with rhythm. The "beat generation" of the fifties went on the road seeking freedom from the demands of a money-grubbing society. But the same period saw the advent of what the social scientist Robert Putnam calls "the long civic generation," the cohort born between 1925 and 1930 that developed a strong sense of political participation.[19]

The hippies of the 1960s abandoned the conventions of their bourgeois origins for a blissful communal life made more tranquil by marijuana and more exciting by LSD. Their militant offspring, the Yippies, sought to wreak havoc in defiance of the Vietnam War. The Yuppies (Young Urban Professionals) of the seventies abandoned social goals and ideologies to seek their individual pleasures in the material rewards of an expanding economy. But in none of these cases did the exponents of these attributes make up a majority of their age group.

Cultural historians sometimes characterize the outlook and artistic expression of decades—the "Gay Nineties," the "Thirties," the "Sixties"—or of the reigns of rulers or presidents (the "Edwardians," the "Eisenhower Years"). But these designate conventionally accepted though arbitrarily defined periods of time rather than the people who lived through them.

Professional demographers prefer to think in terms of age cohorts—people born within a particular slice of time who presumably have some common elements of experience in their historical context. A generation is generally described as an age cohort that has undergone a unique traumatic episode in history—a war or depression whose effects reached and reshaped every element of society.

A psychologist, Lloyd Rogler, notes that

> Young adults who share experiences of cataclysmic historical events and who are also affected by institutional influences impinging on their own problems are disposed to develop common memories. . . . As they recollect and share with age peers the disruptions of their life-cycle transitions, their personal narratives merge into collective memories of the events.[20]

The baby boomers born in the years immediately following troop demobilization at the end of World War II did indeed share a common experience. They encountered a social infrastructure largely unprepared for their sheer numbers, and a society that had turned away from the great collective task of defeating fascism to the pursuit of individual goals of "self-fulfillment." The egotism that marketers celebrated as the "Age of Me" gave way to the anxieties provoked by the increasingly unpopular Vietnam War and led to the campus upheavals of 1968 and afterward. At this time there emerged (along with the already mentioned loosening of racial barriers, new contraceptive technology, and the weakening of traditional gender roles), the so-called counterculture that Theodore Roszak has compared to a "barbaric intrusion."[21] For these reasons, the baby boomers may truly be regarded as a generation with a unique historical identity. Its successors and offspring, voguishly named "Gen X" and "Gen Y," lack these characteristics. So do the newly arrived 13–24 "Millennials," fatuously described as "unlike any other youth generation in living memory."[22]

The notion of "generation" assumes that there can be great discontinuities of experience, when in fact what occurs in the course of ordinary lives is a continuous progression and usually imperceptible change. Individuals' life courses are disrupted by events; the underlying culture they share may be modified but never abruptly transformed. When authors write of the "Greatest Generation" of Americans in the Second World War, the reference is to that small portion of the population living through those years who served in the military, not to the great majority of younger and older people whose daily routines and career lines were affected but who did not share in the special experience of military life. A mother who lost her only son in the war suffered more than a draftee who served a few months at a domestic army base, but it is he, not she, who is included as a member of the wartime generation.

Generations differ in size, and this has large economic, social, and cultural consequences. The American population has been aging, though at a far slower rate than Western Europe's. In 2001, 2.7 million people, the first baby boomers, turned fifty-five. By 2004 the number rose to 3.5 million.[23] As the children of this very large age cohort entered adulthood, a new baby boom began.

The United States, the world's oldest surviving republic, has always thought of itself as a young nation. Its politicians have always contrasted America's youthful vigor with the troubled somnolence of the Old World. American popular culture has always stressed novelty, curiosity, and energy—the signal attributes of youth.

A 2003 Harris poll done at my suggestion asked a national cross section of people what age they would like to be if they could live in good health forever. Nearly two-thirds of those 18–29 said they would like to remain at about their present age. Among those in their thirties, two of five would like to stay in that age range, but an almost equal number would like to be younger. Among people in their forties, only one in five would like to live forever at the age they are, and two-thirds would prefer to be younger. A plurality of those 50–64 would like to be in their thirties, those of 65 and over in their forties.[24]

A renowned marketer, Alvin Achenbaum of Achenbaum Bodga Associates, comments that "Everyone nowadays is really young—or they are until they are sixty, and even then, if they are healthy, they don't want to admit they are old."

But the popular desire to be young, or younger, does not in itself explain the media's orientation to youth.

Marketing and the generations. Marketers have of course been sensitive to the shifts in public tastes and values as the population changes. Characteristically, they seize upon minor social trends, give them some memorable nomenclature, and accord them an exaggerated importance.

The "Pepsi Generation" was invented by the BBDO agency in 1961,[25] but in 1996 a Coca-Cola ad spoke of the "Cybernaut Generation." In 1967 the great adman Leo Burnett hailed the "Critical Generation."[26] Then there were "Youth Power"; the "New Age"; the "Now Generation"; "Cutting Edge"; the "Twenty-Somethings."

Automotive marketers directed their advertising themes to capture young consumers' presumed rejection of parental values and choices. In the mid-sixties came the "Dodge Rebellion"; Rambler introduced the "Rogue"; Chrysler had the "Rebel"; General Motors rechristened the Oldsmobile the "Youngmobile."

Fashion changes accompanied these transformations. Hats and neckties disappeared. High-fashion male models were commonly unshaven, suggesting their defiance of convention.

Thomas Frank, a sociologist, comments on the prevailing theme of late 1960s "countercultural" ads, in which the powers that be coopted the anti-Establishment outlook of young people for commercial purposes. "*Youthfulness* became as great an element of the marketing picture as youth itself."[27] The message was,

> Consumer culture fosters conventions that are repressive and unfulfilling; but with the help of hip trends you can smash through those, create a new world in which people can be themselves, pretense has vanished, and healthy appetites are liberated from the stultifying mores of the past.[28]

The transformation of young consumers was led by a "Creative Revolution" in advertising agencies, exemplified by a new type of "creative boutique" that broke away from what was considered the stodginess and bureaucracy of the big agencies. Those big agencies proceeded to merge into gigantic conglomerates, which not uncommonly absorbed the boutiques themselves. The copywriters and art directors of the print era gave way to a fresh breed with eyes on Hollywood as the ultimate career goal. During this period, with the growing ascendancy of television, the creative function in agencies became more important in the planning of ad campaigns, with clever technique often outweighing an informed appeal to consumer motivations.

"Creativity" was expressed in new hair styles and modes of dress. According to the advertising historian Stephen Fox, "clients were taken on pointed tours of the creative department, to see the miniskirts and jeans, to smell the incense and other suspicious odors, as though to prove how daring and *au courant* the shop was."[29] (I once had to ask the creative department of the organization I worked for to remove a large Vietcong flag that festooned its quarters.)

Today youth remains associated with iconoclasm, novelty, freshness, and creativity. Youth is presumed to set the pace for what is to come in the world ahead.

Newspapers and the trade press typically discuss the rivalries and fortunes of the television networks in terms of their ability to reach young audiences, always described as "highly coveted." When the magazine *Maxim* entered television with two "specials" (long programs produced as unique events rather than as parts of an ongoing series), the *New York Times* referred to its "editorial formula of gadgets, humor, sports and pictorials of scantily dressed young women" that "bonded" it to "the 18-to-34-year-old males whom advertisers prize."[30] Network officials panicked in October 2003 when Nielsen figures showed a drop in the viewing by men 18–24.

There is nothing especially new about this. In 1979 a brewery executive proclaimed: "Get the youth market and you're halfway home. . . . The 18–34 market is very important to us."[31] Another executive: "Getting a freshman to choose a certain brand of beer may mean that he will maintain his brand loyalty for the next twenty to thirty-five years. If he turns out to be a big drinker, the beer company has bought itself an annuity."[32]

Is it true that consumers captured at an early age will stay with a product from then on? This question is central to the transformation of television. I shall return to it in the next chapter.

Are young people the forerunners of market change? Marketers seek young consumers because their product and brand choices are in a formative state and thus more open to persuasion. And since they watch less television than their elders, they are an elusive target. The media research director of a super-agency raises both points to explain advertisers' interest in young people:

The young are much more difficult to pin down, especially on the networks, these days. Of course, everyone wants to be associated with young people; it's human nature. Their habits are not as settled. They're being brought up in a wholly different atmosphere than we were, with fifty channels to choose from. They are harder to reach. It was a great surprise when the reality shows were able to do that. When I look at the TV program guide I always look at the networks first; *they* [young viewers] don't. But most marketers believe that brand loyalty starts at a young age. I'm a Coke loyalist, because I prefer their flavor, but growing up it didn't matter much which brand I used. There's so much choice these days!

An agency CEO interviewed on television agrees that advertising is targeted to younger adults because they watch less TV, but observes that since older adults watch more in total, they can be reached by programs aimed at the younger. Thus broadcasters have every incentive to direct programs at young viewers' tastes while programs aimed at older audiences would turn off the young.[33]

Some ad agency executives consider the emphasis on youth as just another example of ill-informed client demands. One remarks that "operating pressures force people to oversimplify complex phenomena in order to get jobs done. Clients also put pressure on operating efficiencies, which encourages the oversimplifications."

But an observer who has been on both sides of the fence says that advertisers and agency account groups "feed on each other. It's just a commonly held paradigm [that youth is the target]."

A marketing executive for one of the largest packaged goods companies observes that "An inordinate amount of resources are spent on young people. It's hard to get teens' commitment to a brand. Nike, which aims at that market, says there's no brand loyalty among them." He correctly points out that it is an individual's position in life, rather than age, that is critical to the development of buying habits. "The 21–24 age group is a better target than teenagers because when youngsters go to college or get their first job, the classmates or the work group begin to form their consumption choices."

Usage of a product—whatever the brand—makes sense in defining the marketing target. But aiming advertising only at present users of a particular brand ignores the steady turnover of consumer brand choice. In the marketplace, promotions and price deals often drive decisions for "parity products" that consumers correctly assume exhibit no real brand differences.

As a network television executive describes it:

> The mentality of the [advertising] sales department is "We want young demos." If they have a young-oriented show, the better they can see the rest of the schedule. Agency people understand the value of hit shows. The programming people in L.A. are young, and they want to do the shows that appeal to them. Their natural inclination is to do young and hip programs. Their empowerment to do this comes from the premium that Madison Avenue will pay for them. Agencies think advertisers want them to dress hip and look hip.

Paying a premium.   The best proof of advertisers' infatuation with young audiences is their willingness to pay extra to reach them. This was demonstrated by David Poltrack, CBS's executive vice president for research, who dedicated considerable effort to a critique of the thesis that young audiences are more desirable. (The network's self-interest prompted this shrewd analysis. The broadcast networks have a generally older audience than many of the cable networks. The original three networks—CBS,

NBC, and ABC—have an older audience than Fox, UPN, and WB, and CBS has the oldest audience of the three.)

Poltrack teamed with Henry Assael, a marketing professor, to identify the thirteen programs most likely to be viewed by those 44 and over in the 1994–1995 broadcast season, and the eleven programs most likely to be viewed by those 18–34. The average cost of a commercial placed in the youth-oriented shows was 75 percent higher, though the average Nielsen audience rating was 19 percent higher in the shows with a concentration of older viewers.[34]

Poltrack and Assael offer a series of conjectures about advertisers' beliefs: older viewers are less likely to spend discretionary dollars or to try different brands; they are not as attentive or responsive to advertising; younger viewers represent larger families and new ones in formation, so they purchase more. But when these two researchers examined the usage of twenty-seven brands and product categories, they found that income and geographic region played a more important role than age as factors in consumer purchasing.

Moviegoing and Pepsi-Cola consumption were age-related; so (inversely) was the use of indigestion aids. Video-game ownership, fast-food consumption, and the use of Kellogg's cereals were linked to age-related family structure. But these cases were the exception.

A media research director concurs: "You're much better off if you look at the usage figures for the product to define the target."

Youthful decision-makers. Poltrack and Assael have a ready explanation for the apparent irrationality of media planners: "The people who create advertising and buy media are almost all under forty, and have little understanding of the potential of the mature market." This is only a slight exaggeration. Actually, 85 percent of all professional staff employed by advertising agencies are under fifty, and 58 percent are under forty, but media departments are disproportionately staffed with newcomers to the business.

The youth orientation arises from the people who make commercials as well as from those planning the schedules that air them. As an agency media director says, "The people creating the [television commercial] spots are young, and they try for that young feel. This country has an incredible fascination with youth. Every brand aspires to a youthful look."

Other disinterested observers believe that the emphasis on youth arises from the personal predilections of young media buyers rather than from marketing realities. As one puts it, "Media decisions are made by people living in that Manhattan environment which is more hip and youth-oriented than the rest of the country."

One complication is the failure to mesh ad content to its environment as was done in the past, as another critic reports. "For those agencies that have split off the creative and the media operations [as most agencies have done in a quest to boost profits], they're not working together on the media and message strategy."

Outside the agency business, there is skepticism about the rationality of concentrating on young viewers. A marketer who disagrees describes it as "a dated proposition that lives on because media buyers are young, and targeting young people is more appealing for ad agencies."

A network executive seems to concur:

The ad business has always had an oral culture. The kids coming in learn from the ones that were there before them. The emphasis on youth may have started with the boomers, but subsequent generations of media buyers are indoctrinated in the idea that the young audience is the one to go for. We had a top salesman who used to take clients to lunch and to the golf course, and that's how he sold schedules to them. Now a guy from MTV comes in and gives them tickets to a Rolling Stones concert, and that's what they go for.

While waiting to interview the media director of one of the largest worldwide agencies, I observed a continual procession of twenty-something media planners and buyers, all dressed in the sporty informal attire that is now universal in the advertising business. One young man, however, was conspicuous by his jacket and tie. When I asked him why he was so formally dressed, he told me he was applying for a job.

An ad agency executive acknowledges the influence of youthful media buyers:

Absolutely it's a factor. The average age of the people who do the buying is certainly skewed young. They come straight out of the university and hope to find their way up the ladder. I wouldn't let anybody buy unless they've had two or more years in planning. The buyer's average age is twenty-seven; the planners are in their mid-thirties.

A media executive suggests that it makes good sense for media executives to be young: "Anyone who buys anything has to have some empathy with what they're buying." But he attributes the reliance on youth-oriented formulas to poor preparation and overwork.

There's much less training of young people in media planning and buying. The problem is not their age but their absence of training. They're working from nine in the morning till nine at night. They're so overworked that they don't have the time to

sit down and talk to [media sales] reps. People do a lot of media buying through remote control. They're buying by the
numbers from the syndicated research services, not from their
knowledge of the actual media.

A similar point is registered by another informant, who suggests, however, that the final effect is to favor older viewers rather
than younger ones: "They're following guidelines or just buying
eyeballs as cheaply as possible, in which case you're not going to
end up with a young audience."

More generally, though, agency media executives reject the
idea that the youth of media planners and buyers orients them
to young targets. One says, "I think that's overly simplistic. It
suggests that you can't make intelligent judgments without supervision. The senior people are a lot older than that."

An agency media research director:

It's the older people who are making the major decisions and
presenting the plans to the clients. The vast majority of the senior people are in their forties. You don't get too many people
in their twenties. Clients are more inclined to push us in the direction of what they want to do.

Whether or not advertising planners' pursuit of young people stems from their own youthful outlook, many media directors believe there are sound reasons for such a policy. One of
them pooh-poohs the CBS theory that the concentration on
youth is based on illusion. "They're making this argument because they don't reach young adults. It's a self-serving argument.
All the major networks reach the older adults." He goes on to say,

In the perception of marketers in general, there's a conviction
that young adults are still forming their consumer decisions and
haven't yet formed brand loyalties. It's silly to conform to what

Nielsen defines as a young adult. [Actually Nielsen provides no such definition, leaving it to the clients to decide what the appropriate age group is.] Young adults have a much more active life style than people over fifty and are harder to reach. Few media reach the younger consumers.

This last statement is an exaggeration, but it overstates a real and important part of the case for focusing on youth. The marketing argument that young people make more valuable customers is one we must examine more closely in the next chapter.

Who is "young"? Marketers' targeting of young people is actually at odds with their limited place in the consumer economy. People in their twenties represent only 14 percent of the public. Adding those 15–19 brings the total to 21 percent. Of total spending power, 5 percent is held by the 18–24 group, 37 percent by those over forty-five. In the past, older people included a large number of poor ones, but Social Security and private pension plans have steadily increased their incomes. And people of fifty and over control 70 percent of total private net worth.[35]

Changes in the age distribution of the American population are inseparable from the rise in immigration and the growth of youthful minorities. While 20 percent of the white population consists of children under the age of fifteen, the proportion is 26 percent among nonwhites.[36] But marketers, media planners, and television producers who contrast the viewing preferences of young and old seldom acknowledge that the differences they ascribe to age may also really reflect ethnic origin and therefore social class.

If young people are the most desired target group, it would seem reasonable that they could be defined in some generally accepted way. But there is no universally accepted description of "youth."

CBS's Poltrack observes that almost all media plans are targeted to groups as diversely defined as 18–49, 25–54, and 18–34.[37] An advertiser refers, curiously, to "the 14–24 male quadrant." A spokesman for one of MTV's ad agencies says their target is 21–27.[38] MTV lumps the 12–24-year-olds, its key audience, together as "media actors" and "multi-taskers."

It is easy enough for advertisers to revise their definitions of youth in composing media schedules.[39] As a media analyst remarks, "The software is all set so if someone wants to shift from 18–35 to 18–29, they can do it. But they don't want to change. The system is a nightmare."

Marketers express some perplexity over the definition of the "youth market." As one points out, "The definition of 'young adults' can start with young teens and extend all the way up to the mid-forties. It all depends on the nature of the product or service."

The "youth" target is sometimes extended to include those who in a past time might have been described as middle-aged. A media executive hops around as he reflects on the question of who the young people are:

> 18–49 is what they call young people today. 18–54 is new. The 25–34 are not as well targeted. If you want to follow where the people are and where the money is, you want to target 30–65. Still, a huge amount is targeted at 18–49. 16–24 is one demographic. 25–34 is different; they're starting families.

A media analyst believes that the most desired demographic segment, "at least for packaged goods, is women 25–54. For years it was the 18–49 group, but with the population aging, they moved it up."

A network vice president says that "18–49 is a mantra in the ad business." He points to the influence of rivalries among the networks. "Years ago, ABC had the lowest network ratings but their profile was youthful, so they started to push that."

The more inclusive definition is sometimes stressed in trade press and newspaper reports. In the fall 2002 TV season, "ABC, which finished fourth last November in the coveted 18-to-49 category, surged to second place. . . . NBC's winning margin in the 18-to-49 category, a 5.1 rating to a 4.2 for ABC, was the biggest for any network in six years."[40] Another newspaper article describes the contest among the networks: "Fox drew the largest audiences aged 18–49, the demographic most courted by advertisers."[41] (Note the use of "demographic" as a noun.)

The "coveted 18–49 category" includes two-thirds of the adult population—a rather imprecise target! Does this kind of marketing make sense? It does if the objective is to reach the mass market. But it is the lower end of the age range that excites programmers' attention.

Walker Smith, president of Yankelovich Partners, a market research firm, offers yet another explanation for the emphasis on young audiences:

> TV advertising is expensive, so you have to be selling a whole lot of stuff to be able to afford it. This turns out to be only certain kinds of products, typically large packaged goods or consumer services brands. By sheer coincidence, these are *also* products whose biggest consumers are younger!! If your business isn't big enough, TV is unaffordable. But even if your business is big enough, the economics of TV still have to make sense. This turns out to apply to products for which the mass marketing economies of scale are needed to turn a profit.

I asked a select group of senior marketing research executives what age span they would describe as "young adults" in consumer surveys. Eight of the twenty-seven said that no such category could be defined because of the varying nature of the markets for different consumer products and services. The other responses were widely distributed. Four opted for the often-mentioned 18–34 category, and two narrowed it to 21–34. Two took a still more restricted view: 18–24. One wanted to start much earlier and take it to a much later age: 12–45, and another also included adolescents but cut the boundary off much earlier: 13–21.[42] I posed the same question to an agency media director (not part of the same group). He wavered back and forth: "Young adults are 18–24 . . . or 18–34. No, 25–34."

William Moult of Sequent Partners and the Marketing Science Institute admits,

> My view of age has changed as I have aged. I remember thinking 18–34 or 35 was an awfully broad range, and now it looks narrow. And 18–49 seemed way too broad until I reached my fifties. If you ask a wide range of people whether they would prefer to have a doctor younger, about the same age, or older, how would their responses vary by age? When you reach age eighty-nine like my father, you definitely want a doctor who is younger than you. Same for a pilot.

At any age, youthful singles living with parents or in bachelor pads cannot be lumped with their age-mates who have started families and adjusted their spending habits accordingly. The distinction is most important for those in their late twenties and early thirties, but ad schedules designed on the basis of age seldom take this crucial distinction into account. Moreover, differences in consumption patterns between singles and married people have no counterpart when it comes to media preferences, except in the case of magazines like *Parents* or *House and Garden*.

The media director of a huge agency describes how the youth target has changed:

> We were chasing youth when we had the baby boom genera-
> tion and the population bubble, but those people are now in
> their fifties. . . . The young people are harder to reach. If you
> buy TV you're guaranteed to reach the older crowd. In soft
> drinks, sales are set on the east and west coasts, and the young
> people are driving those sales. When we get older, it all tastes
> the same.

A celebrated media executive:

> There are two kinds of advertisers. The big ones selling undif-
> ferentiated packaged goods target women 18–49, and they're
> not interested in anyone over 50. They simplify everything.
> They spend so much money on advertising that they have a dis-
> proportionate effect. The second kind of advertiser has a dis-
> crete kind of market, like European automobiles. They tend to
> be more focused. These people ignore the simplicity of age and
> gender, and market to very discrete groups. Thirty or forty
> years ago it would have been 90–10 for the first type of adver-
> tiser. Today it's 75–25. In twenty years it could be 50–50.
>
> If you're going to grow a business, you have to differentiate
> the product in some way. It's so much harder now that audi-
> ences are fractionated. It's so expensive to reach a broad market;
> it's so much harder to get cheap high reach. If you have a line
> extension [using the same brand name for a different product],
> you have to figure out whom you want to reach. The frag-
> mentation of the media has made it hard to reach everybody.
> 16–24 is one demographic. 25–34 is different; they're starting

families. The 18–34s are less likely to be watching TV; they're spending more time on the internet. If you don't reach the younger people, you're not going to have an audience. The networks have lost more of the younger viewers than older ones. So they're filling the pipeline and going against the customers that are hardest to get and that they're more likely to lose. The reality shows are one of the few things they have done that's bringing in the younger people.

That is indeed why those shows have been so popular with advertisers as well as with viewers. The preoccupation with youth extends from ad planning to actual creation and design of products—even very costly ones. While the average age of a vehicle buyer in 2002 was forty-four, that of the less expensive Hyundai's buyers was thirty-six. Micheline Maynard, a *New York Times* reporter, describes "Generation Y, the under-25 group that marketers associate with extreme sports, blaring techno music and a zealous individuality. Some automakers are building cars meant specifically for young drivers, hoping that the attempt to be cool does not brand them as hopelessly not."[43] Toyota's president, Fujio Cho, says, "If we can capture them at 15 to 24, we can enjoy their business for years to come."[44]

An executive of the media buying service for a huge agency conglomerate concedes that the emphasis on youth is "very prevalent. It's not entirely without justification. If you look at everyone 18–24, on average you'll have a greater acceptability of new brand messages." But he does not target age exclusively. "There's a widespread belief that the older you are, the more you are set in your brand selection. There are people 50-plus who are actually amenable to change. When we look at media, we do our targeting by mind-set. We disregard demography. We do cluster segmentation of consumers based on their attitudes."

A former agency media director, who believes that "there's been an overemphasis on youthful targeting," says that the practice

> ignores life styles. At certain stages people review their brand loyalties, when they change their lifestyle circumstances. Moving into your own home, the empty nest, losing a spouse, all force changes in your brand choices. This should be the focal point, not when people reach some artificial age bracket. At any age people are reviewing their brand loyalties and decisions.

Adapting content to the prime target.   The viewing predilections of young people are well known to the managements of television enterprises, and their programming policies are designed accordingly. They heavily promote programs produced and scheduled with young viewers in mind. But these programs are seen by people of all ages.

A cable television executive believes that "young people tend to sample TV very quickly and make the decisions as to whether they like a show or not." But it seems quite likely that viewers of any age, remote control in hand, pass quick judgments on everything they watch.

Advertising executives readily acknowledge that program standards of propriety have been relaxed in order to attract young viewers. As one says,

> The networks are machines for generating audiences. They put on these shows to keep the average age down, because the younger viewers are the ones that have defected to the new media. . . . Young people would just consider a lot of those shows fresh and interesting. We've already had our full share of vulgar and tasteless programs.

New programs under serious consideration by the networks go through extensive testing in theaters set up for recording minute-by-minute reactions and subsequent interviewing. The composition of the test sample is controlled so that it represents the desired characteristics of the target audience. Two of the three major networks do not even bother to include people over fifty-five in their samples.

Although younger viewers gravitate toward programs featuring violence and sex, these elements are actually counterproductive for advertisers.[45] Research by a psychologist, Brad Bushman, shows that brands advertised on sexually explicit and violent programs are 19 percent less well remembered than the same ads shown on a neutral program.[46] Brands whose ads show violence are remembered 20 percent less, and those with sexual allusions 18 percent less than neutral ads. Violent or sexual ads placed in violent or sexual programs are not better recalled.

We shall be considering the consequences and implications of television's use of violence and sex to capture young audiences, but first we must investigate the validity of the premises that gave rise to this studied effort.

4

The wisdom of wooing young consumers

Do the experts agree on the value of youth? The changing character of television entertainment has responded in large measure to advertisers' pursuit of young consumers. But the premise that underlies this preoccupation is spurious. As I have just described, the pursuit of youth has come about for two reasons: young people are harder to reach through mass media, and their buying habits are still unformed and presumed to be malleable. The first point is well taken. The second requires some scrutiny. How different are the consumption patterns of young people—their affinity for particular products and their preferences for particular brands? We can answer these questions by listening to the views of professionals who have spent their careers pondering such matters and by examining the evidence from surveys of what people of different ages actually buy.

In recent decades, corporations have tried to build on the existing reputations of their familiar brands by introducing variants with different attributes customized to appeal to different sectors of the market. (A commonplace example is toothpaste, which comes with different flavors and attributes under the same brand name.) As product lines are extended, more and more brands in most product categories vie for shelf space in the stores and for the consumer's attention. The result, inevitably, is a greater degree of brand switching among people of all kinds.

Companies spend money to advertise on the premise that the public's willingness to accept a product rests on familiarity and comfort with its name. In recent years, Wall Street has defined a brand's reputation as a valuable intangible asset that can be assigned a monetary value in an accounting statement. The term "branding" became common in marketers' discourse and even entered the public and political realms. Along with this, new importance was assigned to the venerable idea of "brand loyalty"—consumers' willingness to stay with a product that is already part of their experience, one that works for them, one they are willing to stick with.

But it is not easy to find supporting evidence for the idea that people will stay with a brand if their attention is caught at an early age.

While agency and television executives generally accept the proposition that young people are a most rewarding target, students of consumer behavior offer a much more nuanced and generally dissenting view. Among the senior marketing executives who set down their ideas for me, some agree with what I consider to be the conventional wisdom. One observes that "the dictum seems to be followed slavishly." Another agrees that the "young are more open minded, less experienced, than the old." A third says, "Young people tend to be more prone to try new products than old people."

Young people, unburdened by commitments, may indeed be more willing to experiment with novelties. But it is important to distinguish between the adoption of new inventions—disposable razors, e-mail, cell phones—and the acceptance of either new or existing brands that promise minor improvements within an already well-established product category. People aged 18–34 try new leisure and electronic products at a better-than-average rate, but new food and financial products at the average rate.[1] New inventions commonly come at a price that young people often cannot afford to pay. (For instance, between 2001 and 2002 broadband communication grew by 24 percent among those 21–24 but by 78 percent among those 25–64.) A company's fight for a greater share of an established market is another game altogether.

Within what age bracket is loyalty easily "captured"? The answer may extend well beyond youth's first blush. In the words of one informant:

> Consumers develop brand preferences by age 40 to 45, or even younger, depending on the category. But, the emphasis is on preference rather than loyalty.

This is an important point, because for any potential purchaser, different brands range from those always used to those that would not be bought even if they were the only ones available.

A number of the experts draw on their own personal histories as consumers:

Allan Baldinger, of the research firm Ipsos-NPD:

> There are certain highly differentiated brands, where the "get 'em early" strategy is probably a powerful ingredient in their success. I've been 100 percent loyal to Heinz ketchup, Colgate toothpaste, Hellmann's mayonnaise, and a slew of others since

I was a kid. It helps when the price point is low, so that price elasticity is not a huge issue.

The "get 'em early" doctrine, when accepted, is generally hedged with qualifications, as in the case of Martin Yazmir, who heads his own market research company:

In some cases it makes sense to "get them when they are young." For products where tastes are established young and last for a long time, such as cigarettes, it is essential to establish trial and usage at an early age. The same was true for some political movements; get them when they are young and you own them forever.

What of the notion we have already heard expressed by some media planners, that a youthful consumer, once caught, will retain "brand loyalty" forever? This has been called the "lifetime value" concept, and at least one marketer believes that "there is a lot of promise" to it.

Russell Haley, who directed research at Grey Advertising and moved on to teach marketing at the University of New Hampshire, calls it "a rationalization for aiming at young people. They live longer, hence the long-term value of their loyalty is expected to be greater. On the other hand, their brand loyalty is lower (higher switching rates), and so they are more easily lost to competitive efforts."

Marketing professor (and former advertising executive) Melvin Prince says, "Obviously, the life cycle value of a loyal younger customer exceeds that of a loyal older customer, *ceteris paribus*." But he also articulates a different point. Youth is not only more valuable but more vulnerable.

Young adults are more prone to instant gratification and are more impressionable. Their buying preferences are not fully matured, and they are more susceptible to mass and interpersonal influence. Younger adults are more experimental and open in their buying. They are especially receptive to new products.

But Prince also notes that "their importance as virgin triers relative to older age groups is overestimated." And he is quick to offer a qualification: "How valuable is that first experience with a brand? It varies greatly by product category."

The experts define "youth" differently. Some evidently think of swinging singles, others visualize recently formed families with great demands. For example, Paul Gerhold, who became president of the Advertising Research Foundation after a career as an agency research director, says he is

> not convinced that the reason they are considered important is because durable preferences are being formed. The reason could be a lot simpler. Young people just buy a lot more. Go to a large supermarket and watch the carts go through the check-out. The ones that are really loaded are almost always pushed by a young adult, with or without spouse and children. This is a big, big market, and brands have to compete for it. It is also a fast-changing market, quick to accept new ideas and new products. Their decisions don't last forever. Brand sales are short-term crops that call for constant cultivation.

BBDO's Bruce Goerlich agrees:

> Most advertising aimed at young people has nothing to do with their switching potential or "lifetime value" but with their purchase patterns—for example, for packaged goods, families are heavier purchasers, and most families are headed by younger people.

If young consumers' purchasing decisions are indeed so volatile, it seems inconsistent to suppose that their brand loyalty can be won.

As is already apparent, many of those who accept the notion that an emphasis on youth makes sense take care to hedge their statements. This is even more true of most of the other marketers I questioned. They point out that product use patterns vary greatly and that new product trial and brand switching can occur at any age.

Gale Metzger, founder of Statistical Research, Inc., believes that

> Brand relationships are complex and influenced by experience, price, options available, etc. All are subject to those variables without regard to age. Aside from ads, experience drives shifting—think of banking or autos or cell-phone service. For ad targeting, the youth emphasis is overdone. I believe in giving different value weights to different target groups. All will shift brands given a similar stimulus.

Universal-McCann's Robert Coen links product choices to physical needs rather than to age.

> If the product is not very different from brand to brand, the consumer could become set on the use of a particular brand soon after a few satisfied uses, regardless of his age. Theoretically the prime target for any type of marketing persuasion would be the prospect who is most likely to respond. For a hairpiece he would probably be bald.

Market researcher Marvin Belkin, who has "always disagreed with the precept that 'young people' constitute the prime target for branded products and services," insists that "the target is a moving one. Some products migrate. The internet migrated from younger to older people. But Scotch migrated the other way, from older to younger, as single malts gained in popularity."

William Moult believes that

> consumers adopt some sense of loyalty, either to a brand or a set of brands, or a store, for many categories. When this happens for ice cream will not be the same as for cold cream or denture cream. It may happen first for flavors of snow cones, later for brands of snowboards, even later for brands of snowmobiles or snow tires.

The vision of markets as being in a constant state of flux is borne out by research showing that while the number of purchasers of a product characteristically stays about the same from month to month, new customers arrive as others drop out.[2] William Moran, who has directed research for Young and Rubicam and Lever Brothers, relates this continuous "churn" to the effects of constant competition among the manufacturers themselves:

> I often have wondered about the "get 'em young" dictum. It does not make a lot of sense for denture adhesives. As new entries are introduced to categories, some brands are dropped out of some consumers' brand repertoires [the brands a person considers acceptable]. They have to be, as the size of brand repertoires is constant. There could be a danger for a brand to be stuck with youthful impressions when those consumers' tastes change along with the years and/or when new products are introduced that succeed in changing the desired profile of characteristics in the category. Many a once-successful brand has failed to remain relevant—Lux, Pepsodent, Oldsmobile. Perhaps it matters whether a brand's positioning is based on fashion attributes or on dependability and value.

Several other comments emphasize the changes that occur in products as well as in people. One comes from Martin Yazmir:

We live in a segmented world, and age targets are no longer enough to be considered the prime market for many products and services. Targeting by age is reasonable in mass media for some product categories, such as most soft drinks, where the index of consumption is extremely high among teenagers. But if it's bottled water, flavored, carbonated, or still, or drinks positioned as diet, we target differently. If consumption patterns for most products and services are formed early and remain fairly constant through life, then targeting young people would be the right course to take. But that assumes that products and services themselves remain fairly constant over time and that consumer tastes do not change. In reality, products change in order to adapt to new economic and marketing needs. The formulations of foods change to recognize new needs, finding lower-priced ingredients to either increase profits, or lower costs to better compete, or lower prices because of increased competition.

Again and again the theme is sounded that "brand preferences are formed and modified throughout life." Walker Smith points out that

Many products and services don't even become relevant to people's lifestyle needs until later ages—investments, insurance, denture adhesives, luxury automobiles, many fashions, products for young children. The information seeking and learning for these products occurs at older ages, not at younger ages. Moreover, brand preferences can change. Usually it's driven by product innovations. SUVs weaned a lot of baby boomers off Japanese cars. New technologies keep people bouncing around from brand to brand when it comes to consumer electronics. There is absolutely no general rule of thumb that I would recommend a client rely upon to make any kind of significant marketing decision.

Russ Haley extends the list of factors that must be considered when he observes that "the applicability of the Conventional Wisdom varies by category. Switching rates [among brands] are a consideration. Also the number of competitors, their relative size, and their level of marketing expenditures." Haley believes that brand loyalty is developed much like personal values, which change as adolescents reorient themselves from their families to their peers.

Theodore Dunn, who has directed research at the ad agency Benton and Bowles and at the Advertising Research Foundation:

A decision to use Crest at an early age may lead the individual to buy that brand. But he or she may learn that other brands offer the same benefits with a better taste, and switch, and later switch to still another brand which offers other desired benefits. A "hot" Pontiac may be desirable at twenty and a smoother Lexus at a later age. Then there is the matter of individual differences, with some people more disposed to change than others. The formation of brand preferences is fluid and dynamic and not captured in the confines of an age bracket.

Walker Smith comments:

It is true that many brand preferences are formed at younger ages. There is more information seeking and learning at younger ages, and there are no established patterns of behavior to change, only new patterns to be learned. Notwithstanding all of this, brand preferences are formed and modified throughout life. All in all, I think [the focus on youth] is a misconception. There are so many exceptions to this rule that could be cited that the rule itself is, paradoxically, actually the exception!

A number of the comments are introspective, as in the case of Gilbert Sabater, president of Becket, Inc.:

> First of all, some product categories I can't afford to buy when I'm a young adult. Second, how much brand loyalty do we find today among consumers? There was a time when cigarettes and liquor had the highest brand loyalty, but now that a pack of cigarettes will put you in the poorhouse, I wonder. The only products I can think of that demand high brand loyalty are baby products. "Whatever my mother used, I'll use." It has a great deal to do with the product category as well as the choices that are being offered. I would fly most airlines except those I don't trust for whatever reason. The [industry's] biggest fear was to get into the category of "I hate that airline." Same goes for gasoline—the choice is one of convenience, not brand. Except there are brands I won't purchase because of poor reputation or bad experiences in the past.

Critiquing conventional wisdom. The critique of the prevailing conventional wisdom boils down to two propositions—that people's tastes and needs change as they move through life, and that technological innovation and competition are constantly changing the dynamics of the marketplace. Both these propositions call into serious question the pursuit of brand loyalty among the young.

A number of the experts suggest that important switches in consumption, including brand choice, are tied to critical moments in an individual's life course rather than to age per se. Malcolm McNiven, who has directed research for DuPont and Coca-Cola, says that

> The time people are making brand choices is when they are going through a transition of some kind. These changes can be

physical (moving), identity changes (puberty), relationship changes (marriage), responsibility changes (new job, kids), and so on. It seems oversimplified to focus only on age. It is true that young people are going through transitions at a faster pace than older people, but when you consider divorce, retirement, and so forth, it certainly isn't limited to young people. Personal products like toothpaste or deodorant usually have high loyalty components, but a new dentist or girlfriend can change the brand preference instantly. The issue is very complex. Unfortunately, agencies have a hard time dealing with complexity in allocating advertising dollars.

Melvin Prince points out that "brand loyalties may harden quickly, and at some point young adults may be as hard to switch as older adults. Further, older adults can be a viable primary target for brands that serve their age segment well."

Charles Overholser, who has directed research at Young and Rubicam, asks us to

consider the following list: laptop computers; credit cards; brokerage services; cruise vacations; luxury SUVs; internet service providers; prescription drugs. These are leading advertising categories today that barely existed during the decades when the conventional wisdom was created. All of them are more likely to be initially purchased by somewhat older consumers than the famous 18–29 or –34 youth group, many by middle-aged, some by elderly. Even if initial purchase experience leads to loyalty over a long time period (that's a very big if), these categories should nevertheless be targeted to older consumers. The notion that you can profitably build brand preference among people who are not yet in the market for the category is wishful thinking. The world changes too fast.

Other comments stress the effects on brand attitudes of technological or design changes.

> The life cycle of specific consumption items is becoming shorter and shorter. Where there is a great deal of innovation, early awareness and favorable attitudes are constantly being challenged and vitiated by new information and experience. Early "habits" deteriorate quickly under such conditions. The longer a category is used in the course of a consumer's life, the more valuable an early preference habit. The early commitment theory holds best for products that have a clear-cut quality edge over competitors. Products that have a psycho-sensual appeal—fragrances, toiletries, etc.—are more likely to achieve a persistent preference based on early experience. There are damn few brands in damn few categories that benefit substantially from targeting young people beyond their potential for current consumption.

Patrick Robinson directed research for Imperial Oil and the Marketing Science Institute before starting his own consulting firm. He writes:

> With maturation, tastes change and old habits are challenged and perturbed. Soon there is nothing so constant as change: bigger, better, stronger, more exciting, sexier, scarier, whatever. One's formative years and youthful habits fade in importance and relative weight. Tradeoffs, compromise, and maturity are apt to foster new fads, norms, and cultural acceptance. Brand identification, product consumption, and also loyalty—it's a process of market exploration and learning. Marketing's continuing processes of persuasion influence choice and modify buyer/user behavior. Likely, we are *all* set in our ways and "loyal" to some socially acceptable modus vivendi, throughout our lives. But we adopt new

consumption patterns and change reference groups with little or no conscious thought or profound reasoning.

Like many other students of consumer behavior, Robinson regards product and brand-usage patterns as expressions of individual personality:

> How is the "oldster" on his Harley expressing himself any more or less than the youngster wearing his peaked cap sideways? Each is nonverbally showing his "colors" relating to a reference group or archetypal "hero" figure. Change may be incremental or catastrophic, it's all *relative*—constantly evolving dynamically. No one escapes maturation and habit-formation phases—that's life and the process of growing up!

Several commentators distinguish brand loyalty for products that carry high or low emotional engagement. One is Marilyn Strand of J. P. Morgan Chase:

> If people stayed with the brands they were exposed to early on, it seems to me they would be driving more Chevys and Buicks and Cadillacs than Camrys and Mercedes. And drinking more Folgers! But people tend to form and hold early brand impressions about low-involvement products, such as window cleaners (e.g., Windex), cleaners (e.g., Ajax), etc., out of inertia or sometimes an emotional connection. Who wants to bother about selecting a new product if the trusted old one works fine—and besides, my mother/father/someone always used it?

The same point is put by Erwin Ephron, who writes that "For run-of-mill products, young people buy what they've seen their parents buy. For products they are interested in, they have distinct brand preferences."

Another marketing executive observes that "Whenever we have tried fancy segmentation, we have found people of all ages in the various groups we create. It depends on the brands, the categories, and the individuals."

Alvin Achenbaum says that a generalization about the importance of young consumers is made for cereals, beers, soft drinks, snacks, and music. "But even in these cases, younger people often make up a small part of the total market."

> People change brands at every age. Loyalty is not totally based on habit. To believe so is to deny the potency of market communications and price. The motivation to buy a brand is complex and tenuous. The idea that you can get a young person early and they then become loyal at a later age is pure poppycock. In the very early years of humans, 0–12, their needs and motives change very frequently as they mature. With the exception of a few products, what they use is bought for them. Teenagers tend to be peer influenced and very fickle. They are unreliable long-term customers. They go with short-term trends, many of which reflect their youthful ignorance and resentments. From a marketing point of view, until persons have money of their own and lots of it, they are not critical in the purchase of the predominant (overwhelming) majority of goods and services.

Colgate Palmolive's Jim Figura weighs in with what may be the most important piece of information: "Regardless of age group, 25 to 40 percent of people have tried a new brand in the past year in most of our categories."

When are brand preferences set? For most consumers of most products, the choice of a brand is a trivial matter, hardly one invested with deep reflection or strong emotion. Switching one's usual selection because it is not on the supermarket shelf or because an alternative is on sale does not represent an important act, if one assumes (correctly, in the case of most packaged goods) that the product's attributes (as opposed to its packaging and advertising) are virtually indistinguishable from one brand to the next.

Is there any particular point in life when brand preferences are set? TIAA-CREF's George Szybillo snaps back, "For cereals and chocolate bars, by the age of three."

Bill Moran comments,

I don't think it has anything to do with age. It has to do with when an individual first is faced with the need to make such a decision. For recent immigrants to the U.S., it is whatever age they are at the time. Same thing about household appliances—when they get married.

Other comments focus on how consumer preferences change with age. Martin Yazmir notes that

What one likes at sixteen, twenty-one, twenty-five, or even thirty-five is not necessarily the same. The influence of peers and significant others as well as new product availabilities affect preferences, habits, and buying behavior, regardless of age. Additionally, the phenomenon of taste saturation occurs for many food and beverage products. Tastes evolve.

Walker Smith does not believe that

there is an age when people become set in all of their brand choices. There are different ages for different brands and different categories. Coke wants to get to people between twelve and twenty-two. Schwab wants to get to people in their thirties but continues to market to them throughout their lives. Cadillac knows that people won't even consider it until they're in their forties, and in fact Cadillac would love to figure out how to get a forty-year-old instead of their more typical late fifty-something.

Pat Robinson argues,

If chronological age were the whole story, this would indeed be a no-brainer. But it's not that simple. Lifestyle and cultural categories often cut across socio-economic and age-related clusters. Isn't that the way the "Real World" functions and evolves? Make room at the table for the young at heart!

Another respondent believes that

Most people don't become "set" in brand choices at any particular age. They develop preferences, but if they have a need that isn't being met or see a new benefit, they will be interested. Some of the "youth" demographic, for example, has very strong brand perceptions of music labels, fashion labels, etc. But I don't think those same people will be wearing Diesel jeans in twenty years.

Many of the preceding observations refer to brand "preferences." Marvin Belkin is another marketing veteran who believes that "the youth emphasis is overdone." He reiterates the important distinction between preference and loyalty, with all the emotional overtones that the latter word carries:

We grow up with—that is, inherit—brand preferences. Brand relationships are complex and influenced by experience, price, options available, etc. All are subject to those variables without regard to age. Consumers develop brand preferences by age forty to forty-five, or even younger, depending on the category. But the emphasis is on preference rather than loyalty. People do develop a "set" of acceptable brands and if given free choice will select from this "set." But loyalty is fickle. It's a sometime thing.

Alfred Kuehn, president of Management Science Associates, suggests that the key decision is to use the product rather than to choose the brand: "New individuals to any [product] category are in the process of forming their consumption habits and preferences, irrespective of age."

Allan Baldinger hypothesizes that "older folks will show more loyalty than younger folks. But it'll be a slowly building thing, so that one is not likely to be able to say that there is a particular age cutoff at which point they become loyal." He singles out "dramatic category-to-category differences," some of which reflect income. Youth marketing, he says, makes sense in the case of products most used by young people, like fast food, soft drinks, and chewing gum, "especially bubble gum and 'straight' gum products, not tooth whiteners or gums designed to cover bad breath." But, he adds, high schoolers' purchases of clothing, jewelry, and cosmetics "tend to be faddish, rapidly changing, and not really appropriate for establishing brand preferences."

Charles Overholser, who notes that "the presence of children by various age categories may be more predictive than age," also points to the closing of the generation gap:

> Our culture is becoming increasingly homogeneous across age categories, except, probably, for a subculture. There seem to be fewer and fewer differences in behavior, values, and attitudes by age than used to exist.

A corporate marketer:

> When I started at [a Procter and Gamble agency] in the 1960s, I was told there were only two P&G targets, women 18–34 and women 18–49, depending on the brand. The reasons given

were: they were less brand-loyal because of being relatively new to purchasing in many product categories; they had more mouths to feed; and they would be alive longer if you managed to "own" them.

Making a "distinction between loyalty (an 'attitude') and re-peat behavior," he goes on to say that

In a marketplace of enormous product fragmentation and widespread discounting, the price of buying repeat purchase might be self-defeating. For automotive, the 18–24 group has seriously declined in share of new vehicle sales, and the sweet spot of the market has moved up to the 45–55 group.

He draws a distinction between marketers' immediate and long-range tasks:

Blindly going young is confused with planning for the future. I like to look at the job of our clients as selling cars tomorrow and today. A balance must be struck between these goals in all areas of the business—product development and marketing. Granted, Gen Y is the future, for a while, but how early is too early to woo them? I do not place much value in directing marketing at groups that will not really have the means to play for five years.

The pressures of life in a two-wage-earner household may also restrict the willingness to abandon established routines and try something new. Another informant writes:

I am wondering if supposedly being set in brand choices at a certain age is partly a function of the time and effort available to consider other brands. For example, working parents don't have the time or energy to think about which ketchup is better—they just grab the one they always buy because the price is good / the kids like it / there is no risk.

A comment by William Moult seems to sum it all up: "I suspect it is a probability distribution, not an on-off switch, and the 'meat' of the distribution varies by category."

The experts' comments offer the equivalent of a short course in consumer marketing. If we take their judgments seriously—as their employers and clients do—the inescapable conclusion is sharply at odds with the theory that young people are unique in their willingness to experiment in what they buy and that their allegiance, once won, will persist through their lifetimes.

We can check these conclusions against the statistical evidence from consumer surveys. Do they support the key proposition that underlies advertisers' strong preoccupation with young audiences—that consumption preferences and brand choices are formed early in adult life and can have sustained value for the firms that are able to capture them? To test this proposition, we must first examine the reality of brand loyalty itself.

The quest for brand loyalty. The marketing experts' replies to my questions represent a distillation of many years of experience with the whole range of consumer products. Their comments emphasize the difficulty of making generalizations, and this is confirmed by a number of recent studies that shed light on the phenomenon of what is widely and naively termed "brand loyalty." Different brands of products exert varying levels of encouragement for purchasers to fall into a repetitive pattern. The percentage of consumers who say they are likely to stick with one brand in a category ranges from 19 percent for cookies to 53 percent for pet food.[3]

As we have seen, the focus on youth is most clearly apparent in the thinking of marketers of packaged goods—the frequently purchased products sold in grocery and drug stores. Packaged goods account for a third of all network TV advertising, for a fifth of cable TV advertising, and for 10 percent of spot TV [commercials placed on individual channels rather than on a national network]. But the influence of packaged goods marketers is out of all proportion to their share of television advertising, because theirs are highly concentrated businesses, commanding huge advertising budgets and often dominating the planning processes of their advertising agencies.

Studies by the Roper organization in 2000 and 2001 demonstrate that brand loyalty (defined as having a favorite brand) varies greatly for different types of products, depending on the number of brands in that category, the perception of differences among them, and the variation in prices.

Of twenty-three kinds of products studied, only one (soft drinks) showed the greatest brand loyalty among people under thirty—a point several of our experts have already noted. In five cases, brand loyalty rose after age thirty but then remained flat. In two cases it rose steadily with age.[4] In five cases brand loyalty was higher among those over sixty but did not change before then. In four categories there was no relationship between age and brand loyalty.

Actually most people, at every age, are *not* loyal to any particular brand. Nearly half of those 18–29 have a favorite soft drink, but this falls to three in ten among those over sixty. While only one in five of the younger group say their next car will be the same make as the one they have now, one in three older consumers give this answer.

Only a low to moderate proportion of adults actually have one favorite brand in a given category. The Roper study reports that

Adults aged 60-plus are 10 percentage points more likely than those age 18 to 29 to have one favorite brand of countertop cleanser. But even among these older consumers, barely 3 in 10 have one favorite brand. That leaves a lot of room for switching behavior. . . . For a producer of mayonnaise or coffee it makes sense to target younger consumers, since they will indeed settle into a repeat pattern of buying the same brand. But other staple household items (dry soup mix, toilet paper, and canned soup) do not show this pattern at all.

As a number of the marketing experts have remarked, products are used at varying levels in the course of an individual's life span. Some age differences in *brand* usage merely reflect these differences in *product* use. Data from Mediamark (a syndicated research service that uses more than fifty thousand interviews and diaries) reveal a number of differences in the consumption habits of young and old.

Young people show distinctive consumption patterns for some products but not for others. They smoke more than older ones (presumably the abstemious survivors), and their consumption of individual brands of cigarettes (measured by the number who report using a brand within the past seven days) simply reflects the total amount of smoking rather than a particular affinity for Marlboros or Winstons.[5]

Similarly, people at different ages consume different amounts of soft drinks and beer. But in this case some brands show far greater youth appeal than others.[6]

Unlike beer and cigarettes, toothpaste is a product that almost everyone uses, but some brands and different product formulas for the major brands are favored more by young people than by older ones.[7] Every toothpaste brand shows almost random variations in its use among different age groups, without any detectable pattern. Shampoo preferences also show random patterns.[8]

Age differences are most clearly apparent among automotive makes. The big Detroit automakers fare less well than the Japanese manufacturers among the young.[9]

Of course "homemakers" (female household heads) are less often found among the young (who include many childless women) than among women of other ages. But in the case of household cleaners, age differences do not form any particular pattern.[10] Among cold breakfast cereals, long-dominant brands show far more strength among older women than among younger ones.[11] Each of the two leading brands of orange juice has its greatest strength in a different age group.[12]

To sum up, the evidence from consumer surveys that link buying habits to age is highly consistent with the judgments of the experts who have spent their careers studying market behavior. For certain products such as beverages and cigarettes, young people are a particularly desirable marketing target, but these are exceptions to the general rule. Their fealty to a particular brand cannot necessarily be won easily if they are captured at an early age. Yet the contrary proposition, asserting the special value of younger consumers, continues to have a strong influence on advertising decisions. Consequently it affects the very character of television, geared as it is to give advertisers what they want.

Other media—film, music, and videos—pursue young people for perfectly rational reasons. As we shall see, their content interacts with that of television. In every medium, producers are motivated to satisfy youthful predilections by testing the limits of what has conventionally been considered acceptable. But television is by far the most pervasive force in mass entertainment. I have argued that its emphasis on youth is based on faulty marketing premises. We must now examine the consequences of TV's transformed content and the ensuing policy debates.

5

Protecting the innocent

How the media went over the edge. In its misguided pursuit of young audiences, television turned "edgy." Other media have gone the same route for more valid reasons. This "edginess" has had an important but unintended side effect. When violence and sex are introduced to lure young adults, these elements are also, inevitably, exposed to audiences who are younger still. Much of the widespread concern about the nature of popular culture centers on its presumably corrupting effect on children. Adults are expected to differentiate fact from fiction and to make their own well-informed and rational judgments about whether media offer a true representation of reality. Children cannot.

The violence that infuses many media productions has attracted young audiences eager for high-powered fictional action. At the same time it has aroused appalled reactions from those who see it as a threat to society, especially to minors.

Dave Grossman, a military psychologist, points out that "Producers, directors, and actors are handsomely rewarded for creating the most violent, gruesome, and horrifying films imaginable, films in which the stabbing, shooting, abuse, and torture of innocent men, women, and children are depicted in intimate detail. Make these films entertaining as well as violent and then simultaneously provide the (usually) adolescent viewers with candy, soft drinks, group companionship, and the intimate physical contact of a boyfriend or girlfriend. They understand that these adolescent viewers are learning to associate these rewards with what they are watching."[1]

Ironically, the violent films that often bring in large audiences are rarely the ones that critics rate highly. Of five thousand violent films on broadcast or cable television in 1995–1996, only 3 percent received a four-star rating for quality.[2] But box office returns rather than Oscars or critical plaudits are the goal of film investors. Children are rarely in their sights except as sources of revenue; nonetheless children are usually in the audience for most feature films and television programs, with large and unexpected consequences.

Children's use of media. The media are far more important for children than children are for the media. Although surveys asking different questions and using different methods generate somewhat different figures to describe the same phenomena, they consistently show how important a presence the media are in children's lives.

Children's use of the media reflects both their parents' habits and the influence of older siblings and playmates. The average American child spends more than forty hours a week consuming media, mostly TV programs, videos, and movies.[3] Although television viewing has been trending steadily downward among children under twelve for the last decade, they still spend 61 percent more time watching TV than doing homework. And what they're watching isn't likely to be "Sesame Street." At 10:30 on a weekday evening about one in seven is watching the tube—almost half as many as at the peak of prime time.

While young children are taken to the movies, listen to musical recordings and radio, and even play video games, it is television that accounts for the bulk of their media exposure.[4] The average child aged 2–7 watches TV for about two hours a day; those 8 to 18 watch an average of three and a quarter hours.

CBS, NBC, and ABC have been television's main protagonists in the continuing battle over children's viewing, yet they now account for only a quarter of the TV time spent by those under twelve. The bulk goes to cable channels, which carry some of the sexiest and most violent films.

One factor in the transformation of television content has been a shift in the control of program production. In TV's early years the networks produced their own shows, sometimes in close collaboration with the sponsors. Beginning in 1970 the FCC's "finsyn" (financial interest and syndication) rules limited the amount of programming that the networks could own. After the rules were dropped in 1993, the networks quickly reestablished a strong position in program production. Fewer and fewer large production companies came to produce a growing portion of the original programming shown on the tube. While independent producers accounted for 30 percent of prime-time programming on the top four leading networks in the 1992–1993 broadcast season, by 2003–2004 their share had fallen to 2 percent. In the same period the share of prime-time programming in which the networks themselves had a stake doubled, from 32 percent to 67 percent.[5]

When the FCC established the "Family Hour" in 1975, it took some early prime time away from the networks and turned it over to local stations, presumably to serve their communities.

A television executive who was in charge of programming for a major network at that time says, correctly, "They filled it with crap." The family-viewing rules affected the timing of both news and late-afternoon children's programming. Network affiliates that moved their evening news programs to an earlier hour also more often deviated from the suggested network schedules in rescheduling their children's shows to less propitious times.[6]

But the broadcasters have been increasingly challenged by the growing importance of cable programming, with its higher component of violence and sex. This has changed the nature of what children view. Half of the top thirty cable programs are professional wrestling matches, and teenagers rank the two leading wrestling series among their top six favorite shows.[7] Violent syndicated shows are often scheduled on weekend daytimes and early evenings during the week, when children are watching.

Families with children are most apt to subscribe to HBO, because of its children's features. But the greatest amount of time that parents and children spend viewing together is with HBO films, which are the most violent of all.

Nearly half a century ago, CBS, under the presidency of a psychologist, Frank Stanton, established an Office of Social Research that studied television's effects on society and politics. Its director, Joseph Klapper, often mused about the premature maturation of children exposed to the strange follies of adults as displayed on the tube. That was in the days when network managements spoke of television as a "family medium." Correctly or not, television is now perceived as an important agent of change in the process of growing up. As an advertising executive puts it,

Kids grow up faster today. A seventeen-year-old is much more like an 18–24 used to be. They grow up faster and they mature later.

In theory, programs unsuitable for children are scheduled after they are expected to be in bed. In fact, however, the level of violent and sexual content is no different at 8 p.m. than at 10 p.m.[8] And many children can choose their own viewing times and programs.

In early childhood the television set is a baby-sitter, tuned to cartoons and other kiddy programs. (This appears to have harmful consequences in some cases, regardless of what is being watched. Submersion in television at an early age has been linked to attention deficit disorder.[9]) Half the parents (and even more among those who are themselves heavy viewers) acknowledge that they are likely to leave their young child alone with the TV on if they have something important to do. But most of the time, they say, the child is watching with someone else (usually a parent) in the same room. In the case of video games, which are seen less favorably, a parent is less likely to be present.[10]

Two-thirds of little children under four can turn on the television set by themselves, and half know how to use the remote control to change channels. Half are likely to ask for a particular show. Virtually all the children (even those one year old) own a toy or other product based on a film or television character.[11]

The remote control makes channel-flipping a normal part of the TV viewing experience for children as well as adults and increases the difficulty of exerting parental supervision. It inevitably entails exposure—however briefly—to the full range of content.[12] Even though children and teens are less likely than adults to be in the audience for violent programs, the average violent film has more child viewers than the average nonanimated children's program on the networks.[13]

A substantial portion of television sets are within the direct control of children. Two-thirds of all children, and a third of those 2–7, have a TV set in their bedrooms.[14] As might be expected, TV use is greater among these children. There is little difference in media habits among boy and girl toddlers, but their program choices change as they grow.[15]

Congressional inquiries into the effects of televised violence have focused on children's programming, but five-sixths of what children watch is mainline programming aimed at adults. (Incidentally, adults account for a large chunk of the audience for what might be considered kiddy shows.) In 1995, for instance, 17 percent of the viewers of Disney's "Aladdin" were children under twelve; but so were 11 percent of the audience for "Roseanne," 9 percent of those who watched "Melrose Place" (a steamy—by the standards of that era—soap opera), and 7 percent of the viewers of "Murphy Brown" (the program denounced for its "immorality" by Vice President Dan Quayle when its eponymous heroine became an unwed mother).[16]

Nearly nine of ten parents of four-to-six-year-olds report that their children imitate positive behavior they have seen on television. But a substantial amount of imitation is bad rather than good. Three of five boys are said to have imitated aggressive behavior. In keeping with these ambiguous observations, two of five (43 percent) parents think that television and video help their children's learning; 27 percent think it hurts.[17]

On Saturday morning, over three-fifths of children are watching TV.[18] But there are actually more children 2–11 watching at 9 p.m. on Saturday (33 percent) than at the peak morning "children's" hour of 10 a.m. (28 percent). Even at 10:30 p.m. on Saturday, in 1995 a fourth of the youngsters were watching TV. In 1997, on weekday nights, 15 percent of the 2–5-year-olds and 20 percent of the 9–11-year-olds were watching at 10 p.m.

TV viewing in the family setting. Children watch a lot of television where household use of television is also high.

In a third of homes, parents say that a television set is on *all* the time.[19] The amount of time spent with television is closely associated (negatively) with education and social class, and therefore with race. In black households the television set is on for twice as many hours as in white ones.

Understandably, the parental controls exercised in better-educated, higher-income families are tighter and better informed than in those lower on the social scale. This makes it all the more difficult to disentangle the effects of television content on children's behavior from the larger influences created by the home environment. A fifth of all households account for two-fifths of total viewing time. The acute problems associated with televised violence are concentrated in those impoverished, disorganized families already characterized by rage and aggressive behavior, where viewing levels are highest and where parental control is weak or absent.

Children with lower grades in school and those who are least happy and most apt to get into trouble are the heaviest media users. Since poor families watch far more television than wealthy ones, they more often have a bedroom set, even though they are less able to afford one. (The TV is on "most of the time" among 56 percent of black households, 42 percent of Hispanic, and 39 percent of white.) Three-fifths (58 percent) of all children live in homes where the TV set is on during meals, and 49 percent live in homes where there are no rules about watching TV.

For many years television viewing was a family activity, centered in the living room, where the TV set was the focal point of attention. In 2003 only 11 percent of homes had but a single TV set, and 60 percent had three or more.[20] As most households acquired additional sets, viewing became much more of an individual activity. This gave children autonomy in their TV viewing and reduced parental supervision.

The media executive Gene De Witt goes so far as to say, "There is no longer a family television audience. Most homes have multiple sets, and most people watch their own programs."[21]

But this is an overstatement. Many programs, especially in prime time, are watched as a family activity (or perhaps, better said, inactivity). Young children often are with their parents in front of the principal set in the house.

Most parents assert that they watch TV with their children half the time or more often,[22] and three of four say they always or usually know what the children are watching.[23] About half say they have specific rules about when the children can watch TV.

But parents' reports differ from those of the children involved, who typically report far less parental control. Nine of ten parents say they have rules about the content of television programs and videos their small children are permitted to watch; about seven in ten say they set time limits. Whatever controls the parents believe they exercise, diaries kept by children over seven indicate that parents are not present 95 percent of the time they view TV. Even children 2–7 watch TV *without* their parents 81 percent of the time.

A fifth of children say they watched TV alone the previous day, and three-fourths report watching with someone else (a sibling in two-thirds of the cases, and a parent in almost half. Five percent watched both alone and with others.)[24] Seven of ten parents insist they are watching with their children all or most of the time.[25] Who is to be believed?

Fantasy reality and true reality.   Even for adults, television and film often blur the distinction between fact and fiction. (Consider the pseudo-documentaries of Oliver Stone.) Marie-Louise Mares, of the Annenberg Public Policy Center, observes that very young children don't really understand the story of what they are viewing.[26] Little children happily watch the same video over and over. The pleasure comes from the familiarity induced by repetition.[27]

Television programming largely deals with fantasy, but live coverage of major news events inevitably becomes part of children's TV experience, sometimes with traumatic effects.

Broadcasters' routine self-censorship of disturbing imagery mitigates the impact of TV news' depictions of the world's disagreeable realities. The photographer Peter Howe, reviewing some of the gruesome scenes of wartime casualties he had photographed, comments on television's relatively sanitized perspective of the 2003 war in Iraq:

> As a nation we seem to have little compunction to exposing our children to hours of fantasy violence while at the same time wanting to protect them from the reality of the violent world in which they live. . . . In the thousands of images I looked at while authoring a new book about war photographers, I never saw anything that compared with the sight of one dazed soldier holding his severed arm in *Saving Private Ryan*.[28]

Viewers watching the collapse of the Twin Towers on September 11, 2001, frequently used the expression, "It was just like a movie!" Indeed, the imaginary catastrophes produced by Hollywood's special-effects departments sometimes outdo the horrors that occur in the real world. Immediately after the attacks on the World Trade Center and the Pentagon, over half (54 percent) of parents said they had restricted their children's viewing of news programs.[29] (The proportion was higher among college graduates, who might have been expected to use the breaking news as a subject of family conversation.) Nearly half (46 percent) said their children had expressed fears—a proportion little different from that in the 1991 Gulf War (43 percent), which hardly represented a threat to American homes.[30]

Just as news reports of the world's real violence makes fictional violence seem more admissible, so the appearance of sexual episodes as major news items has reduced the shock effect of fictional sex. There were such lovingly described episodes as the cases of Lorena Bobbitt, who cut off her husband's penis, of sportcaster Marv Albert, who was tried on charges of sexual assault, and of boxer Mike Tyson's rape convictions. The barriers finally came down when Monica Lewinsky appeared on the scene.

Changing notions of childhood.   The idea of protecting children from objectionable elements of media content arises from the presumption that they live in a state of innocence that is easily corrupted. This gets down to the question of when childhood begins and ends. Just as in the classification of adults, the lines between infancy, childhood, and adolescence are hard to draw. Different societies have different expectations of when children are to enter the adult economy and assume adult responsibilities. I have seen five-year-old children working rug looms in Morocco. Boy soldiers of nine and ten armed with Kalashnikovs terrorize villagers in half a dozen African countries.

The historian Philippe Ariès argues that the notion of childhood is a creation of the modern age.[31] In earlier times, he maintains, the high rate of infant and child mortality discouraged the development of close feelings between parents and their offspring, and children were put to work early to help sustain the family's precarious existence. The crowded circumstances of the home further discouraged intimate parent-child relationships.

Only with the beginnings of modernity in the seventeenth century, according to Ariès, did the idea emerge of children as a fragile and protected species whose character was to be shaped by learning—though learning was too often accomplished through regimentation. With the decline of infant mortality, child-rearing practices changed, and bonds of affection replaced stern patriarchal discipline.[32]

Recent scholarship has challenged this view of childhood as a transient stage in human history. It stresses the persistence of family structure and parent-child relationships throughout history and across cultures that differed in many respects (like the age of marriage, the location of the first home, and the number of childbirths per woman).

Nicholas Orme, contradicting Ariès, maintains that the primary change in the seventeenth century was the increase in surviving historical evidence.[33] Another historian of the family, Linda Pollock, agrees: "As far back as we can tell, most parents loved their children, grieved at their deaths, and conscientiously tended to the task of child-rearing."[34] One need only look at the friezes depicting loving families on Roman marble sarcophagi to find supporting evidence for this view.

Whatever the historical truth may be, childhood in Western countries and in modern times is generally regarded as a period in life that should be dedicated to play and learning and sheltered from the unpleasant deeds and coarse behavior that adults indulge in. Almost all the uproar over film and television's undesirable effects on children was for many years centered on their violence; lately it has turned to their language and their depiction of casual sexual relations. An important element of television content—advertising—has been largely immune from hostile assault.

Marketing to kids. A by-product of children's extensive media exposure is that their hours awake, like those of adults, are saturated with commercial messages. Some are squarely aimed at them, selling sugary cereal, soft drinks, candy, games, and toys. (The ad industry spends $12 billion a year on ads directed at children, mostly through television. By some estimates, a child sees twenty thousand commercials a year.) But since most children mostly watch adult programming, much of the advertising they see is for general consumer goods, including a substantial amount aimed at adolescents and young adults. Advertising has actually been merged into other programming content, as "product placement" puts packaging front and center in television drama and comedy.[35]

R. J. Reynolds used a genial cartoon character, Joe Camel, to deliberately transform the Camel cigarette brand in 1988 by appealing to adolescents and using the character as a prop to win "peer acceptance-influence."[36] Camel's share among smokers under twenty-four tripled.[37] The rate at which nonsmoking teenagers started to smoke rose from 51 per 1,000 in 1988 to 77 in 1996—the years when the Joe Camel campaign was at its peak.[38] But it is hard to attribute this enormous general increase to the ads for one brand.

Adolescents aspire to adulthood and model their behavior on that of those who are somewhat older. Inevitably, therefore, their entertainment tastes are hard to differentiate from those of young adults. This means that advertising schedules targeted for people in their twenties—by beer advertisers, for example—scoop up large numbers of younger viewers as well.[39] Alcoholic beverage advertising on television appears on programs whose teenage audience is 15 percent higher than the proportion of teenagers in the total TV-viewing population.[40]

Adolescents, presumably, approach the messages they see with a certain degree of dispassionate judgment. But this cannot be said of younger children. TV speaks to them with parental authority, and it is only after years of schooling that they learn to recognize the feigned enthusiasm of pitchmen, just as they learn to distinguish the difference between dramatic fiction and the reality of the news.[41] There is no powerful constituency lobbying for limits on television advertising, which now occupies over a fourth of air time. Loud voices have, however, been raised to protest television violence.

The extent of TV violence.   On TV, as in film, violence is ubiquitous, depicted as a commonplace form of human interaction. By one estimate, a child graduating from elementary school will have seen 8,000 murders and more than 100,000 other acts of violence on network TV.[42] Researchers using different definitions of television violence have turned up widely varying counts of the number of incidents per hour, ranging from 9.7 to 38.[43]

The level of violence in TV fiction exceeds that in "reality" or nonfiction programs, including news, "tabloid news," public affairs, and documentaries.[44] Nearly two in five fictional programs include some element of visual violence, with higher proportions in syndicated shows and in evening hours.

A series of studies conducted between 1994 and 1997 found that violent episodes occurred in three of five programs (not including news, sports, game shows, religious broadcasts, and infomercials).[45] Violence occurred in 54 percent of the shows on broadcast networks, and in 86 percent of those on premium cable.

Although graphic or gory depictions are rare on TV, violence is glamorized, often associated with attractive characters, and condoned. In fact, the perpetrators are almost as attractive as the victims. Three-fourths of the violent actions are unpunished.

Perhaps this is understandable, since in over half the instances the victim appears to suffer no pain or physical injury. (Only 13 percent of violent programs show suffering or other long-term consequences, and only 4 percent have an anti-violence theme.) Good characters who engage in violence are punished only 15 percent of the time. Violence is typically shown as part of a pattern of repeated behavior.

In three of four cases, it is violence with no remorse, criticism, or penalty. Three of five (58 percent) include repeated displays of violence. Sympathetic characters, heroes, and role models initiate two of five violent incidents. (This is especially true in cartoons, where heroes use their superhuman strength to attack villains who threaten the peace.)

Of those characters who perpetrate violence, 45 percent are bad and 24 percent good, with the remainder showing mixed or neutral attributes. Good and bad targets occur in equal proportions (31 percent). The targets are generally individuals rather than groups. In 40 percent of the cases, violence is committed without a weapon; guns are used in 25 percent of the incidents. Only 15 percent of the episodes show blood and gore (in movies and on pay cable the proportion is almost double, 28 percent in both cases). Most violence is motivated by the desire for personal gain, in anger, or by the need for protection.

About half the episodes show "events that could possibly occur in the real world." Violent programs divide almost evenly between live and animated action (almost all of this in children's shows; nine-tenths of the fantasy violence occurs in children's programs).

Few programs show the long-term consequences of aggression. A large part of the time (in 43 percent of the episodes), violence is associated with humor. It's fun! (George Gerbner, a communications scholar who has devoted much of his career to the subject, refers to "happy violence." He notes that the highest-rated programs are seldom violent.)

The research team, headed by Jeffrey Cole, that conducted the large-scale analyses of programming between 1994 and 1997 took pains to note that "not all violence is to be treated equally." They identified eight hundred "high risk" scenes in which the perpetrator was attractive, the violence apparently realistic (to viewers under seven), justified, and unpunished, and the victim suffered minimal consequences. These scenes occurred most often in programs addressed to children, especially cartoons.

Another research team looked at violence in what they called "reality shows" dealing with actual happenings—as opposed to fictional ones, and distinct from the genre of "reality shows" that have become popular since their study—and found wide variations among subtypes of programs. Violence occurred in all the police shows, in 86 percent of "tabloid news" shows, and in 72 percent of documentaries, but in only a fourth (26 percent) of other news programs and in 15 percent of talk shows.[46] Eighteen percent of all the "reality shows" (as they defined them) included talk about violence, though they did not actually show it.

Much of the violence shown on television occurs in the movies that are an important part of its content. Of 114 feature films aired in the 1996–1997 season, 34 contained violence, as did 12 percent of made-for-television movies. Most violent prime-time programming genres are actually more violent than PG-13 movies,[47] but feature films continue to contribute a disproportionate share of violent content.

Violence was also featured in a new kind of "real-life" video, some using outtakes from TV and films. "Jerry Springer: Too Hot for TV" contained thirty brawls in fifty-four minutes. A video adapted from "Cops," a Fox TV show, was promoted with a call to "See for the first time what the censors hold back. It's gritty, graphic, outspoken and outrageous real-life footage." Other Fox shows included "When Animals Attack," "The World's Scariest Police Chases," and "The World's Most Dangerous Animals."[48]

The high incidence of violence is not the only respect in which television presents a distorted view of American reality. In the spirit of true political correctness, the realities of crime statistics are ignored. Three-fourths (77 percent) of the victims and 76 percent of the perpetrators are white. Five percent of the perpetrators are black, though in reality blacks and whites are charged with equal numbers of murders. In TV drama, 71 percent of the characters are human, 12 percent animals, and 10 percent supernatural creatures. As I noted in Chapter Two, one-fourth of American families consist of a married couple with one or more children. But only 11 percent of prime-time television characters are parents, and of these only three of five are married.[49] Women are identified as married twice as often as men.[50]

Such a weird caricature of American life, constantly repeated, can easily be conflated with reality by impressionable minds.

Why all the violence? In the early 1950s a crusading psychiatrist, Fredric Wertham, publicized the subject of media violence's influence on children; he blamed comic books for youthful misbehavior.[51] Since then, film and television violence have attracted the attention of child advocates, social scientists, and government. Actually, the debate over the effects of film content has been under way since the 1930s, when social scientists investigated "Our Movie-Made Children" under the aegis of the Payne Fund.[52]

The age of television coincides with an enormous rise in criminal and aggressive behavior in the United States, though a host of other factors have contributed to this development.[53]

What explains the ubiquity of violence in American mass media? It attracts audiences, but this is only a partial and superficial explanation. The media economist James T. Hamilton likens televised violence to other social ills that represent the aggregate effect of innumerable minor and thoughtless acts. He considers it to be "a problem of pollution. Many public policies, ranging from zoning to air pollution controls to residential garbage collection, are driven by the notion that individuals do not always internalize the cost to society of their actions." Such problems, says Hamilton, generate "negative externalities," costs borne by different people than those who do the damage.[54]

Hamilton advances an ingenious and more profound explanation for televised violence. He draws a parallel between the economics of television and that of other industries, like automobile manufacturing, whose balance sheets fail to include their products' social costs. Just as the environmental damage wrought by automotive fuel inefficiencies must be borne by society as a whole (especially by future generations), so the psychological damage done by media violence is never reflected in the balance sheets of media corporations.[55] "Even if broadcasters jointly would be better off reducing levels of television violence, however, each individual broadcaster has the dominant strategy of continuing to broadcast television violence."[56]

Is violence bad?   Do the fictions that punctuate the unremitting succession of commercials on the TV tube really make a difference? Of course they do. A very large number of academic studies substantiate the commonsense observation that media violence arouses expressive feelings in children who watch it.

A recent broad synthesis of the scholarly literature makes a number of points:

Children as young as four distinguish between good and bad characters in television programs. But young children do not easily distinguish between fact and fantasy.

Viewers are more likely to model their own behavior on that of characters who are perceived to be attractive. These are the ones who behave helpfully to others.

Aggressive response to violent programming is greater when viewers can identify with the perpetrator or the victim of violent action and when that action is shown to be justified. Violence is more frightening when it is unjustified or directed at innocent victims.

The use of weapons increases the aggressive response. Scenes of real-world violence arouse more emotion from adults than clearly fictional scenes.

When violence is shown to produce successful results, it stimulates aggression; the reverse occurs when violence is punished. Expressions of pain by a victim inhibit aggressive response in the viewers.[57]

The evidence on the harmful affects of televised violence has been reviewed in reports by such authoritative bodies as the American Medical Association, the American Psychological Association, the Centers for Disease Control and Prevention, and the National Academy of Sciences. A comprehensive summary of the scholarly research was published in 2003 under the auspices of the American Psychological Society.[58]

The summary indicates that violence is low on public television (18 percent).[59] The level is highest in movies (90 percent) and drama series (72 percent). Children's series have a surprisingly high level (66 percent) because of the buffeting about of cartoon characters, but music videos (31 percent), reality-based programs (30 percent), and comedy series (27 percent) rank low.

The analysts of content concluded that "violence is frequently used in contexts that are most likely to stimulate learning and imitation." They came up with some sensible recommendations to programmers: "Be creative in showing more violent acts being punished; more negative consequences—both short and long term—for violent acts; more alternatives to the use of violence in solving problems; and less justification for violent action. . . . When violence is presented, consider greater emphasis on a strong antiviolence theme."[60]

Such well-intentioned and sensible counsel seems totally unrealistic in relation to the pressure-cooker realities of program development, in which scripts are commissioned and massaged, productions are cast and rehearsed, and actors and directors ad lib under fierce time and budget constraints.

The researchers warn that uniform rules (for example, on air times) are hard to apply intelligently. They note that "many younger children identify strongly with superheroes and fantastic cartoon characters who regularly engage in violence. Furthermore, younger children have difficulty connecting nonadjacent scenes together and drawing casual inferences about the plot."

Just as smokers often reject the idea that smoking is bad for their health, the chronic viewers of televised violence are most likely to reject the idea that there are unhealthy consequences to what they enjoy. People 18–34, who are described as "prime consumers" of violent shows, are least likely to believe that these harm society or are a major cause of breakdown in law and order.[61]

The National Television Violence Study corroborates previous research which shows that repeated exposure to televised violence desensitizes viewers and increases their fears of real-life violence. As the Council of the American Psychological Association put it in 1985, "Viewing televised violence may lead to increases in aggressive attitudes, values, and behavior." These changes carry over into adulthood.

In fact, television viewing as an activity appears to be associated with anti-social actions, quite apart from the content of what is viewed. (This may merely be an incidental result of the relationship between social class and the amount of viewing.) To cite just one recent illustration, a 17-year study that tracked children in 707 families in upstate New York found that adolescents and young adults who watched television for more than 7 hours a week were more likely to commit an aggressive act later on. This was true even when social and demographic factors were considered, and it was true of all TV viewing, not just of violent programs.[62] "Merely viewing 15 minutes of a relatively mild violent program increases the aggressiveness of a substantial proportion (at least one-fourth) of the viewers."[63]

More aggressive children prefer the company of similar children. In another recent contribution to a research literature that has mounted to thousands of articles and books, a 15-year study of 329 children, originally aged 6 to 9, found that the boys who as children were heavy viewers of violent television shows were, in adulthood, twice as likely as their lighter-viewing contemporaries to push, grab, or shove their wives and three times as likely to be convicted of crimes by their early twenties. Girls who were heavy television viewers were similarly twice more likely to have thrown something at their husbands and more than four times as likely to have punched, beaten, or choked another adult.[64] The combination of sex and violence has been shown to be particularly dangerous.[65]

As I have noted, mass media producers have always insisted that they merely reflect society's values and have no part in shaping them. The television industry for many years disparaged the vast quantity of hard evidence linking its fictional violence to anti-social actions in the real world. As recently as February 2004, Gail Berman, president of Fox Entertainment Television, told a congressional hearing that "the evidence is inconclusive." The industry sponsored research of its own, raising questions about the connections, much as the tobacco industry did for years to raise doubts about the compelling data that showed that cigarette smoking caused disease. In similar fashion, the over-whelming evidence linking fuel emissions to global warming has been called into question by the makers of SUVs.

The dense and dry statistics and sometimes qualified find-ings reported in academic journals do not readily lead to pub-lic awareness. There is "a disturbing discontinuity" between news reports and scientific evidence on the effects of media vi-olence.[66] Two psychologists, Brad Bushman and Craig Ander-son, analyzed 636 newspaper and magazine articles dealing with media violence and aggression. A mere 6 percent clearly "stated that media violence was a cause of societal violence." Only half the articles advised parents to discourage children from violent media. *Newsweek* and the *New York Times* both published arti-cles that cast doubts on the linkage but failed to publish au-thoritative rebuttals.

"Over the past 50 years," write Bushman and Anderson, "the average news report has changed from claims of a weak link to a moderate link and then back to a weak link between media vi-olence and aggression. However, since 1975, the scientific confi-dence and statistical magnitude of this link have been clearly positive and have increased over time."[67]

Not everyone believes that fictional violence is harmful. One psychologist, Christopher J. Ferguson, argues that "humans are a violent species" and that "violence is a basic fact of human na-ture," as demonstrated by its prevalence among all primates. He argues that "people in the United States and other industrialized nations may actually be equally violent," but Americans "may simply have better access to more efficient tools with which to kill."[68]

In rebuttal, Anderson and Bushman point out that "drinking a large number of alcoholic beverages prior to driving does not always lead to fatal accidents. Then should driving while under the influence of alcohol not be illegal?"[69]

Social science findings, like those of any scientific inquiry, rarely measure up to the legalistic requirement that guilt be proven beyond any reasonable doubt. Marjorie Heins, a former ACLU attorney who heads the Free Expression Policy Project, writes, "Most of the studies measure aggressive attitudes or behavior, not violence—and there is a big difference."[70] But there is ample evidence that threatening behavior may arouse as much anxiety or more than actual violence.

Heins then goes on to pursue a different tack: the rare cases of individuals who imitate bizarre behavior they have seen on the tube, with tragic consequences.

> Holding publishers, authors, producers—or newscasters—liable for the "copycat crimes" of deranged individuals, when thousands or millions of others exposed to the same work were not moved to violence, has dire consequences for free expression. . . . There is no coherent way for raters to decide what violent content is harmful or inappropriate, and labeling all violence, from war movies to Shakespearean dramas, would target a vast amount of valuable expression.

But instances of "copycat" violence are few and far between. Only eccentrics would call for censorship of *Macbeth* or *All Quiet on the Western Front*. Most media violence cannot be justified by claims to artistic integrity or historical verisimilitude. The violence is there because its makers believe it will make money for them.

The strange case of cartoons. Intelligent analysis of the content of violent television programming always centers on the issue of context—who does what to whom, under what circumstances, by what means, and with what consequences.[71]

Is the formulaic violence of children's cartoons, in which animals and caricatured humans punch, beat, and mutilate each other, to be equated with the violence in fiction that uses real human actors? Most of communications scholars' analyses of content proceed on the premise that the two formats cannot be distinguished.

Is it really violence when the Road Runner or Mighty Mouse outwits, tortures, and flattens a monstrous assailant? Through the years, broadcasters have steadfastly ridiculed studies of television content that apply the same criteria to the doings of cartoon characters as to those in Westerns or detective stories. Child psychologists counter that Santa Claus is a real-life being for very young children in their most impressionable years. The distinction between fiction and reality does not become very clear before the age of seven. There is ample evidence that cartoon violence makes young children more aggressive, just as realistic violence affects older viewers.

Televised cartoons became increasingly violent with the introduction of a new generation of Japanese imports called *anime*, modeled on fast-paced, extremely violent video games. (Crudely drawn, these cartoons cost $100,000 per episode to produce, compared with $500,000 for a typical cartoon made in the United States.) As Jim Rutenberg of the *New York Times* describes one: "A pug-nosed thug kicks in an elderly storekeeper's face. Then he punches a young heroine in the eye and cracks her in the small of the back with a heavy bar stool. Her limp frame collapses to the ground as he stands over her with his gun drawn and pointed at her head."[72]

Mike Lazzo of the Cartoon Network, which along with the WB and Fox networks now fills much of its weekday afternoon and Saturday morning children's schedule with such Japanese imports, observes that Japan has a very low rate of violence. "These cartoons are made and air in a country with one of the lowest rates of violence in the world." Pokémon, one of the milder of these programs, was at one point the most popular show on American children's TV.

Demonstrating how different media borrow from and reinforce each other's violent content, Joel Andryc, Fox's executive vice president for children's programming, points out that "Today's kids have grown up on the video games, they've grown up on Sega and PlayStation. . . . They don't give a second thought to this kind of animation. . . . The kids can relate to these characters. They see how someone can empower themselves and fight a monster and save the world."

But it is precisely because "kids can relate to these characters" that they have the potential for wreaking harm.

Public reactions to media content. Parents consistently reveal disquiet in their perception of television's influence on their children. Two of three think media content is generally inappropriate, and four of five think it teaches them "violent, antisocial behavior."[73] Similarly, nine of ten (89 percent) believe that sexual content "encourages children to become sexually active at younger ages." Nine of ten also agree that hearing coarse language in the media contributes to children's parroting the phrases.

Another survey reports that three-fourths of parents worry about "negative messages in the media."[74] Nine of ten agree that "TV is fine for my child as long as he/she is watching the right shows and in moderation." But nine of ten parents also agree that

"When it comes to bad language and adult themes, it seems like TV programs are getting worse every year," and nearly half (47 percent) agree that "Wherever my child turns, he/she sees crude or sexual messages in the media." Parents who say they supervise their child's viewing closely are also more likely to say they have been shocked by something on TV.[75] And parents split evenly between those who worry that their child watches too much TV and those who say "it is not an issue in my household."

Half the public thinks "pressuring the entertainment industry to produce movies and music with less violence and sex" would be "very effective." A different survey reveals a deeper current of concern—a widespread feeling that the impersonal powers that control television content are not amenable to change or influence.[76] Seven of ten parents say they have been shocked or offended by something they saw on TV. But there is a widespread sense of fatalism about the power wielded by the mysterious forces that control programming. If ten thousand people were to call a TV network to complain about a broadcast, opinion splits evenly between those parents who think the executives in charge would pay attention and those who think it would be ignored.

This sense of resignation explains broadcasters' reports that they get little or no reaction to programming that they themselves consider outrageous.

The particular worries of parents are reflected in the opinions of the public at large. Televised violence may not be uppermost in the public's mind, but a variety of surveys show it to be a matter of considerable anxiety.[77] Yet while people are concerned about TV violence's effect on children, they do not feel it affects them personally. Only 9 percent agree with the proposition that "when children watch TV programs containing violence, they get rid of some of their own aggression." A majority reject the notion that violence should never be shown.

Three-fourths of the public believe that TV entertainment programs are a major cause of violence in the society.[78] The same proportion worry about "negative messages in the media."

Since 1971, seven of ten people have consistently agreed that entertainment TV portrays too much violence,[79] but the percentage who say that TV news is too full of violence has increased from two of five to two of three. While two-thirds of the public are "very concerned" about what children see or hear on television, almost the same proportion say this of movies and video games too. Among parents, three-fourths are "very concerned" about what children view on the internet.

The disapproval expressed in surveys does not necessarily mean that the public regards media violence as a burning issue. A network research executive suggests, "Rather than ask whether there is too much violence on TV, ask about its salience to viewers." The subject is certainly not one of those most frequently mentioned when opinion polls ask people what they are most concerned about. It is, however, a hot subject for an activist minority.

From violence to sex. In many countries, "adults only" labels are applied to violent rather than obscene content. In the United States, televised violence has been a contentious subject for four decades. While the amount of it appears to have stabilized (perhaps having reached the limits of tolerance), attention has shifted to the increased amount of sexually explicit episodes, street language, and portrayals of natural functions. The transformation came about very quickly.[80]

Two in five people say they are most bothered by the amount of violence on TV, a fourth by the amount of sex, and a fourth by both equally. (Only 8 percent say neither bothers them.)

Nearly two-thirds (63 percent) of parents express "a great deal" of concern about sexual content on TV, 59 percent each about violence and language. Half think that the sexual and violent elements in TV affects children's behavior "a lot." But there is no consensus as to whether the government should intervene to change things. The public divides evenly (48 percent to 47 percent) on the question of introducing "new government regulations to limit the amount of violence and sexual content in TV shows during the early evening hours."[81]

In the space of only a few years, sex has become a prevalent component of TV. Dale Kunkel and his associates analyzed the content of 1,114 television programs for the 1999–2000 broadcast season. Two-thirds (68 percent) of them included some sexual content (up substantially from 56 percent in a similar study two years earlier). In 65 percent of the shows there was talk about sex (most often about a couple's own sexual interests), and 27 percent (with an average number of 1.8 scenes per hour) showed actual sexual behavior, including 10 percent that implied or showed intercourse (typically covered with a sheet or blanket).[82]

Sexual content is more evident in prime-time network programming than in other television fare. Three-fourths (75 percent) of network programs contain such content, 29 percent showing sexual behavior.

Over half (56 percent) of the scenes coded as "sexual behavior" involved passionate kissing. Another 6 percent were described as "intimate touching," as in an episode of "One Life to Live" on ABC: "She kisses his chest, moving her head lower and lower towards his lap as the scene fades." Illustrative of "depicted sexual behavior" is a scene from Fox's "Ally McBeal" in which the heroine enjoys a sudden acquaintance with a car-wash worker: "The brief flashes show them discreetly nude, having intercourse in many different positions inside the car wash."

Women typically initiate flirtation, though actual intercourse is more of a mutual affair.

Teenagers are depicted in 9 percent of the scenes involving intercourse—up from 3 percent two years earlier. Except for what the researchers classify as "reality programs" (defined as game shows, documentaries, and public affairs programs rather than as the contrived contests that have more recently become popular), over half the shows of every genre or type include some sexual content. Sitcoms average 7.3 such scenes an hour. Between 1997–1998 and 1999–2000, the percentage of comedies with sexual content grew from 56 percent to 84 percent, and the number of scenes an hour from 5.8 to 7.3.

Like violence, sex has become a ubiquitous ingredient in television programming, just as it is in the movies. But neither violence nor the growing prevalence of sexually charged programming and films has appeared on the scene by chance, or even by popular demand. It has been brought in as a studied effort to attract the young people for whom it is correctly believed to have a special appeal.

Generalized opinions about types of programming content are often at variance with the same individuals' actual viewing habits and their spontaneous comments about specific shows. A 1991 study for one of the broadcast networks found that half the public agreed that there is too much sex on TV. But these people were identical to those who disagreed with that idea in their viewing of specific TV programs and their evaluation of them. Asked what they liked and disliked about fifteen different shows, violence and sex came up significantly in only one case each. (On violence there were actually as many positives as negatives.) For a longer list of programs, sexual content was overwhelmingly found acceptable, and only a small minority (between 5 percent and 10 percent) said they were offended by movies on "sensitive themes."

This extraordinarily permissive attitude in part reflects the social changes I reviewed in Chapter Two. But it also suggests that the public has become inured to television's changing standards and has accepted them as normal ways for people to behave.

Steven Bochco, television producer: "The audience that watches my 'NYPD Blue' and hears 'scumbag,' 'douche bag,' and 'prick' isn't going to reach for the remote if it hears 'bullshit.' When you're surrounded by junkies and whores in a jailhouse bullpen, the word just goes by naturally."[83]

With reactions deadened by the ubiquity of vulgarity, sex, and violence, and increasingly skeptical about the sense of responsibility among the powers that be, the public no longer responds indignantly to breaches of traditional restraints.

The "cutting edge."   In the endless competition for audiences, media scrutinize one another, borrow ideas, and test the limits of what the public and advertisers will accept. The process accelerated when television broke the film industry's entertainment monopoly and moviemakers responded by introducing more content that the networks would not air. TV, in turn, was forced to relax its standards. Cable, with both uncut Hollywood films and newer channels provided for young viewers, went farther beyond the former norm. Pay cable, relieved of advertiser pressure, went farthest. And at every step of the way, the most conservative elements of the industry were forced to reappraise the limits they had imposed in the past. Many of the industry's own executives are alarmed by what they see, but they are themselves caught up in the process of making the changes happen.

In a day-long discussion among television and film creative executives about how far the limits of acceptable content could be stretched, the points that are raised are not very different from those that would occur to any group of ordinary viewers. The subjects of the audience's age, or of young viewers' special vulnerabilities, never surface. There is a lot of talk, however, about how the business has changed. "[In the good old days] doing a show was about trying to tell the story of people in person, to tell the truth. It was all about going to places where none had gone before." The vogue term "cutting edge" comes up repeatedly in the conversation.

A producer: "'Cutting edge' is doing something that's daringly different. Not just about violence and sex and profanity. The reason why [a network] wanted to take the risk of putting on [a disturbing series] was to show that the networks could do cutting-edge drama. So they let down the barriers in depicting drug use. Prison rape. Violence. The ratings for the show sent the message that cutting edge doesn't matter."

A network executive: "In the past you had three mom-and-pop businesses [the broadcast networks] all playing by the same rules and giving the public some good noncommercial programs. In the present competitive environment nobody can do that. They all have their eyes on the quarterly balance sheet. In this environment there's no loyalty to shows. MTV with a one [percent of audience] share can make more money than any of the [broadcast] networks."

The important thing, in the view of one veteran television executive, is "Choosing the subject. 'All in the Family' [featuring the bigoted working-class character Archie Bunker] pushed the envelope. It all depends on the way the subject is portrayed. It has an impact on every creative person."

Another participant in the discussion chimes in: "The more the rating, the more money. The more money, the more power to make more of the things you want to make—what's getting put on TV that nobody is going to view but everybody's going to write about."

A writer/producer: "We simply evolve with the times. Your responsibility is to tell compelling stories. You want something that gets attention, and the more it gets the more it's going to make advertisers take notice."

A television executive: "Every art is a business. The money doesn't understand the audience. [On pay cable] you have a direct contact between the viewer and the network."

A film star blames the network programming departments: "In [the pay cable program] 'Sex and the City,' a character talks about 'a man coming in my mouth.' It's a matter of taste. The problem is not the [network] standards people. It's the meeting with the network executives [to plan a show]."

A network executive counters: "The networks really want the best shows they can get. There's a high turnover among programming executives."

A star actor-producer: "There's a belief that quality is dangerous. TV is at a stage where everything can go to excess."

A television producer complains of the insufficiency of talent to meet the demand: "You can't schedule twenty hours of network programs, and nobody does."

In a separate conversation, a network researcher suggests that television is not really fulfilling the public's appetite for even more of the same: "National polls have never asked, 'Do you think there is not enough sex on TV?'"

Cable's transforming influence. Unlike violence, sex and salty language are rarely central elements in media content. They are almost always ornamental and peripheral, and therefore easy enough to control.

A television functionary describes how simple it is both to introduce scenes, language, and episodes, and also to eliminate them. A movie is transformed as it is adapted for different purposes: "Everything released for theaters is forty minutes shorter than the director's cut. You take another twenty minutes off for TV. For showings on planes it's cut further. New dialogue has to be dubbed in when films are cut." He brings up the subject of how pay cable has set the pace. "People are taking greater risks as 'The Sopranos' and 'Oz' steal the audience. The networks fight back by introducing pornography. It's done to appeal to the audience in the 18–48 group. I think people get tired of it. The reality shows are an odd phenomenon. People don't get tired of sex, but they get tired of watching other people having sex. The parents are not going to be watching the sex-based reality shows."

Unlike broadcast television, whose programming formulas have always been set to appeal to the broadest possible audience, cable channels have flourished by going after specific subgroups of viewers. Those like MTV and Comedy Central, serving "the youth market," have from their inception introduced language and scenes that would not meet the big networks' acceptability standards.

MTV is owned by the same media conglomerate, Viacom, as CBS. With its fast-paced musical formula aimed at young people, MTV is seen with ambivalent feelings of envy and disapproval. "MTV is the cutting edge. We did a documentary on adoptions that showed a pregnant woman chain-smoking. There was an argument over that, but that's the way it was."

A network executive: "I never thought I was risk-taking. I watched MTV and asked, 'Where's the stewardship?'"

Television content delivered by cable or satellite is free of the federal regulation that (at least theoretically) affects terrestrial broadcasters' operations. Cable system operators (who in many cases, like Time Warner and Cablevision, also operate cable networks) are awarded their franchises by local governments. (In the past, bribery scandals have spotlighted the intimacy of the operators with local politicians.) But the cable networks (or "content providers" in industry jargon) are not subject to any outside governmental controls, although they, like the broadcasters, use the radio frequency spectrum. They may be restrained by the knowledge that system operators must face community pressures, but since many of those operators offer pornographic pay channels, the issue of censorship hardly ever arises. As the studies of television content have demonstrated, premium or pay cable has gone farthest in stretching the limits. This has had profound effects on mainline television.

A cable TV executive: "TV is made in the same studios that movies are made. [NBC president] Bob Wright recognized that HBO was doing things, and that the more broadcasters could get to what HBO was doing the more attractive they would be to the public."

Another informant notes that "HBO wasn't the first [to alter the standards]. Public access got away with it. [Cable system operators are required to dedicate certain channels to members of the local community, including some with bizarre agendas and tastes.] HBO has higher production values and more responsibility."

A television executive sees the escalation of sexual content leading up to an inevitable collapse:

As the networks cut back, the only way to do it is to crank up that stuff higher and higher. Unless they go out on a limb you will see a reaction to it. We're a puritanical nation. When this all came out there was a great hue and cry in the creative community: "We're going to do better!" But the people who control the purse strings just want the money. I think they do it [introduce prurient content] in an effort to win more viewers. Some in the artistic community try to clean up the material, but others don't.

On "The Sopranos," they have the type of serio-comic material that's required. Sex and nudity or off-color language used in natural situations makes sense. In movies it's done in cases where the film doesn't have a lot of value, but I don't think it's done to a huge extent. Everything in life is organic and changes all the time.

A pay cable executive observes: "The whole media industry has opened up as far as what people are exposed to. It started with Hugh Hefner and *Playboy*. The whole industry has become more liberal."

A vice president of a rival pay cable network: "The big change came in news and in sitcoms in the sixties. The movies had to respond."

Another pay cable executive, asked how pay cable's output differs from theatrical films: "We're picking up slack where the theatrical [film] producers have been left behind. It's of theatrical quality and something we're very proud of. We have product that deals with social issues. Theatrical films have been geared to producing what we call popcorn. Very rarely do you see Hollywood movies that are geared to the young adults or middle America."

Permissiveness and porn. As the entertainment media relax the limits on their sexual content, their distinction from pornography has become more and more difficult to discern. What made *Last Tango in Paris* a work of cinema art was the quality of the acting and direction, the intimations of individual character that distinguished it from the garden variety of films showing sexual intercourse. Sexual depictions become pornography only when they are declared to be illicit. It does not require complete nudity for men to become aroused by full-length photographs of good-looking women. To a Muslim fundamentalist, a woman's uncovered face is impure and provocative. This doctrine is removed only by degree from the common restriction in Western society on the public portrayal of sexual acts—though simulations that do not actually display the sex organs are now generally deemed acceptable.

As the sociologist Charles Winick describes it,

> Both the President's Commission on Obscenity and Pornography (1971 [in the Nixon administration]) and the Attorney General's Commission on Obscenity and Pornography (1986 [in Reagan's administration]) felt that it was not possible to define pornography clearly. . . . The President's Commission recommended that the laws on obscenity should be repealed, because the material represented an insignificant social problem and had no negative effect on its users. The report of the Attorney General's commission urged that the obscenity laws should be strictly enforced, because the material had significant negative impact and constituted an important national problem."[84]

Compared to the substantial amount of academic literature on the effects of television violence, there is far less evidence on the effects of pornography. It has been demonstrated, however, that the combination of sex and violence is particularly disturbing.

Stacie A. Cass and Margaret Bull Kovera point out that the relationship between child pornography consumption and active pedophilia has not been demonstrated because the Child Pornography Prevention Act of 1996 forbids the use of the material necessary for research. They believe that "child pornography may elicit responses similar to the secondary effects produced by violent adult pornography."

The commercial sale of pornography has long been associated in the public mind with the actual sale of sexual favors, though Winick observes that

> There seems to be no relationship between sexually explicit materials and prostitution; consumers of these materials are not likely to be customers of prostitutes, because of differences in the gratifications provided by the two activities.[85] . . . Empirical studies have failed to find any consistent correlation between availability of and exposure to explicit materials and sex crimes against women.[86]

Pornography in 2001 was a $10 billion to $20 billion industry, depending on whose estimates are accepted. (Forrester Research estimated it at $50 billion and the *Boston Globe* at $100 billion.) A billion dollars a year is spent on telephone sex, with an average call lasting four to seven minutes. The internet has given pornographers substantial new opportunities.[87]

The pornography business flourished after World War II, with "adult" bookstores and movie theaters in deteriorating city centers. (The 1972 film *Deep Throat*, made for $25,000, grossed well over $100 million). Films were soon replaced by inexpensively produced "adult" videocassettes that could be enjoyed at home or in the privacy of a hotel room. A Playboy Press book proclaimed "Sexual Freedom; Freedom of Nudity; Freedom of the Toilet; Freedom from Hang-Ups; Freedom from Censorship; Freedom of Pornography; Freedom of Obscenity; Freedom to Fool Around."[88]

Many of America's leading corporations have tapped into this large and lucrative business. DirecTV, with 8.7 million subscribers, sells $200 million a year in sex films. EchoStar, also controlled by Rupert Murdoch's News Corporation, is number two. Time Warner's Channel 35 is dedicated after hours to commercials for prostitutes. Liberty Media's On Command is the major supplier of pay-TV sex films, which generate far more revenue for hotels than minibars.[89] AT&T owns the Hot Network, with hard-core sex films transmitted through its cable lines. Tracy Hollingworth, a spokesman for AT&T, says, "We call it choice and control. Basically, you use your remote to block out any programming you don't want. But if you want it, we offer a wide range of programming that is available in the market we're in."[90]

While Hollywood released about four hundred films in 2003, eleven thousand sex video titles are produced each year, and they account for two of five rentals on the West Coast and in the Northeast. Winick comments that "The VCR is especially popular for viewing sexual content because it permits the user to speed up, slow down, replay or freeze images."[91] There are more than 700 million porn video rentals and sales a year, generating $4 billion in sales.[92] A typical release sells 2,000 units or less. A film that costs $50,000 may easily bring in five times as much. *Playboy* has moved from X ratings to XX and XXX, promising even more rewarding erotic experiences.

Explicit presentation of sex in the media may have no detectable consequences. Nonetheless it represents a violation of the personal privacy that for centuries has been regarded as appropriate for one-on-one relationships, and therefore belittles their emotional significance.

Marketing entertainment to youngsters. Since the media are replete with violent, sexually charged, and vulgar elements, their exposure to juveniles is both inadvertent and unavoidable, given the widespread access to material intended for adults. But media companies have not been satisfied with such incidental or accidental contact with underage audiences. They have actively sought them out.

In September 2000 the Federal Trade Commission accused five major conglomerates with combined annual sales of $25 billion—BMG Entertainment, EMI, Sony Music Entertainment, Universal Entertainment, and the Warner Brothers Music Group—of deliberately marketing violent and sexual content to juveniles. The FTC report[93] posed "two questions about the marketing of violent entertainment material: Do the industries promote products they themselves acknowledge warrant parental caution in venues where children make up a substantial percentage of the audience? And are these advertisements intended to attract children and teenagers? . . . For all three segments of the entertainment industry, the answers are plainly 'yes.'"

The FTC report is only one of many government-produced or -funded research projects that over the years have periodically focused congressional attention on the problems of mass-media content and its influence on children. Invariably these studies have invigorated the continuing clamor of private groups calling for the imposition of governmental controls on what the media disseminate.

The 2000 report found that while the entertainment industry had taken steps to identify content that might not be appropriate for children, the companies in those industries still routinely targeted children under seventeen in their marketing of products that their own ratings systems deemed inappropriate or that warranted parental caution because of their violent content. Marketing and media plans expressly targeted children and promoted and advertised products in media outlets most likely to reach them. Labels placed on content to discourage juvenile customers (which I discuss later) were found to be largely ignored in practice.

The report found that "most retailers make little effort to restrict children's access to products with violent content. . . . The surveys also revealed that unaccompanied children ages 13 to 16 were able to buy both explicit recordings and Mature-rated electronic games 85 percent of the time."

According to then FTC chairman Robert Pitofsky: "Companies in the entertainment industry routinely undercut their own rating restrictions by target-marketing violent films, records, and video games to young audiences."

The commission recommended further action by the industry to enhance self-regulatory efforts, but it made no legislative recommendations to Congress. It asked the industry to establish or expand trade association codes that prohibit target-marketing to children and impose sanctions for violations, and "increase compliance at the retail level by checking identification or requiring parental permission before selling movie tickets, video games, or recordings carrying labels intended to keep juveniles away." The report also urged producers to "increase parental understanding . . . by including the reasons for the rating or the label in all advertising and product packaging."

According to Chairman Pitofsky: "Because government intrusion in decisions about content raises important First Amendment concerns, self-regulation continues to be the preferred solution to problems in this area." But self-regulation in the entertainment industry has come about only because of the threat of government action that organized citizens' groups demand.

Pro-social content.   Parents' organizations, distressed by the rise in what they consider to be anti-social television programming, have clamored for broadcasters to do more on the positive side. Beginning in September 1997 the networks were required to present three hours a week of educational programming geared to children under sixteen. This rule is being treated as flexibly as it was in the days when "Amos 'n' Andy" was squeezed in under the heading of "public service."

NBC offered "N.B.A. Inside Stuff," as teaching "life lessons." It also included such educational shows as "City Guys," about urban school boys; "Hang Time," featuring a girl on a boys' basketball team; and "Saved by the Bell: The New Class." Fox offered a seven-year-old cartoon, "Bobby's World."

A Fox affiliate (WLFL) claimed in regulatory filings that episodes of "Geraldo" with such titles as "Underage and Oversexed," "Overweight Kids and Their Mothers," and "When Love Doesn't Make the Grade" were educational-instructive for children sixteen and under."[94] Other broadcasters satisfied the "educational and informational" requirement with "The Jetsons."[95] WB showed reruns of "The New Adventures of Captain Planet." MTV presented a parody of a gangsta-rap video by "Weird Al" Yankovic. In his words, "CBS said, 'Well, all of our shows are educational.' So I said, 'You know what? Now it's educational!'"[96]

Margaret Loesch of Fox Kids Worldwide insisted: "There's no sense putting on programs to educate and inform kids if kids won't watch them." But except in the case of CBS, Saturday morning educational programming did not lose audiences when it was introduced. Public broadcasting, potentially the most important way to introduce pro-social content, struggles to survive on less than $1.50 per capita annually. (The BBC gets $27.)

It is hard to conclude that government-imposed efforts to make the media a strong positive force in children's upbringing have been successful. Far greater energy and attention have been focused on the media's negative aspects.

Censorship and restrictions. On any occasion when media content arouses contention, it also becomes a matter of governmental investigation, political debate, and proposals for government action. The precious freedom of expression guaranteed by the First Amendment has never been applied literally. At every period in American history it has been restricted by the demands of public order and safety, the ordinary individual's right to immunity from scurrilous personal attack, the protection of children from corrupting influences, and the requirements of public decorum.

The eighteenth-century demand for freedom of expression was inseparable from the other requirements of political democracy. It was—and is—considered essential for unpopular opinions to be safeguarded from silencing by the prevailing majority. That principle has held up well over the past several hundred years, though it has sometimes been difficult to translate it into specifics. (The Supreme Court did not define free speech until 1919.)

Restricting expression has a long history. The rulers of society have always found certain ideas and images to be unacceptable, have punished those who articulated them, and have clamped down on their further circulation. Information that might be freely available to an elite inner circle (as in Communist dictatorships) is withheld from the masses because of its potential for political subversion. Utterances that appear threatening to the state or to established religious authorities and doctrines are not the only targets of censorship. They are difficult to disentangle from those that appear to violate the prevailing codes of propriety.

It has never been easy to distinguish outrageous political statements from outrageous statements of other kinds. This was exemplified in the trial of the "Chicago Seven" in the wake of the rioting outside the 1968 Democratic party convention. The

Yippie leaders on trial hurled expletives at the judge as a political demonstration.

Bans on unorthodox political utterances have been justified as an extension of bans on morally offensive behavior. Bans on what a regime classifies as morally offensive are more easily defended if they are invoked to protect the innocence of children. Censorship of this kind appears to have developed fairly recently in Western society. What we today consider the pornography of ancient Greek vases and Pompeian paintings, or of nineteenth-century Japanese prints, was apparently acceptable in those cultures. By contrast, throughout the Middle Ages the Roman Catholic church was fervent in its repression of heresy. Its Index of proscribed literature, a response to the iconoclastic spirit of the Reformation, was inconceivable before printing was invented.

The subsequent development of mass media brought the problem of censorship to a new level of importance. The diffusion of unacceptable thoughts was no longer limited to a literate few but affected increasingly large segments of the population, and was therefore all the more threatening to the established order. With the beginnings of film, recordings, and audio, the spread of ideas moved beyond the limits of literacy.

In recent years, in the land of the First Amendment, textbooks have been censored to eliminate references to Mickey Mouse and Stuart Little (on the theory that mice are upsetting to children), urban blacks (reinforcing stereotypes), women teachers, secretaries, and librarians (same reason), jungles (conveying a "regional bias"), owls (evoking death in some cultures), and dinosaurs (because they raise the subject of evolution, which President George W. Bush considered a debatable theory. In 2004 the word "evolution" was not permitted in Texas textbooks). Passages have been deleted from Shakespeare's *Romeo and Juliet* because of their presumed sexual allusions.[97]

There are longstanding precedents for this sort of action, including examples of self-censorship. In the 1819 edition of their fairy tales, the brothers Grimm removed "every expression inappropriate for children and stories like 'How Children Played Butcher with Each Other.'"[98] In his *Family Shakespeare,* Dr. Thomas Bowdler (1754–1825) eliminated "those expressions which can not with propriety be read aloud in the family." Years later, in 1844, in a similar vein of self-righteousness, an American, Anthony Comstock, began crusading against liquor stores. He broadened his attack on immorality in 1868, persuading Congress to pass "An Act for the suppression of trade in, and circulation of, obscene literature and articles of immoral use." As a post office official, Comstock regulated the distribution of dime novels sent through the mail.

Laws forbidding the passage of obscene and pornographic material from the postal system and other channels of distribution reduced the flow of such materials in the early twentieth century. These laws were designed to safeguard the morals of the general public rather than to protect children specifically. Custom dictated propriety in the language and visual images used in the press; court decisions barred unacceptable vocabulary in literary works like *Lady Chatterley's Lover* until they were lifted in the 1933 *Ulysses* decision. Radio broadcasting labored under the burden of its status as a federally licensed enterprise, whose valuable franchises were placed at risk by any transgression of the rules.

During the twentieth century, both judicial and administrative rulings have progressively removed obstacles to free expression. In *Roth vs. United States* (1957) the Supreme Court defined obscenity as content "utterly without redeeming social importance."[99] In *Miller vs. California* the Court decreed in 1973 that each community could set its own standards. The New York

State Regents rescinded an order to censor literary works that included passages that some groups considered offensive.

Extralegal harassment has continued, however. Vigilante groups have moved aggressively to curtail the dissemination of whatever they don't like. A prime example was the Legion of Decency, founded by Catholic clerics in 1934 and, after a period of frenzied visibility, disbanded in 1965. Yet the practice lives on. The bookseller Barnes and Noble was subjected to a boycott campaign by an anti-abortion group, Operation Rescue, which sought to prevent the distribution of art books that contained pictures of unclothed cherubs.

It has sometimes been difficult to draw the line between such grotesque instances of pressure and the legitimate demands of groups defending abused minorities. For most of the twentieth century the media shamelessly indulged in racial stereotyping and caricature. (D. W. Griffith's film *The Birth of a Nation* was perhaps the most vicious example.) With changes in racial attitudes these gave way in some instances to hypersensitivity. Occasionally media censor themselves when protests are aimed at ethnic stereotypes or slurs. Arabs protested the film *Aladdin*, so Disney dropped a lyric that went, "When they cut off your ear if they don't like your face / It's barbaric, but hey, it's home."

Consumer boycotts don't work, but pressure on advertisers often does. Historically, advertisers have wanted the largest possible audiences. I have earlier cited examples of campaigns employing titillating or gross imagery and double-entendres. But most advertisers have been highly conservative and have leaned on the television networks to control objectionable content. In October 1997, Isuzu and Weight Watchers withdrew their commercials from an ABC program, "Nothing Sacred," which aroused a handful of well-orchestrated protests from a small Catholic organization. Pressures lead to counterpressures. Bill

O'Reilly, right-wing commentator on Rupert Murdoch's Fox News Channel, called for a boycott of Pepsi-Cola products in 2003 because the company ran a commercial featuring the singer Ludacris, known for obscene and profane lyrics. After the advertiser withdrew the commercial, it faced another boycott from the Hip-Hop Summit Action Network, led by a rap producer, Russell Simmons. He pointed to the company's use of another performer, Ozzy Osbourne, also noted for his obscenities.

Special-interest groups have had occasional but limited success in suppressing particular media outlets, but they have been highly successful in activating government inquiries into larger questions of media content and its effects. This has led media industries to take collective measures of defense, designed to ward off government intervention rather than to change the content itself.

Mindful of the First Amendment, Congress has consistently sought to steer away from government-imposed controls on what media present, and has encouraged media organizations to police their own efforts. The first and most notable example of such self-regulation occurred in the film industry.

6

Labeling films

Youthful moviegoing.   Although young people are light viewers of television, they are the most avid consumers of the other channels of popular culture—music, video games, and especially the movies.

In all the entertainment media, star power has been the most important attractive force for people of all ages. When children and young people aged 8–21 are asked with whom they would like to have dinner, 50 percent name a musician or singer, 42 percent an actor, 32 percent a comedian, and 29 percent an athlete.[1] Eleven percent mention a talk show host and 5 percent a newscaster. Statesmen, scientists, and philosophers don't make the cut.

Mass enchantment has allowed performers (including professional athletes, whose stellar status is endowed by television) to demand ever greater and often outrageous compensation, secure in the knowledge that the costs will eventually be passed on to theatergoers or television advertisers (and thus on to the public in the form of higher prices for the goods it buys). The escalation of talent costs has forced the film and television industries to turn instead to comparatively inexpensive formulas—movies and television shows based on "concepts" rather than "star power."[2]

Producing feature films and television programs are closely linked enterprises, often under common ownership, using the same facilities and a common pool of talent. Television reaches larger audiences, but film carries greater glamour and prestige. A film executive: "Everyone would rather work in movies than in TV. That's where the big money is. The A-list is the movie business. In the Academy Awards, you're dealing with American gods and goddesses."

The producers of TV shows have always been alert to the trends in feature films and heavily influenced by them, though there are enormous differences in the experiences of watching movies in the theater and in the home. Feature films, as we have seen, are a staple of television and have a post-theatrical life on videocassettes and DVDs.[3] This makes their total audience far broader than in the theater. The median age of VHS renters and buyers alike is forty-one; for DVD buyers it is thirty-seven; for renters thirty-six.[4] But it is the theater box office that has dominated Hollywood's thinking.

Hollywood's fictions are a powerful source of the public's fantasies; its realities are also a major national preoccupation. As in such countries as India and the Philippines, American film actors like Ronald Reagan, George Murphy, and Arnold Schwarzenegger have easily transformed their celebrity into successful political candidacies. The success of films at the box office is often assigned higher news value than important events affecting millions of lives. Magazine covers—not just of fan magazines—are festooned with the photos of actors.

According to the *Los Angeles Times*'s astute media observer, David Shaw,

Motion picture executives say that a movie's gross seems to have become more important to the media—and as a result to their readers, viewers and listeners—than what the movie is about or whether it's any good. They also say reports on opening weekend grosses become a self-fulfilling prophecy, strongly influencing the ultimate success or failure of movies in the marketplace and—perhaps more important—shaping what kinds of movies are made. . . . Reporters say they devote time and space to box office reports because the lines between Hollywood and Wall Street have become increasingly blurred.[5]

Unlike television, which has directed its attention to young people because advertisers want them, the film industry wants them for their own sake. Younger people actually represent a declining portion of movie theater admissions. In 1980, 80 percent of the moviegoers twelve and older were under forty; by 2002 they had fallen to 67 percent.[6] This still leaves them as the overwhelming majority of the theater audience. Teenagers and young adults under twenty-four make up 18 percent of the total population but almost 40 percent of total movie theater admissions.[7] If we add those 25–34, the figures rise substantially.

If we leave out children under 12, youngsters 12–17 account for 28 percent of all movie admissions. Young adults 18–24 and 25–34 account for an additional 29 percent. These numbers jibe with the film industry's assertion that young people represent three of five admissions. This way of defining the market does not properly place in perspective the enormous difference in outlook and taste between a "young person" of twelve and one of thirty-four.

As might be expected, the highest attendance rate for theatrical films is among teenagers of high school age, 15–17, who go to the movies an average of 1.5 times a month.[8] Youngsters of 12–14 go 1.27 times a month, and those of dating age, 18–24, about once a month. The older youth group, 25–34, has a frequency of .76 times a month. These are averages, which obscure large variations and important differences between those in any age bracket who rarely go and those dedicated fans who account for a substantial part of the aggregate attendance. About a fourth of adolescents and young people 18–24 report no moviegoing at all in the past month, while about 10 percent of the teenagers and 6 percent of those 18–24 go once a week or more often.

One fourth of the youngsters 12–17 say they usually attend a film on its opening weekend, and another fourth (24 percent for the 12–14s and 30 percent for the 15–17s) say they go within the first two weeks after the opening weekend. Another one in six say they go after the second week.

The emphasis on the initial response to movies heightens the importance of avid young fans. Patrick Goldstein, a *Los Angeles Times* columnist, observes:

> The media have made the opening weekend gross so important that studios now make movies specifically designed to have those features most likely to guarantee a big opening weekend. If you have an adult movie and a movie for 15-year-old boys both opening the same weekend, the movie for 15-year-old boys will win the ballot of the box office every time. They go to more movies and they're eager to see the movie the first weekend to be able to tell their friends they've seen it. Grown-ups can wait.[9]

A film executive: "The shortest way to box office success is to appeal to adolescents. They'll go to see the same movie multiple times. Film is a fine art. Movies are a business."

Young people particularly like film comedies and attend horror films at double the average rate. Twice as many moviegoers aged 18–34 as those 35–49 say they like "vivid horror scenes" and "vivid sex scenes." They are also much more attracted to "wounding and killing scenes" and to scenes of fires, explosions, and crashes.[10]

In 2004 young people accounted for the huge box office success of actor-producer Mel Gibson's *The Passion of the Christ*. Its computer-generated special effects depicted the Crucifixion with excruciatingly protracted scenes of bloody sadism. Surveys by the film's distributors, Newmarket Films, found that much of the audience was made up of young people attracted by the reports of its gory nature. It was promoted on websites appealing to horror fans. Bob Berner, Newmarket's president, reported that "The R rating is limiting younger kids, but it is getting teens and college kids."[11]

A film studio head:

You try to reach a young audience. Much moviegoing is a dating phenomenon, so a majority of films are aimed at the younger audience. A drawback to making a picture whose primary appeal is to a younger audience is that you may lose older people, who are inclined to be more critical. The younger audience will forgive flaws. The adults read reviews, so a film better be good to attract them. Teens count for a huge percentage of the audience. There's the "If you do it, they will come" theory. Is it strictly teens? Is it teen-friendly? Reviews don't mean anything to teens.

As always, this filmmaker thinks of the audience in terms of the people who go to the theater, rather than of the much larger number of people of all ages who see movies at home. In 2004 the American public spent $10.7 billion at the box office but

$25.8 billion on home videos. And the studios garnered another $4.5 billion in fees from the television stations and networks that reached an even larger general audience. But the wider public is not the focus of the film industry's interest.

The ethos of Hollywood.   Close observers of the film business offer the same kind of critical assessment that Hollywood often makes of its own institutions and personalities in its satirical self-portrayals. In Goldstein's account, "Many of the movie people whom reporters have to deal with lie constantly and compulsively about almost everything, refuse to speak on the record about even the most routine matters and delight in anonymously circulating unflattering, damaging and often untrue rumors about their colleagues and competition."

A producer told Anita Busch, editor of the *Hollywood Reporter*, "Let me be honest with you, though that's not in my nature."[12] After Busch called a film (*Fight Club*) "exactly the kind of product that lawmakers should target for being socially irresponsible," Fox, the studio that produced the film, canceled $200,000 worth of advertising in the newspaper.[13] A *Los Angeles Times* contributor, Richard Natale, asked a studio head why a movie had done well. She answered, "Because it's a very good movie—but that's off the record." Goldstein adds, "To them truth is what makes a good story, period. They spend their days making it up as they go along."

A studio may indulge a successful director's desire to create an "art film" that is destined to be a box office flop. But even this indulgence reflects the wish to retain that director on a leash. Michael Cieply, a longtime film industry reporter, believes that "Hollywood is not so much driven by cold, hard financial calculations as by personal relationships—by hatreds, rivalries, egos, sins and crimes."[14] Yet those personal relationships beloved by gossip columnists are rarely permitted to outweigh the "financial calculations" that keep the industry flourishing. When MGM's Dore Schary sought to indulge his penchant for serious films, his rivals complained, "We used to be in the entertainment business but we have sold our souls for a pot of message."[15]

The movie moguls who founded the studio system could indulge their personal instincts. But this no longer applies, as a film executive confirms:

> This is not the day of Louis B. Mayer. There's no gut feeling any more. You're dealing with a conglomerate business. I can read a script and tell you whom it's going to appeal to. But it's not a science. The typical process is, when you green-light a picture you have the marketing people, the financial people. You have a model of whether it's going to be making money. You can't make serious pictures because they won't appeal to a young audience.

In contrast, a writer-producer for both films and television rejects the principle of targeting:

> I can honestly say I almost never think about the "audience" when I am creating a show. What I mean by that is that any assumption as to what the audience's tastes might be at any given moment in time has always seemed to me to be presumptuous and arrogant at best and foolhardy at worst. I have always approached the creation of a television show as an act of personal expression (forgive me—I *know* how pretentious that sounds), and I proceed under the assumption that if something fascinates or amuses me, there is always the slim possibility that it will fascinate or amuse someone else. I fear any greater sense of calculation will be sensed by whoever might watch and will

immediately render whatever I have tried to create unworthy of the viewer's time and attention. Besides, audience calculation has always seemed to me to be the unique province of network executives.

In his view, movies have lost their spirit and inventiveness.

There was a period in American filmmaking that began in the late sixties and ended in the early eighties that seemed to me to be filled with risk-taking. It was an exciting and breathless time to be in love with the movies and is really the reason I decided to do what I do for a living. This contrasts with television during that same period, which in general was highly formulaic and designed to be easily digestible and completely inoffensive. I do believe that since the early to mid-eighties an argument can be made that the two mediums—American mainstream films and American network television—have in fact switched positions. Movies have become "safer," more "calculated," and far less personal. Television, on the other hand, seems to me to have become more challenging, idiosyncratic, and daring.

Films and the Motion Picture Association of America. The controversy over the content of movies, its increasingly aggressive departure from traditional mores, and its effect on children has become sharper since television arrived on the scene, but it has a long history. For many years the Motion Picture Association of America (MPAA) code kept a tight lid on content. When the association was formed in 1922, Will Hays, former head of the Republican National Committee, was brought in to run it. In 1928 the first film "talkie," *Lights of*

New York, dealt with bootlegging, and in 1933, a film director, Clarence Brown, observed:

> We took the position that motion pictures should reflect American life, and cocktail parties and speakeasies were definitely part of that life. . . . It was the motion picture, showing that in spite of prohibition, liquor was an immense factor in American life, that had a great deal to do with changing sentiment on that question.[16]

But films had to satisfy the Production Code Administration of the MPAA, set up in 1934, which gave the seal of approval required to distribute a film in the nation's theaters. This imposition of censorship aroused both indignation and derision.[17]

Underlying the Code's procedure was the assumption that films attracted a family audience and that children required protection from adult depravity. But when World War II brought with it a much more mobile population, contact with foreign cultures, and a heightened level of education, thanks to the GI Bill for veterans, the accompanying changes in behavior led to demands to loosen standards. The studio heads then feared that restrictions might crumble altogether and produce a backlash in the form of government regulation.

Films that fell below the Code's threshold were thus labeled X. They either played in houses on central-city sex store strips or "combat zones," or struggled to find theaters willing to exhibit them. In later years such notable films as *Last Tango in Paris*, *Midnight Cowboy*, and *A Clockwork Orange* were rated X.[18] Although this was not the Code's original intention, the X was appropriated by makers of pornographic films.

Movie attendance plummeted when TV became the main channel of entertainment, heightening the film studios' urge to go where television did not or could not as a publicly regulated medium. Hollywood's shift in standards had a sound marketing rationale. As television grew, the theatrical film audience changed character. It consisted more and more of young people in their teens and twenties who wanted to sit in the dark on a date. Throughout the 1950s, Hollywood began to cater to their taste for the risqué, for street language, for fast action and brutal violence—elements of content that the television networks still considered unacceptable. (Hollywood pursued other strategies as well: lengthening films, going to color, widening the screen, introducing stereo sound.) The process was a spiral. As the audience became more youthful, Hollywood's productions aimed to satisfy its preferences, thereby alienating its older public. And as older people stopped going out to the movies, the audience profile became even more youthful.

Here I must distinguish again between the *theater* film audience and the audience for films. Movies became an increasingly prominent element of television programming, especially as the number of independent (non–network affiliated) stations grew. Without a feed from the networks, their air time had to be filled! The rise of the VCR further expanded the exposure of films to an adult audience outside the theater setting. The VCR also eliminated the theater showing of X-rated pornographic movies, which had enjoyed a steady growth, and shifted the viewing of these films to the home TV set. These films also found new distribution through pay-TV channels.

As this type of content became more readily available, the producers of mainline films grew more eager to test the limits of what could be released for conventional theater showings—more sexually explicit scenes, frontal nudity, vulgar language, gory and sadistic violence. These had an impact on the prevailing culture, though producers insisted they were just responding to changes in popular tastes.

The movie rating system. The film industry's Hays Office operated on a simple go/no-go procedure, though its enforcers were continually battling and negotiating with movie producers over specific elements of scripts and scenes. Under a new president, Jack Valenti, a former public relations adviser to President Lyndon Johnson, the Motion Picture Association moved away from a simple choice between accepting and rejecting a film and developed a new system for labeling it, based on its presumed fitness for children of a given age to see.

Valenti describes the situation thus:

When I became president of the Motion Picture Association of America in May 1966, the slippage of Hollywood studios' authority over the content of films collided with an avalanching revision of American mores and customs. By summer of 1966 the national scene was marked by insurrection on the campus, riots in the streets, rise in women's liberation, doubts about the institution of marriage, abandonment of old guiding slogans, and crumbling of social traditions. It would have been foolish to believe that movies, that most creative of art forms, could have remained unaffected by the change and ferment in our society. The result of all this was the emergence of a "new kind of American movie," neither amiable nor fixable.

The first issue was the film *Who's Afraid of Virginia Woolf?*, in which for the first time the word "screw" and the phrase "hump the hostess" were heard. . . . I was uncomfortable with the thought that this was just the beginning of an unsettling new era in film, in which we would lurch from crisis to crisis, without any suitable solution in sight.

The second issue . . . was the Michelangelo Antonioni film *Blow Up* . . . the first time a major distributor was marketing a film with nudity in it. . . .

Finally in April 1968 the U.S. Supreme Court upheld the constitutional power of states and cities to prevent the exposure of books and films to children that could not be denied to adults. It was plain that the old system of self-regulation, begun with the formation of the MPAA in 1922, had broken down. . . . I had sniffed the Production Code constructed by the Hays Office. There was something about this stern forbidding catalogue of "Dos and Don'ts" the odious smell of censorship. I determined to junk it at the first opportune moment.[19]

Valenti proceeded to meet with representatives of the studios, the National Association of Theater Owners (NATO), independent film distributors, and film industry professional groups. The new ratings system he introduced in November 1968 represented the motion picture industry's reluctant acceptance of its critics' premise that content had consequences.

The system provided for four categories: G (for everyone), M (for mature audiences, but with no restriction on admittance), R (restricted for children under sixteen—later raised to seventeen—except those accompanied by parents), and X (changed to NC-17 in 1990, with no one under seventeen admitted). The M label was later changed to GP and then to PG (advising Parental Guidance). In 1984 the category was split into a PG and a more restrictive PG-13. The expectation was that theater owners would restrict juvenile attendance at films labeled R, and that parents would be cautious about bringing youngsters to those rated PG-13.

In G-rated films, "some snippets of language may go beyond polite conversation, but they are common everyday expressions." The PG rating "is an alert for examination of a film by parents before deciding on its viewing by their children." This description can hardly be taken seriously. What parent would go to a movie to pass judgment on it and then come back the next day with a twelve-year-old child?

As Valenti describes it,

> The entire rostrum of the rating program rests on the assumption of responsibility by parents. If parents don't care, or if they are languid in guiding their children's moviegoing, the rating system becomes useless. . . . Indeed, if you are 18 or over, or if you have no children, the rating system has no meaning for you. Ratings are meant for parents, no one else.

The ratings themselves were and are assigned by a Rating Board of eight to thirteen members located in Los Angeles. They serve for periods of varying length and are full-time employees of the Classification and Rating Administration (CARA), which is funded by fees charged to producers and distributors. The MPAA president chooses the chairman of the Rating Board, "thereby insulating the Board from industry or other group pressure." The president and his chosen chairman of CARA select the jury of "average American parents" who assign film ratings. "There are no special qualifications for Board membership, except the members must have a shared parenthood experience."[20]

Valenti explains,

> The criteria that go into the mix which becomes a Rating Board judgment are theme, violence, language, nudity, sensuality, drug abuse, and other elements. . . . There is no special emphasis on any one of these elements. All are considered. . . . I take no part in rating decisions and do not overrule or dissuade the Board from any decisions it makes. . . . No one is forced to submit a film to the Board for rating, but the vast majority of producers/distributors do. . . . Any producer/distributor who wants no part of any rating system is free to go to the market without any rating at all

or with any description or symbol they choose as long as it is not confusingly similar to the G, PG, PG-13, R, and NC-17.

The Rating Board's decisions are subject to review by an Appeals Board, made up of one member from each of the MPAA companies plus an equal number of representatives from the National Association of Theater Owners.[21]

For twenty years (1974–1994) CARA was headed by the historian Richard D. Heffner, who testifies that "My mother didn't raise me to count nipples." He compiled a fascinating account of his experiences for Columbia University's Oral History Project.

Age-based ratings or content descriptions?   Unlike the Hays Office's censorship, which could prevent a film from being distributed, the new rating system was intended to guide parents rather than direct them. Heffner recalls, "I importuned Jack Valenti to drop the word 'code.' All we are saying is that most parents think this film should be rated G or PG or whatever. A code implies that you may not do this, and that doesn't apply."

By Heffner's account, "There were so many things done to fool the public. I stayed all those years out of arrogance, thinking that I could be a little Dutch boy with my hole in the dike and that I could outsmart them."

Heffner learned that "In Hollywood, the bottom line is *always* the bottom line." His continuing struggle with Valenti centered on his insistence that the real purpose of the rating system was to supply parents with the information they needed to make their own judgments rather than with only a simple designation.

He says he was driven by the urge to

give parents real information about the films their kids are going to see. . . . What is really at stake here is the question of the workability, the validity, the real potential of voluntarism in a country like ours that is driven by the profit motive. . . . You had to explain something about the *reasons* the Board put those ratings on those films. Otherwise it was meaningless.

Heffner estimated that including explanations along with the ratings would add only $20,000 to $40,000 a year to CARA's multi-million-dollar budget. In his view, "Jack had always double-talked his way around that whole business, saying, 'You couldn't give *sufficient* information, so don't give any information at all.' . . . His objective was not to have change at all; no change."

The studios' advertising and publicity people were leery of offering explanations that did not match their marketing strategy.

If they were trying to push a film, publicize a film—because they thought this is the only way to sell it—in terms of it's being the hottest, sexiest film ever made, and we came along and offered the reason for the rating of that film as "Language" (and didn't talk about the sexuality because we didn't think that lowered the film to the level of R), we would screw up their publicity and promotion plans.

As one film executive wrote, "An expanded rating system is likely to hurt the motion picture business . . . rather than help it. . . . Continued research into the ratings area can only lead to a 'no-win' situation, at least from a business point of view."[22]

Valenti opposed explanations for X-rated films, though he finally acceded to explanations of violence but not of sex. As Heffner describes it, "At the studios, the chieftains were quite willing to accept the rating explanations. . . . But it was their ad people, their marketing people, who put the kibosh on it."

Pressure from theater owners in 1979 and 1980 led to an experiment in areas of Kansas and Missouri in which ratings were accompanied by explanations. An evaluation of the experiments, based on a survey, led to the conclusion that "as parents became more familiar with the availability of this information, they would avail themselves of it. They would become more aware of it as time went on. And . . . hateful, hateful, hateful—they would use this information, probably, to keep their children from going to see certain movies."

In 1990, explanations for the rating on a particular film were introduced, "available to the parents at the theater (by telephone or at the box office), in certain media reviews and listings." (It also appeared later on the MPAA's website home page.) The X category (mistakenly identified as pornographic, though it was also applied to other types of objectionable content) was later re-named NC-17.[23] Explanations, to which Valenti objected, were finally introduced in 1994 for the small number of films in this category.

Going for PG-13. Valenti concluded from a survey that "Even though parents know that they have lost control over their children, they want to believe that they have put forth their best efforts in advising their children." That was his guiding principle for the rating system.

Since the present system began in 1968, movie violence and vulgarity have increased enormously. A third of the films that year were rated G, though a few years earlier almost all movies were aimed at a general family audience. Hollywood's output shifted in short order to the more restrictive categories. Of 786 feature films rated in 2002, 4 percent were G, 9 percent PG, 19 percent PG-13, and 69 percent R. One received an NC-17 rating. Of 2002's 20 top-performing films, 13 were PG-13 and none of the other 7 were rated R.

The Rating Administration was involved in a continuing struggle with producers eager to get the label that would guarantee maximum ticket sales. Battles arose as the filmmakers strove to avoid both the G rating (with its implication that the film was directed to children) and the NC-17 (which implied that its content might be excessively offensive). Elements of content were eliminated or added during shooting or in post-production in order to get the rating that the producers assumed would best fit their marketing plans.

In Heffner's telling,

> Valenti said, "We have got to get stronger material into our films because TV is competing with us." He wanted our ratings to be softer and more permissive. There's harsher material in film now, particularly in unrestricted ratings—G, PG, and PG-13. They're unrestricted because all you're saying is that some parents may consider it unsuitable.

PG-13 quickly became the studios' most sought-after rating, with its suggestion that a film is sufficiently daring to be unsuitable for those younger than the teenagers who make up a disproportionate share of theater audiences.

Heffner reports that Valenti first wanted to make PG-13 a restricted rating, then put out a release saying it would not be. PG-13 "ultimately was a way of getting restricted films out of the restricted area."

Before PG-13 was introduced, Valenti wrote: "Joel Resnick, president of NATO . . . and his colleagues believe that implementing a no-admission policy would be too difficult a daily task for theater owners to diligently monitor."

According to the *New York Times*'s Hollywood correspondent, Bernard Weinraub, "the unspoken rule is that a PG-13 film may contain one four-letter word, so long as it's not used in a sexual way. A PG-13 is now almost slavishly sought after."[24] A film researcher agrees: "Producers really want the coveted PG-13. It opens it a little wider. When they make a decision about a movie, they'll try for that rating."

Ratings inevitably require subjective judgments of a film in its totality rather than arbitrary quotas of specific scenes or incidents.

Heffner points out that "seconds go by slowly on the screen. They drag by. So even if you say something is only five seconds, it still can contain a lot of content . . . violence, sex, or whatever."

The desensitization that psychologists have observed in laboratory experiments seemed to be working in the case of the Rating Board. According to Heffner,

> the Board got brainwashed . . . by generally seeing too much of this violence, and by seeing individual violent films too often. . . . Interesting, the more sex you'd see in a movie, I think it was quite clear that they [the Board] got touchier and touchier about it. The more violence they saw in a movie, I think the more they could and would accept the violence without thinking, "My God, this is too strong!"

A top television and film studio executive offers a very clear analysis of why and how films are doctored to fit a restricted label:

> The preteens want to be teens, and the teens want to be adults. The adventure of seeing an R film is intriguing to them. There's no possibility of controlling it, and yet everybody pays lip service to it.
>
> There are no X-rated films these days, or even NC-17. They go unrated. The classification [NC-17] exists, but no one releases pictures under that label. There's a picture out now called *Irreversible*—the most violent, sado-masochistic picture I have ever seen, and it's unrated. PG-13 was invented by [the director-

producer Steven] Spielberg and Valenti. The studios release a lot of pictures under the label of PG-13, when in the past a lot of them might have been rated R.

He reiterates the point that content is altered to get the right kind of rating attached to it. "Studios will fight if they have an R and revise the film so it gets a PG-13 label. Certain pictures are so explicit sexually or so violent, and the studios tweak them down to fit under the PG-13 umbrella." In short, the creative integrity of a film's writers and directors must give way to marketing requirements.

When we did [a film with strong appeal to children], we didn't want it to go out as a G because it would sound too soft. If you don't want a picture to be perceived as strictly for family audiences—which will drive off the teens—insert something to make it PG-13. We know that artists like [the director Martin] Scorsese don't compromise. Others will never make an R-rated picture because the potential box office [in PG-13] is greater than an R. The broadest-appeal pictures are in the PG-13 area. You're shaving off part of the audience by going to an R. Generally G pictures will lose the teenagers. Seventy percent or two-thirds of the admissions are the under-25 group. [As we have seen, this is an overstatement and a misperception, but it seems to be widely held by those in the business.] The dating teens are the frequent moviegoers. That's why the summer is geared to that audience. You release your strong product geared to that audience. Memorial Day to Labor Day is 40 percent of the business.

Another producer-director makes the same point:

In theatrical films, particularly those financed by a major studio, it is almost always a contractual point that you are making a film that *must* receive a specified rating (PG-13 or R in the case of the films I have been involved with) and that failure to do so puts you in breach. In this sense, the composition of the audience, and by extension, the content of the film, is predetermined by the contracts negotiated before the script is written or the film is shot.

Research indicates that the more "inclusive" the rating, the greater potential audience size. It is interesting to note, however, that of all the "inclusive" ratings (G, PG, PG-13), the one that seems to be the most desirable is PG-13. Could it be that this is because while it allows anyone who wants to to see the film, it suggests that there may be material that isn't suitable for everyone? The lesson here: Nothing sells like forbidden fruit, as long as you're allowed to buy the fruit you're forbidden.

Robert Towne, who wrote the script for *Chinatown*:

If we weren't doing an R-rated film, we weren't going to reach the audience we wanted—the audience that would make the film a success. We were getting audiences away from the television to go out and see something they couldn't see at home. These films had adult content. Now you're absolutely under pressure to make PG-13 films.[25]

Does a film's box office success depend on its rating? The question is tricky. As a film researcher explains,

By definition, films rated less than R, especially G-rated films, attract more child admissions and therefore yield a lower average ticket price than R films. Thus if you have an R-rated film that grossed $50 million at the box office, and a G-rated film that grossed $50 million at the box office, there is a very good chance that the G-rated film yielded 10 to 20 percent more admissions—provided the G-rated film was not adult-themed, if such a thing is possible.

An independent film producer contends that "The Rating Board is far more tolerant of violence than of sex."

Heffner thinks the presence of sex has already reached its high point. "The violence is going to get worse because that's the area where they can trump themselves. What can you do with sex when you have already gone to Paree? With violence you can never end the escalation."

An independent film producer: "I would be for censorship if I could do the censoring. There's a discriminatory factor. The studios get away with things that independents won't, especially at the Appeals Board level, because they have the clout."

A film producer insists that filmmakers are sensitive to popular tastes: "There are people in the media who really strike out and become prominent because they have the pulse of the population. If you don't keep up, if you're not in tune, you're just out of it."

Negotiating ratings. Heffner provides a concrete example of how content is deliberately debased so that it will be rated more restrictively.

> We all voted G for *Chariots of Fire*. And I called [the producer] Alan Ladd, told him that he was the proud possessor of a G rating, and he tells me that therefore they're changing something, so don't give it a rating, and they will resubmit in another form. And I tell him, "I just hope they're not going to add stuff for the sake of getting a PG." But that's what they did.

David Puttnam, the studio head, wrote angrily to Heffner:

> The film *Chariots of Fire*, contains the expletives "hell" and "bloody hell" three times in its opening three reels, and in addition a reverse shot of a naked male and two slow-motion action shots of runners taking appalling falls. One would have

hoped that these would be enough to qualify the film for a PG, and that it would have been unnecessary to arbitrarily add the word "shit" in an entirely gratuitous way in order to achieve that rating. You will be better versed than I in the rationale as to how a G rating can adversely affect an adult picture.

Heffner wrote back,

Do you really mean to suggest that my Rating Board colleagues and I should have told a flagrant untruth to our constituents, American parents of movie-age youngsters? . . . That we should have warned parents to exercise Parental Guidance when we believed they needn't, but rather could take even their youngest children to see this splendid production without the concerns that of necessity accompany most moviegoing today?

Heffner wrote of a 1981 film, *Lion of the Desert*,

A few scenes of particularly strong, particularly graphic violence do add too much for a PG. Like the tanks rolling over and squashing the blood out of people crushed beneath them. Like the men shot in their heads. Like villagers graphically executed in a manner that just hasn't entered the PG classification before. Like the knife thrust into an officer's belly. For good or for bad, we bend over backward in war pictures, as perhaps we clearly do in James-Bondish pictures, not to apply our R rating too quickly. In the one, war is clearly hell; in the other, perhaps one could say that fantasy is fantasy.

But the Appeals Board voted to change the rating to PG. On another occasion an R was given to a nudist-colony film which, Heffner thought, looked

like life in a penile colony. . . . Six months later we got another nudist-colony film, only this time it's not only all hanging out but it's being used vigorously. Every sexual organ around the place. And naturally we said X. The guy said, "You can't give us an X. You gave an R to that other film that had all that nudity in it." And it's that kind of thinking, that level of thinking, that contaminates the atmosphere. I guess it does wherever the only thing really at issue is the buck.

In one interesting episode, Michael Winner, the producer of *Death Wish*,

> kept insisting that we *couldn't* give it an X; it had to be an R because his first film was an R. Jerry Weintraub [the agent] has been very important over the years in getting the stars he represents, the singers, the musicians he represents, and others too, to "perform" for politicians for whom Valenti wants to do favors, so that in turn he can curry favor with them. His job is to get legislation passed, or avoided. And you do that by making friends of these people in Congress, state legislators and governors, etc. And the way you can help them out, scratch their backs, is to get artists who will give concerts for them, raising funds for them or "servicing" them in other ways.

Valenti insisted that Heffner go to see Weintraub at his home about *Cruising*. "Billy Friedkin [the director] insists, . . . 'I know it's X, but we have to have an R or else.'"

In a phone conversation taped by Valenti, Weintraub says of Heffner, "I'm going to blow this fucking son of a bitch right out of the water. This guy is playing around with my livelihood. He's playing with dynamite. I'm going to put Mr. Heffner away." Valenti called Heffner in the middle of the night to play back the tape.

Frank Price, head of Columbia, seeking a PG for *Blue Lagoon*,

> sent along at least one letter from a psychologist who said the kids screwing was "healthy love" and nothing sordid about it.

And there *wasn't* anything sordid about it. It was quite lovely. Whether it was the boy masturbating or the nude scene prior to the sex scene between the two of them, all very lovely, but not, in most parents' thinking, to be available to kids of *any* age at all. We gave it an R.

Heffner continues:

Having a rule that was so rigid that it had to be overturned could take us out of the situation of looking at each thing particularistically. . . . When Woody Allen used the word "fuck" in *The Front* at the end of the film, in the context of that film [about the effects of Hollywood's political blacklist in the 1950s] the word could be accepted in PG. The film didn't have to be made R. But now the industry had created a larger context of its own, a context in which film after film after film (as if the rule was that you *had* to have "fuck" in a PG-rated film) was throwing the word in and creating a context in which I finally said "enough is enough."

Heffner suggested an X for "shit like *Frankenhooker*" and films like *Life Is Cheap . . . but Toilet Paper Is Expensive*, a Wayne Wang "classic."

Studios' battles, lost at the Rating Board, were sometimes won on appeal to their colleagues on the Appeals Board. An extremely violent film, *King of New York*, given an X, was defended by a psychologist who worked in a large inner-city hospital where 60 percent of the patients were being treated for drugs or gunshot wounds. She said, "It's a perfect picture of urban life," objectionable only to "nice, white, middle-class Midwest families." The Appeals Board changed the rating to R.

Some of the arguments centered on the issue of whether a film's eventual outcome outweighed the social derelictions it portrayed sympathetically. In *Nine to Five* (starring Jane Fonda), this group of funny and nice gals, as a matter of course, were smoking pot at lunch. You can't tell me that doesn't legitimate that value. . . . What should the Rating Board have done about that film's drug use? Was it "gratuitous"? To me . . . absolutely. What else? But not to the film's creative people. Was "redemption" there? I didn't see it, did you? . . . What about all those other films being discussed now where the filmmaker cries out "Redemption! Redemption!" . . . but we say, "Bullshit!"

Carl Gottlieb, a screenwriter: "A big opening weekend . . . requires explosions, shattering glass, exploitative nudity, and a lesbian scene that the lead actress can talk about on Leno [the late-night talk-show host]."[26]

The application of the MPAA ratings scheme has become steadily more permissive, leading to what Kimberly Thompson and Fumie Yokota of Harvard's School of Public Health term "ratings creep." Comparing the content of films in each rating category in 1993 and 2003, they report that "today's movies contain significantly more violence, sex, and profanity than movies of the same rating a decade ago."

Given the history of the current movie ratings system, it comes as no surprise that four of five parents polled say they do not trust it. One in five say they "completely trust" it.[27]

Although administering the system is no easy task, movie producers find it no less of a headache. A top studio executive:

I think [the rating system] is kind of effective. It's a warning system for people who are involved with their children. There are probably a minority of people in middle America who do use it. It doesn't work at the theater level because you're dealing with multiplexes with fourteen or sixteen theaters, and policing it is impossible. A kid can buy a ticket for one show and go in to see another. In the big cities it's almost impossible.

This observation receives confirmation from the 2000 Federal Trade Commission report, which found that just under half the movie theaters admitted children aged thirteen to sixteen to R-rated films even when not accompanied by an adult.

A film producer believes, however, that controls are getting tighter at the theater end: "There was a time when an R rating meant nothing. Now it does mean something. When a kid tries to get in, he's turned away. In New York they're checking IDs at the box office. A lot of films that would have been rated R are now being re-edited to get a PG-13." But at the other end of the scale, he also agrees that "dicey elements are introduced into films that might otherwise merit a G. PG-13 is the holy grail."

A film industry researcher agrees that theaters are tightening up:

> It used to be easier for kids to get tickets for an R-rated film, but there's been more control in the last three or four years. Kids have found different ways of getting in. They get someone older to buy a ticket, or they buy a ticket for another show in the same multiplex and go into the one they want to see. X means what was PG-13. It opens up the appeal so that kids don't feel they're going to a baby-rated film. With an R-rated movie you're limiting access. With PG-13 anyone and everyone can get in. A lot of parents take their eleven-year-olds to a PG-13. Anything that's rated G, you need some kind of pedigree. If it's made by Disney or Pixar, parents feel they can trust it. Where you get into a problem with Gs is if the story isn't appealing. PG is still available to the teens.
>
> You can ask people what the ratings are of some movies and they won't know unless they come to the box office. They all know that animated movies are G-rated.

Organized protest only arouses the curiosity of the youthful audience. "Some groups censor themselves. Church groups send out flyers warning their members about certain films. If they condemn a film, it can bring crowds to the box office."

When violence, foul words, and bedroom scenes are routinely introduced to lower the rating rather than to advance the plot or delineate character, the reason is simple: there is a payoff at the box office. Sit through the previews—"Approved for All Audiences"—of coming attractions in any movie theater. What does the exercise of film craft have to do with their often-displayed brutality and licentiousness?

The transformation of Hollywood's output over the past thirty years had complex origins, which I have already reviewed. But the film-rating system played its own part in modifying standards of speech and behavior, dangling the prospect of forbidden fruit before a youthful audience.

High school students faced with a fictitious set of movie titles and plot synopses showed the same levels of interest regardless of what MPAA rating was attached.[28] But when it comes to the acid test, any teenager can testify that it's simply not cool to see a film rated less than R.

The film rating system opened the way for content to be de based intentionally to gain the label that assures maximum appeal to the young audience—the movie business's principal target.

The former head of a major film studio:

The motion picture code boils down to a very simple thing. It's a defensive measure by the business to head off efforts by states or localities to censor films. If you have a board in Chicago and another in New Orleans, it would be a nightmare. So a national code was adopted, and it has generally worked to hold off what would be an impossible situation. It's made it possible to have national distribution. There has always been a lot of fussing about the Motion Picture Association ratings. And they've been modified. There was a whole thing about the X rating. Harvey Weinstein used it very well to get some free newsprint and not spend so much on advertising. That was changed to NC-17 by Spielberg. X was generic. The suits [that is, the business office] were coming against it. NC-17 was more specific.

There have been various effects, but they change every time. The G rating was once considered the kiss of death. It meant it was a boring picture. So throw in one or two bad words or some violent action and make it a PG. Probably the same thing still applies. With the teen audience, they have less interest in a G. Even the preteens. If you add something to a film that might be G rated, it will be more popular. With [a film version of a popular Broadway musical] we thought it would have a G rating, so we changed it to make it a PG. We were looking at how we attract the maximum audience to it. If G carries the connotation of boring, you avoid that at all costs. There are times when you wrestle with something. There can be a big commercial difference between a PG-13 and an R. It does have some impact. If you had a picture where you add a word or two or a scene where a change would get you a PG-13 rather than an R, you would trim this or that.

A producer who has worked both in films and television suggests that

In television there was a history of regulation, a concern with public-interest criteria that was always lurking in the background. That was never true in Hollywood. The people who created it came from the garment industry and grew up without that sense of public interest, convenience, and necessity. Can you have regulation of content without censorship? I don't know.

A film industry observer: "As long as one can make two bucks instead of one buck by being crude, it will be done. Voluntarism doesn't work. What isn't the answer is 'hands off.'" Yet "hands off" may well be the best solution.

Of the forty-four movies rated R for violence in the FTC's 2000 study, four of five were targeted to children under seventeen. Two-thirds of the marketing plans expressly stated that children were the films' target audience. Plans for the other one-fifth of the movies were extremely similar.

In their quest for the juvenile audience, the film studios have routinely tested children's reactions to their products, including those with patently unsuitable content. Three-fourths of the R-rated films had been test-screened for children as young as nine. Commercials and promotional trailers were also tested among children.

The FTC report cited the research plan prepared for an R-rated film (*I Know What You Did Last Summer*) by the National Research Group, which does much of the major studios' testing: "Attendance at the original dipped down to the age of 10. Therefore it seems to make sense to interview 10- to 11-year-olds." (Actually the survey sample also included nine-year-olds.) One film promotion commercial tested among teenagers featured "a needle toward clamped eye." A research memo reports that "the standout scene continues to be the blonde hitting her head into the mirror."[29] A report on the test of another film: "Scenes liked most: Chief justice dies in front of Blind Justice statue. Former chief justice dies. Hanging with cannibals. First judge saves Dredd from cannibals."[30]

After the publication of the FTC report, the MPAA said its new goal was "not inappropriately specifically targeting children" in promoting R-rated films. The industry seems to have acted accordingly.

In its 2001 follow-up report, the commission checked the studios' marketing plans for six violent R-rated films and three violent PG-13-rated films and found no evidence that their marketing was aimed at children. Teen magazines carried no ads for R-rated movies. Three of four film websites (among thirty-four examined) displayed the films' ratings, and almost all of them provided the reasons. The FTC's conclusion was that the motion picture and electronic game industries had "made some progress both in limiting advertising in popular teen media and in providing rating information in advertising."

The commission's review found that rating icons and descriptors in the print ads were often smaller than the industry code requires; that television ads never included the content descriptors; that only a little more than half the websites reviewed displayed the rating clearly and conspicuously; and that just one-fourth displayed the content descriptors anywhere on the site.[31]

But the problem of film marketing to juveniles is not just a matter of placing icons in ads. It lies in the changed nature of the films themselves. In this respect, films have been the bellwether for other media.

7

Labeling television

Testing the limits. Film, like the press, is essentially an unregulated industry. The broadcast media, on the other hand, acquire their enormously lucrative franchises from the government and are therefore subject to rules set by the Federal Communications Commission. Until 2004, violations of these rules had rarely been treated severely. Between 2001 and 2003 the FCC issued only 17 warning notices to stations, though it received a quarter-million complaints in 2003 alone. In 2004, after receiving 200,000 viewer protests (many perhaps organized by right-wing clerics), the FCC announced an investigation of a well-publicized episode at the halftime break of the Super Bowl football game, in which a performing partner bared one breast of the singer Janet Jackson. The broadcasters responded heroically to this outrageous revelation (described ingeniously as a "wardrobe malfunction" and later celebrated in at least one St. Patrick's Day parade poster as "Thanks for the mammaries!"). They introduced five- or ten-second delays in airing such spontaneous occasions as the Grammy awards and Nickelodeon's children's show "U-Pick Live." NBC eliminated a hospital drama's brief display of the breast of an eighty-year-old woman dying of cancer.[1] An Indianapolis radio station removed the words "urinate" and "orgy" from a broadcast by the right-wing commentator Rush Limbaugh.

The furor over the Super Bowl caper led to a $550,000 fine against CBS by the FCC and to the introduction of legislation to punish "indecency." One, the Clean Airways Act, passed by the House of Representatives 391 to 22 and supported by the White House, would raise the maximum fine from $27,500 to $500,000 for holders of broadcast licenses, and from $11,000 to $500,000 for entertainers. A Senate bill added violence to the punishable offenses, thereby ensuring that this election-year legislation would go nowhere. But the Senate did pass a "Defense of Decency" Act on the same day that Vice President Dick Cheney told Senator Patrick Leahy, "Fuck yourself!"

Some time before the Jackson incident, the FCC had declined to press charges when the singer Bono repeatedly used the word "fucking" as he accepted the award for "best song" in a live NBC airing of the Golden Globe awards. (The commission noted that the term was employed "fleetingly" as an adjective and not as a verb.) NBC's expression of regret for the incident came a year later, only after the subject of "indecency" had become a congressional preoccupation. After the FCC backtracked and ruled that the Bono episode violated standards of decency (though it did not impose a fine), the network and other broadcasting organizations invoked the First Amendment and petitioned for yet another reversal.

The commission had never fined or suspended a television station's license because it was charged with indecency, though it had acted in a few cases involving radio. In the wake of the 2004 Super Bowl episode on television, the giant radio chain Clear Channel paid a negotiated fine of $1.75 million because of a broadcast by "shock jock" Howard Stern that dealt with anal sex.

Before then the FCC's fines had usually been mere love taps. In 1988 it had fined Stern's WXRK radio show in New York $7,000 after his Christmas show featured "lesbians filled with lust." It once levied a fine of $35,000 against WQAM, Miami, for airing songs that were "lewd, inescapable, and understandable." In 2001, Emmis Communications, the owner of WKQX, Chicago, was fined $21,000 for carrying skits on pedophilia, incest, and masturbation.

A more powerful institution was involved in another landmark case. In 2002 the FCC levied a $375,000 fine against Viacom's Infinity Broadcasting's WNEW-FM, New York, after it broadcast a live report of a couple having sex in the vestibule of St. Patrick's Cathedral in New York City. Infinity fired its "shock radio" stars, Gregg Hughes and Anthony Cumia, who had engineered this exploit, but they later quietly returned to the air. *Radio and Records'* Al Peterson asked, "If it had happened in a subway, would anyone have noticed? Remember, this was the third year of this contest."

Those are rare instances. The commission and its staff, with a workload that is barely manageable, have generally gone easy on violators of "decency" standards, leaving enforcement to individual station managements.[2] Radio talk-show host Bob Grant was fired by WABC, New York, after he said of Commerce Secretary Ron Brown, whose plane had crashed, "My hunch is that he is the one survivor. . . . Maybe because, at heart, I'm a pessimist." Hired by New York's WOR-AM two weeks later, he referred to the city's black mayor, David Dinkins, as "the men's room attendant." Another talk-show personality, Doug Tracht, of WARW, Washington, said of a hip-hop artist, "No wonder people drag them behind cars"—referring to the notorious killing of a black man in Texas who was pulled behind a pickup truck.

Censure of such transgressions is much more likely to come from private individuals and organizations than from government. Arbitrary political criteria are often invoked to determine what content is offensive. In television, the Cartoon Network withheld twelve Bugs Bunny cartoons from a planned broadcast of the complete series because they showed what were presumed to be stereotypical or derogatory stereotypes of blacks, Indians, Eskimos, or Japanese. (French, Italian, and Irish caricatures remained.) Cartoon characters shown smoking were eliminated from other broadcasts. Such politically correct sensitivities have had no parallel in the handling of violence, language, and sex.

Television and the V-chip.   Between 1950 and 1982, two-thirds of all television stations pledged adherence to the code of the National Association of Broadcasters, which committed them to "advancement of education and culture," responsibility toward children and the community, and the upholding of general program standards. (It also restricted the amount of time devoted to commercials and promos.) In 1982 the FCC forced the code to be abandoned on the grounds that it represented collusion. The networks' offices of standards were left to pass judgment on content. That task steadily became more difficult. As the boundaries of propriety were loosened in film, they were also tested in television. The big three television networks, which for years had held 90 percent of the prime-time broadcast audience, were challenged by effective competition from cable channels whose staple content was feature films. These received only mild forms of censorship. Television program production had largely moved to Hollywood and had been integrated with feature-film production, employing many of the same actors, writers, directors, and producers. The growth of multi-media conglomerates accelerated this process.

A former leading film and TV executive:

[Movies and TV] are two different industries. There are areas of overlap. But the GPs [general practitioners] in each of those businesses are exclusive to that business. They're either making motion pictures or they're making TV shows. At the time of the three networks and the separate motion picture studios, you had two distinct businesses. What could get on in motion picture theaters wouldn't get on TV. Language could be used, more violence and sexual scenes. They could be edited for TV, but it wasn't the original. Then came cable TV, which started buying theatrical films and running them unchanged.

One reason why theatrical films could put in more language or sex or violence was that they had to give the audience something they couldn't see on the home screen. It was a sales advantage as well as a creative advantage. Now comes cable and HBO, and they start putting on the pictures and competing for the theatrical audience. The movie audience was not cut down; they just started slicing it up. Then the movie business started going still further. It was a cycle, a spiral. One of the solutions of commercial TV was to become much more accepting of sexual scenes and situations because they couldn't compete on the violence. [Because it's more expensive to produce?] Yes, because of the money. Sex they could do; it isn't expensive to produce, so you can do it in a sitcom. It reaches the point where you have done all you can do, and you try to make the best pictures you can, but it's hard to bring people in without shock value.

Both films and television programs were vigorously promoted with commercials and promotional announcements that invariably selected the most violent elements of content; these were larded into otherwise inoffensive programming. As the changing rules of conduct depicted in feature films gradually worked their way into television, daytime soap operas became ever more open in their depiction of amorous intrigues, and incest and masturbation became acceptable subjects for prime-time comedy.

It did not take long for such changes in the definition of what is permissible to generate public displays of disapproval, as manifested in the opinion surveys I have already summarized. Such attitudes were quickly translated into organized opposition. Growing pressure in Congress led to the adoption in 1996 of certain restrictive provisions in the Telecommunications Act, which President Clinton announced he would veto unless it provided for a new piece of technology, already pioneered in Canada.[3]

Starting in 1998, all new television sets have been equipped—at added cost—with a silicon "V" (for violence) chip that allows parents to eliminate children's access to unsuitable programs. Although it was mandatory for all new television sets to include the V-chip, few owners of existing sets chose to install them. Appliance retailers did not advertise that the sets they sold contained a chip, because consumers didn't care.

The use of the chip depended on a system of labels that could activate electronic triggers to block out selected kinds of shows. The 1996 act carried the threat of an FCC-run rating system if the industry's own labels were unsatisfactory. As a result of this law, TV, already regulated by the FCC and periodically under the scrutiny of congressional inquiries into violence, was the first medium after film to introduce a rating system of its own.

That rating system, adopted by most of the broadcast and cable networks in 1996, derived from the familiar terms used by the Motion Picture Association of America. They are age-suitability designations: TV-Y for programs that are deemed acceptable for children of all ages, and TV-Y7 for children of seven and over. There are also TV-G (all ages), TV-PG (parental guidance suggested), TV-14 (unsuitable for those under fourteen), and TV MA ("mature audiences," a euphemism for unbridled mayhem and lechery).

The labels closely followed the criteria established within the film industry. Given the intimate relationship of film and TV producers, it seemed natural that MPAA's president, the golden-tongued Jack Valenti, should become the television industry's spokesman on this subject. He chaired the industry task force that negotiated the labeling agreement.

When the television rating system was proposed, Richard Heffner and Charles Champlin (a former *Los Angeles Times* arts editor) addressed the TV industry's claims that ratings would "drive away advertisers and turn off viewers." They recalled that Valenti "similarly stonewalled against more information about content in the film rating system on the specious ground of 'creating confusion,' similarly for the same reason, that it might turn away customers."[4]

Heffner and Champlin attacked Valenti's "trial balloons" and "calculated leaks," which "imply strongly that the TV rating system will be like the movie rating system. . . . It is an ingenious plot—innocence by association." They pointed out that the film exhibitors had been the enforcers of the rating system and that no such protection at the box office would exist for television. "The movie rating system works because it is driven not by altruism but by the specter of imposed censorship. Yet since they were adopted in 1968, the ratings have led to heavier doses of violence, sex, and hair-curling language. There is every chance that the TV rating system will have the same effect." Indeed it has!

The broadcasters accepted the V-chip and the labels because, as one of them puts it, of their "overriding concern that [they] obtain the ATV [advanced or digital] spectrum free and quickly." But the acceptance was accompanied by overwhelming skepticism, which persists to the present day. Media tycoon Barry Diller said the ratings "will prove too unwieldy to succeed. . . . It can't work." NBC's programming genius, Brandon Tartikoff, said it would drive the best writers and producers "away from free, over-the-air TV and over to pay cable."

The broadcasters initially opposed the V-chip on First Amendment grounds, pointing out that voluntary controls of the sort that they have since set up could be a precursor of censorship. But they gave way to overwhelming political pressures. As Ted Turner put it at the 1996 White House meeting where program labeling was announced, "We are voluntarily having to comply. We're either going to do it or we're going to be done for." Turner thought the V-chip would make television more bland. "It's going to result in more Brady-Bunch-type programming." These assessments did not change after the chip and the ratings were introduced.

A veteran television executive: "The V-chip is the greatest waste of time and money in the history of the world, next to the Star Wars project."

A pay cable TV executive: "Nobody pays attention to the labels, and nobody uses the V-chip. There's a well-educated moral minority for whom the V-chip is important. It's well intentioned. In the inner-city schools even interaction between parents and teachers is nonexistent, so how do you expect controls to work?"

Professionals within the television business are uniformly doubtful that the V-chip and content labels have had any influence on viewing habits or programming content.

A high-level film and television executive thinks that while film ratings serve a purpose, it is a mistake to label television:

I believe in the [film] rating system because it serves those parents who care and who need advice. Valenti was brilliant for inventing the rating system, which replaced what was censorship [by the Hays Office]. It protects American prudery and also American attitudes toward violence, which are highly permissive. I think it's enormously effective in advising parents in a very disparate society where everybody's values are not the same as mine. Enforcement is another issue. The theaters are lax. I didn't believe in adopting it for TV because I feel that [the long-standing network] television standards were more effective than the ratings. They had the social effects we wanted. The parents know what they must control.

Deciding how to rate.   Until he retired in 2004, Valenti still chaired the TV Parental Guidelines Overnight Monitoring Board, which receives questions and complaints about individual shows. The board has twenty-four members, including six from the cable industry, six from the broadcasters, and six from "the creative community." The remainder are drawn from outside the industry itself, from child advocacy, medical, religious, and educational organizations.

While panels of parents from outside the movie industry assign the film ratings, the TV networks rate their own programs, using their individual—and different—criteria. The labeling icons are applied to specific programs by their producers; even Valenti expressed doubts that ratings assigned by program producers and distributors would carry credibility. Robert Gould of the National Coalition on Television Violence called this "the fox guarding the chickens." But who else is equipped to handle the formidable assignment of rating two thousand daily hours of television programming, not including sports and news?[5] By contrast, MPAA film ratings are made by a jury that rates an average of two films a day.

When the television rating system was first proposed, the MPAA wanted to limit it to labeling by age groups. As in the case of feature films, Valenti objected to any coding by content. He cited a Peter Hart survey which showed that parents "overwhelmingly" approve an age-based system, though there was apparently no effort made to inquire about their reactions to content descriptions.

The American Psychological Association and twenty-six other professional organizations insisted on content, rather than age limits, as the labeling criterion. Before the rating procedure was set in motion, a Roper survey for the Media Studies Center[6] showed that 73 percent of parents preferred content labels and only 15 percent wanted age labels. Seventy-two percent of parents (and, curiously, 62 percent of adults in households without children) said they were "likely" to use the V-chip to block out certain programs.[7]

Three of four parents preferred a labeling system that would allow *them*, rather than the industry, to judge the suitability of programs for their children. Presumably that would mean giving them a considerable amount of detailed information— far more than either the exigencies of programming or the realities of parental control would make practicable. Before the V-chip was introduced in the United States, a series of small-scale experiments in Canada had indicated that parents were uncertain whether the broadcasters' standards would match their own.

How much information about a program can the public reasonably be expected to use? Tim Collings, one of several who claim to have invented the V-chip, has tested a complex system that scores violence, sex, and language for each program on a six-point scale. This, he believes, would make it easier for parents to customize the selection of programs to be blocked out. But does the average parent have both the will and the skill to master the procedure for doing all this?[8]

While the industry resisted anything but the "clear and simple" age-based system, child-advocacy organizations considered the age labels an inadequate guide for parents and insisted on more specific identifiers for offensive content. The advocacy groups charged that the TV industry preferred to keep the rating standards *un*clear in order to avoid losing viewers. The groups wanted to label programs TV-PG if they contained words like "damn" or "hell," if they included "punching, shoving, or comic/slapstick violence," or "mild sexual interactions" like hugging and kissing. The networks argued that this would restrict some of their most popular sitcoms.

In the end, Valenti lost the fight. Since 1997 the networks (except NBC and the Black Entertainment Network) have also been marking descriptions of objectionable program content: D (for suggestive dialogue), L (for coarse language), S (for sex), and V (for violence). There is also an FV (fantasy violence) label for children's shows. As the Kaiser Foundation's V-Chip Education Project describes the results, "some V-chip TV sets have separate on-screen menu displays for both age and content categories, while others may display both age-based and content-based ratings in the same screen." An analysis by Collings found that only a fifth of the programs carried any content advisories to accompany programs marked PG in the age categories.

How the V-chip works—or doesn't. The V-chip uses line 21 of the vertical blanking interval in the television signal to transmit the program's rating. Blockers are run by remote-control units with codes that parents can set, though in some units the code is wiped out when the power is cut off. Some blockers can only cover channels 1 through 99, and some only up to four channels at a time. Some can be set to cover only certain periods of time.[9] Once the chip is programmed to block programs with a designated rating, the signals from those programs are stopped and replaced by an on-screen message.

A complex series of steps is required to program the V-chip to block certain kinds of shows through the remote control. To activate the chip, a parent must first display the ratings menu, then program the settings to be blocked—a cumbersome process. A parental lock code, or personal identification number, must also be created and entered each time the chip is to be turned off. A further complication is that TV sets using closed captions face interference from the encoded program ratings.[10]

A network executive comments:

What the label has done is to get information to the viewers, but it hasn't forced them to use it. Parents don't know how to activate the V-chip. It took me two weeks to set up the V-chip to block certain shows. It was a nightmare to figure out. Then each set manufacturer has a different display, which makes it difficult. You can't ask your neighbor because she may have a different kind of set. The setup is difficult. There was a good intention, but the execution was not effective.

Massachusetts Congressman Edward Markey had first proposed the V-chip in 1993. According to former FCC general counsel Henry Geller, "Congress chose the V-chip approach because it recognized that only the responsible parent would use the empowerment in a straight programming approach, and it wanted a 'magic bullet' that would be more widely effective."

Markey and his principal House colleagues in the battle for the V-chip agreed in a letter in 1997 to give the industry a three-year reprieve from further legislation on labeling content, so that the system could be appraised. Markey thought the V-chip could work with any kind of program indicators, and felt that a single uniform code was unnecessary.

Central to the concept of the V-chip is the idea of "parental control."[11] The MPAA's Valenti talked about "a renaissance of individual responsibility." President Clinton, meeting with industry leaders, announced that "They're handing the TV remote control back to America's parents!"

This is like saying that the way to reduce young people's use of drugs and handguns is for parents to be more *caring*!

What possible reason is there to assume that parents who have until now failed to steer their kids away from the wrong kinds of programs will suddenly begin to exercise discipline? The TV producers and broadcasters who resisted content labels were absolutely right when they said these would complicate life for the typical household. The V-chip is a technological nuisance that taxes the average person's ability to program and manage—especially as, in case after case, parents find themselves second-guessing the standards that the programmers apply.

New York Times TV critic Walter Goodman observed, "Pasting on ratings is like decorating a garbage dump."

Objecting to the labels, CBS president Peter Lund argued that they "could actually backfire by serving as a lure to the very children we are trying to protect." This judgment is sound. A television producer testifies to the effect:

[Establishing] TV ratings was a fairly cynical move. Everybody knew that it was useful for propaganda means. Years ago I had wanted to do a production of [Ralph Ellison's] *Invisible Man*.

We had some arguments with the standards and practices department, so we came up with a disclaimer at the start of the program. It turned out to be one of the highest-rated programs we had. The warning label becomes a sales tool.

Dick Wolf, producer of "Law and Order," said at the time content advisories were being introduced: "If all these shows have warnings on them, you could have a situation where producers are saying to standards people at the networks, 'I've got a warning. I can say whatever I want. I can kill as many people as I want.'"[12] This is precisely why labeling content has proven to be counterproductive. In the heavy viewing, disorganized, low-income households where parental controls are seldom exercised, an exclusionary rating makes the most effective program promotion.

Just as young people are invariably present at any matinee showing of an R or NC-17 rated film in a suburban multiplex theater, they are in front of the TV set when the V-chip is in place. Even in those rare cases where parents can master the art of programming the chip and actually bother to do so, any resourceful eleven-year-old who can program a VCR or log on to the internet can figure out how to bypass it. With several sets in most households, each set requiring its own programmed chip, how many parents are likely to follow through?

The law requires identification of "video programming that contains sexual, violent, or other indecent material about which parents should be informed before it is displayed to children." In adopting the law, as Vicky Rideout of the Kaiser Family Foundation observes, "Congress never defined 'violent video programming,' which could include news, documentaries, cartoons, fictional drama . . . educational films about the Holocaust or the Civil War, and Shakespearian drama. There's nobody who has any incentive to promote the V-chip."

What labels should be applied?   Explaining NBC's refusal to label programs, its president, Robert Wright, pointed to "one cable network['s] . . . made-for-television movie which included nudity, vulgar language, and gratuitous violence. The movie was inappropriately rated TV-14, even though it had further content labels." NBC chose to use its own advisories, such as, "This program has some violent scenes."

John McCain, chairman of the Senate Committee on Commerce, Science, and Transportation, attacked NBC's "inexplicable intransigence" in not going along with the content labels. He overtly threatened license renewals for the network's main source of profit, the owned-and-operated stations, and perhaps for its affiliates too. Refusing to concede, and with the lobbying clout of its owner, General Electric, behind it, NBC promised to make its age-based icons larger, to selectively flash "advisory" warnings such as "Parental Discretion Advised," to air more public-service announcements urging parents to guide their children's viewing, to conduct more frequent audience surveys, and to post program labels on NBC's website.[13] The heated exchange was soon forgotten.

Some producers contend that restrictive labels that call attention to a program's sensational elements are not an inherent attraction, and that audiences are drawn to excellence. A TV producer:

> The audience will tend not to watch the bad stuff, and they'll watch the good stuff. If you have a bad series, the sex isn't going to help you. In 1969, Twentieth-Century Fox decided that Russ Meyer was going to be their savior with his soft porn. They flopped. The audience still watches good pictures.
>
> The program content designation is weird. The reality stuff is the worst ever—organized prostitution—but it's rated PG.

The networks are willing to put on whatever they want to put on. They feel compelled to go further than premium cable. They don't realize that people don't watch "The Sopranos" or "Sex and the City" because of the language and the violence but because they're good stories. If the networks think they can build an audience just because they put in more sex, they're wrong. Showtime's mantra is "no limits." They have gone out of their way to say, this is what you can't see elsewhere. I think if they do cut back, there would be no effects.

A TV executive:

A natural vulgarity is part of the growing-up experience to-day. No real people asked for this system to be put into place. It was all contrived to appease the politicos. Parents are not monitoring children's diets, let alone their TV habits. Most parents also have some intuitive understanding that the kids are going to choose a balanced diet. There's a much greater effect from the violence on news programs that are exempt from the labeling rules.

The difficulties that the movies encountered in making judgments were also apparent from the start in the labeling of TV programs. At a meeting sponsored by the Freedom Forum's Media Studies Center, audience members were asked to review short segments from four television shows and rate them both by age category and by content. There was, according to the Center's research director, Lawrence McGill, "an almost complete lack of consensus as to how a given segment should be rated, regardless of the rating system."

Valenti: "We are not dealing with Euclid's geometry, where the equations are pristine and explicit."[14] Roland McFarland, vice president for broadcast standards and practices, ABC: "Is it a punch? A gunshot? A gunshot plus killing? These are all subjective interpretations. The classic discussion here is around shows where there's heavy jeopardy involved but no real on-screen violence." A Showtime film that showed "frontal nudity, simulated sexual intercourse, and frequent coarse language" was rated TV-14 but carried the network's own labels: "Brief Nudity, Violence, Adult Language, and Adult Content."[15]

As in the case of films, ratings assigned to TV shows can arouse an indignant reaction from the creative side. In 1997, when ABC proposed to add an on-screen warning notice that the show "Ellen" had "adult content," its star, Ellen DeGeneres, a lesbian both on-screen and off, threatened to walk out, calling the action "blatant discrimination."[16]

Although children are in the television audience at all hours, they do generally go to bed before their parents do. For that reason there is a court-imposed "safe harbor" for "obscene" and "indecent speech" between 10 p.m. and 6 a.m. (However, the Supreme Court invalidated a provision of the 1992 Cable Act that required leased-access channels to place all "patently offensive" content on a channel that would be available only to viewers who asked for it.)

The head of standards for a major network: "Because TV is a mass-audience medium, we are trying to reach the largest number of viewers in a particular demographic. There is no one audience, per se. We are trying to reach a different audience at 8 p.m. than we are at 12:05 a.m."

But programs (especially on cable) are scheduled to run at different times on the East and West Coasts, making it difficult to position them at a time when children are less likely to be in the audience. Programs that are broadcast after 9 p.m. on the East Coast appear at an earlier hour in the West. In the words of one producer, "You get an early audience for a late-evening show."

Apart from sports and news, important components of television remain outside the labeling system. Unedited movies on premium cable are not rated; those on ordinary cable TV display the original MPAA rating. Syndicated programs, of which only a minority are reruns of network shows, occupy five times as much air time as the networks fill, though their audiences are much smaller. Many of these programs carry no content ratings.

The ratings of an original TV show are not assigned until after it is produced. A half-hour sitcom that is intended for an 8 p.m. audience will normally have a different content than a one-hour drama broadcast at 10 p.m. As one television executive points out, "The content determines the rating, not the other way around."

But the labeling factor enters into the equation when a show is planned and produced, just as it does in the case of feature films. A network standards head offers an ambivalent appraisal:

> The appeal or audience size of a show is likely to be greater if it is assigned a more restrictive rating. It depends entirely on the program produced. For example, [a police series] is a highly successful one-hour drama that is in its tenth season. Every episode to date has been rated TV-14, and nearly every episode is preceded by an advisory, usually notifying viewers of adult language, adult situations, and/or partial nudity. Last season, another one-hour drama by the same producer was rated the same way and carried similar advisories but did not have the same ratings success. The rating doesn't make the show more appealing per se.

This last statement contradicts the earlier one that a restricted rating adds to a show's appeal. But the very contradiction reflects the mixed feelings that television executives exhibit about the whole labeling procedure.

Labeling program content is, in principle, a popular idea, which is no doubt why politicians love it. In practice, however, it hasn't worked. Although the V-chip was mandated in an effort to clean up the medium, it has had the opposite effect—by encouraging more use of violence, explicit sex, and foul language in the endless pursuit of larger audiences.

Have labels made a difference? How do the program labels affect the public's opinions and practices? Only two parents in five had noticed the age-based designations a month after they were introduced, but half said they understood the new "ratings system" very well or fairly well.[17] Seven of ten adults in households with children (according to a Roper poll) said they would block certain programs; but so did six of ten in households without children! How much faith can one put in these well-meaning assertions? The V-chip is even less commonly used than the VCR's recording capability, while a growing proportion of programs are rated V, S, D, and L.

By accepting the V-chip and the labeling system, the television business bought time and deflected attention from the real problem: its steady descent away from traditional decorum. The V-chip has opened the gate to other forms of automatic screening for content, as already occurs on the internet.

A television producer remarks that "The most powerful anti-censorship device is the remote control." But a program blocked (presumably) by the V-chip remains inaccessible even with this device. Personal digital recording systems like TiVo have made the swift elimination of commercials even more efficient than the "fast forward" features of the VCR and DVD. Might it be appropriate to label programs that harbor politically controversial topics? How about blocking those that carry commercials for products that a viewer may find offensive—or simply of no interest? (No, we mustn't be carried away.)

TV's intimate political connections make direct government intervention into content unlikely as well as horrendous to contemplate. Powerful senators may be moved by personal conviction, but they are also influenced by forces whose efforts to change TV's formulas go well beyond children's programs.

When President Clinton met with broadcast and movie industry leaders, he told them to "recognize that their creativity and their freedom carries with it significant responsibility." It's not just their creativity and their freedom that demand an acknowledgment of the public interest. It's their free license to use the public airwaves and right of way to coin incredible sums of money.

From the start, the subject of television program labels raised significant questions: Does it make sense to label only some of the available programming when much of it is excluded from the present rating system? Is it feasible to label all potential content, including film libraries and imports? Should labeling be applied only to entertainment programs, or should it be extended to news, documentaries, and talk shows? Do restrictions of any kind open the way to other forms of censorship?

Some of the most troublesome questions center on the interpretation of content elements that are not easily definable. For example, the effects of violence can be assessed only in relation to its context, its realism, the plot, the motivation of the characters, the consequences. Suspense, music, and sound effects can acutely arouse anxiety without any violence at all on-screen. Children aged 7–11, with only a limited notion of probability, can be even more affected by the fear of a threatening event than by seeing one actually depicted.

Context is also important in judging sexual scenes and rough language. But if one believes on general principles that children should be kept away from such content, their context may well seem irrelevant.

The difficulties of applying general principles to specific cases have been understood for a long time. A quarter-century ago the Surgeon General's Advisory Committee on Television and Social Behavior commissioned the Social Science Research Council to look into the possibility of setting up a "violence index." After much study and debate, a blue-ribbon committee of psychologists, sociologists, and educators concluded that "it is questionable whether the production of a violence profile would contribute to a reduction in actual violence."[18] That understatement applies to the labels that are now in place.

When the new TV labeling system appeared, only a fourth (27 percent) of parents thought it would be very helpful.[19] This unenthusiastic response has been borne out by what has since occurred.

For the first year after the V-chip was introduced, 150 families with children 7–10 were tracked in a study directed by a communications scholar, Amy Jordan.[20] A control group of 40 families had, on their own, acquired a set equipped with the chip; of these only two knew they had it, and neither one used it. An experimental group of 28 families, in whose sets a chip had been installed and programmed by the researchers, agreed to use the device. Of these, 70 percent never used it, 22 percent tried it but gave up, and 8 percent were still using it at the end of the year, though half said they would be likely to use it in the future. It was hard to program the device; there were more than 40 buttons on the remote control used in the experiment. The average assessment of the controls was a bit over 7 on a scale of 1 to 10. It was pointed out that children could watch programs on other sets in the home. (Typically there were four sets.) The labels themselves were confusing to viewers; 94

percent didn't know what TV-Y or TV-Y7 meant, and 96 percent didn't know what D stood for.

In March 1997, shortly after the new guideline labels were introduced, a Roper survey for the networks found that 84 percent of parents had heard of them. But when asked what had "considerable influence" in determining what programs their children should watch, over half (53 percent) selected the response, "Whether I am familiar and comfortable with the program's content." Forty percent said it depended on whether the program was one the child liked.[21] Thirty percent said they were influenced by the program's content label. Another survey found that three of four parents wanted to judge the suitability of programs themselves and not have the industry do it.[22]

Of course, it is the industry's producers who are supposed to assign the labels. This duty is often skipped or applied haphazardly. A year after the content labels were introduced, the Kaiser Family Foundation studied 1,147 randomly selected programs. (NBC programs, which did not and in 2004 still do not use the labels, were included in the count.) Ninety-two percent of programs with sexual content did not carry the S label, and 79 percent of those with violence did not carry a V. Four of five (81 percent) of violent children's shows did not carry the FV label.[23]

A report from the Annenberg Public Policy Center in 2000 found little change in the way parents controlled children's television exposure. Few understood the meaning of E/I (educational/instructive). Such entertainment shows as "Oprah," "Who Wants to Be a Millionaire?," and "Judge Judy" were widely perceived as "educational."

In 2001 a national survey of eight hundred parents, also conducted by the Kaiser Family Foundation, found that 7 percent had used a V-chip to monitor their children's viewing, though 40 percent had a V-chip-equipped TV in their homes.[24] Of parents whose sets had a chip, over half (53 percent) did not know they had it, and three in ten (30 percent) chose not to use it; 17 percent had used it to block programs.[25]

Over half (56 percent) of the parents say they had used the TV ratings to control their children's viewing (28 percent often), a proportion similar to those who had used the advisories on music (50 percent) and video and computer games (59 percent) but far less than the 84 percent who say they have used movie ratings. Forty-eight percent find the ratings "very useful," and 44 percent "somewhat useful."[26] Only 5 percent know that D stands for suggestive dialogue.

In the same year, five years after the V-chip was introduced, a study made by one of the networks found that less than one-third of parents had an accurate understanding of its purpose. Over half (56 percent) were unaware of it. Two in five (41 percent) had heard of it, but only two in three of these could describe its function. Altogether, a fourth (27 percent) were aware of the chip and could accurately describe what it does. Only 1 percent of adults had used the V-chip; the proportion rose to 6 percent among the one in eight who had it. Nine of ten among those who actually had it had *never* used it.[27]

It is clear from the evidence that the labeling system is completely understood and put to use in only a small minority of households. These are the very households where parental judgment and discipline over children's media exposure would be exercised without any labeling system in place.

A television executive comments on the awareness of labels in the age of the remote control, when much viewing occurs after a program has started: "I don't see the advisories or ratings when I tune in in the middle."

This is an important point. Less than half of all the viewers for an average show are tuned to it for the first minute, when the labels ordinarily appear.[28] The producer of a successful, long-running television show points to the apathy of the audience, its indifference to the labels and to the very elements that brought their introduction in the first place:

> Film and television are two different businesses. Some movie theaters won't allow some films rated R. On the TV side, on pay-per-view the networks love the advisories because they imply this is what you can't get on free TV. They have used it to pump up their [audience] ratings. On the network side, there's extraordinary inconsistency in the way the advisories are applied. On daytime soap operas, which are the worst, you get very similar shows, the same content, with different ratings assigned by different networks. The first year we had labels, no one was paying attention. There was political pressure to do this, but no pressure from parents. Valenti has an 800 number for the MPAA to receive complaints. There aren't any. No one is really concerned about it. The labels are almost perceived as noise. But when the audience is upset, as when a sportscast is interrupted for a special event, they know how to reach the networks.

By 2004 it was abundantly clear that the V-chip had hardly been used and actually had had the opposite of the intended effect. Nonetheless, following the FCC's freshened sensitivity to "indecency" after the Janet Jackson incident, the broadcasters, with the aid of the Advertising Council, launched a campaign to promote its use. The V-chip's chief proponent, Congressman Markey, continued to maintain that

> the legislation has worked for significant segments of the population who have young kids and are informed about it. In order to get usage higher, it will require a much more vigorous

public education campaign on the part of the broadcast and cable industries. Also, it is worth noting that for the most part the ratings still are not carried in the TV guides printed in the paper. This reduces public awareness considerably.[29]

Markey told a conference on the subject,

The more information parents are given, the more likely it is that parents are going to use it. . . . If you have little or no information about it, you have little or no likelihood that you're going to use the technology. . . . So we have to find better ways of informing parents about it.

But Markey was more realistic on the point that touches my main thesis in this book:

Parents . . . are not going to stop Hollywood or the broadcasters from putting on the programming they intend putting on because they're targeting 18-to-34-year-olds, young adults, to watch programming that is—let's put it like this—not aimed at the highest possible intellectual, cognitive reach that human beings are programmed to achieve, right?

Right. People 18–34, who are described as "prime consumers" of violent shows, also are less likely than those 35 and older to believe that these harm society or are a major cause of breakdown in law and order. Attitudes rationalize actions.

Films on TV and their labels. Feature films occupy a large part of television time and present an even larger part of its violent content, especially on cable. A broadcast executive says,

There are no real cable codes, and they don't edit film. When they say, "This film has been edited," they're referring to the technical conversion of the wide screen to the TV format. Not the content.

James Hamilton analyzed 11,603 movies broadcast between 6 p.m. and midnight between February 1995 and March 1996. (This included films on premium cable channels, which had a greater number of violent films as well as more films that were low-rated by critics.) A majority (57 percent) were rated as violent.[30] Thirty-seven percent used "adult language," 50 percent "adult situations," 25 percent nudity. Fifteen percent had all these indicators. Rated by the Motion Picture Association designations, 3 percent were G, 13 percent PG-13, 20 percent PG, and 32 percent R.[31] Of the prime-time films broadcast during this period, 14 percent carried viewer discretion labels.

Violent theatrical films that carried warnings were interrupted for longer commercial and promo breaks than nonviolent ones, or, for that matter, violent films without warnings. Violent films with warnings carried a higher proportion of promos, suggesting that not all the available commercial time was sold. (Made-for-television movies did not show such differences.)

Films with warnings carried more commercials for sports, leisure, and alcoholic beverage products—products consumed by men 18–24 in childless households, as Hamilton notes. They carried fewer ads for products whose users are older. Hamilton concludes that "networks may have been less willing to give viewers detailed information about violence since this would raise the probability of advertiser backlash. . . . Broadcasters may be more likely to give a film a TV-PG than a TV-14."

Hamilton finds a different pattern for violent program series than for violent films. "Advertisements for violent series in general are for products used more by females, older consumers, and those with lower incomes relative to advertisements for products on violent movies." In other words, the violent shows brought in the advertisers who want youthful audiences.

Forbidden fruit.   Warnings reduce viewing by children 2–11 by 14 percent, Hamilton found. For adolescents, however, the effects are quite different. Whatever is placed out of bounds, in television as in film, carries an irresistible allure.

A writer for television:

> My guts tell me there has been no effect [of content labeling] at all. It doesn't affect my kids' [eight and ten] viewing. The kids self-censor themselves. They walk away if there's too much kissing; they just leave the room. On a show like "NYPD Blue" it [the restrictive label] just helps the [audience] rating. [Producer] Steve Bochco has gotten a lot of mileage out of that.

A research team led by Joanne Cantor tested a number of different types of labels: the age-groupings used by the MPAA, and three sets of content indicators—those used by the premium cable channels, by Canadian broadcasters, and by the Recreational Software Advisory Council for video games. (I shall describe those in Chapter Nine.) "Advisory" notices ("Parental Discretion Advised" and "Contains Some Violent Content") were also tested, as were "simple recommendations of age-appropriateness" and mentions of merit awards for programs.

In a carefully constructed experiment, Cantor and her associates asked 297 children in Madison, Wisconsin, to choose from lists of fictitiously named television programs and short plot descriptions of an episode, as well as from a list of both real and fake film titles.[32] Parental advisories or MPAA ratings were randomly attached. Just over a fourth of both younger and older girls chose programs with the advisories. They were more of an attraction for boys. (The advisories attracted two of five younger boys and half the older ones.) There was no particular difference when the advisory was general or warned specifically about violence. Older boys were most attracted and older girls least attracted to films rated R.

No added attraction came from age-suitability indicators that did not imply parental controls. The MPAA restrictive labels (PG, PG-13, and R) made older children more eager to see programs, while the G label diminished their interest. Not one older boy showed interest in a G-rated film. Among younger children, the warning "Parental Discretion Advised" made boys more interested, girls less; both boys and girls were turned off by the premium cable codes of "MV: Mild Violence" and "GV: Graphic Violence."

The authors concluded that "information about violent content per se is a less potent magnet for children than the exhortation that the child should be prevented from seeing it." What aroused interest was not the promise of violence but the prohibition on access to the movie.

The lure of the "forbidden fruit" was especially strong among children of all ages who watched the most television and who were most aggressive to begin with.

Cantor and her colleagues point out that "there is little indication of what type of content to expect in a movie rated PG or PG-13." While two-thirds of the films in those two categories contain what is euphemistically called "adult language," half have violent scenes and two-fifths are sexually explicit. This simply underscores two fundamental questions: Until what age should the juvenile audience be protected, and against exactly what? Such questions defy quick and easy answers.

The presence of the rating icons may not significantly alter children's viewing habits, but it provides the rationale for lacing run-of-the-mill television programs with ever more questionable elements. After all, the kiddies have been warned away.

Although some producers feel, in the words of one, that "The more restrictive rating no longer increases a show's appeal," more seem to agree with a cable TV executive who concludes: "The ratings make these things [gratuitous sexual dialogue and nudity] more likely to happen."

Or, as a broadcast television executive explains: "The ratings are really providing an inducement to watch. They say, 'The scenes coming up are really going to be raunchy.' The lower the income, the more the tube is on. The rating system for movies works better because there is some discipline and control over the younger person."

The producers of TV programs naturally disagree, at least for the record. Rosalyn Weinman, a sociology professor who became a producer of "Law and Order":

> The forbidden fruit thing doesn't make sense. Logically it should be even more forbidden fruit, more enticing to them, if you gave more detailed ratings. Teenage boys turn on HBO [which, like Showtime, presents advisories at the start of programs] and see 'Brief Nudity,' and they turn to Showtime and see 'Graphic Violence,' and they decide, do they want striptease or a Bruce Willis movie? . . . On the one hand they say we sanitize violence and there's not much pain and suffering shown. On the other, they say we sensationalize it. You can't have it both ways.[33]

But it is not the pain and suffering that attracts young viewers. It is the action.

Pay cable. In a statement that hardly jibes with the evidence, a broadcast network vice president claims that

"Violence isn't an issue for network TV any more. We don't do that any more. It's on video and cable."

Cable networks, with content immune to oversight by the FCC, have stretched the ground rules of propriety in ways that the broadcasters still hesitate to follow. The cable networks, like the broadcasters, are somewhat constrained by their conservative advertisers. Nearly half of cable households subscribe to one or more premium channels. These channels, unlimited by advertiser or FCC constraints and responsive only to viewer demand, carry a higher component of violence and sex than "free" cable.

The cable networks have instituted their own versions of program labels, though these are not uniform. The leader, Time Warner's HBO, uses its own Parental Guidelines: TV-Y (appropriate for all children); TV-7 (directed to older children); TV-G (for general audiences); TV-PG (parental guidance suggested); TV-14 (parental guidance strongly suggested); TV-MA (mature audiences only). The list of content advisories is: AC (adult content); AL (adult language); GL (graphic language); MV (mild violence); V (violence); GV (graphic violence); BN (brief nudity); N (nudity); SC (strong sexual content); RP (rape).

Of 188 MPAA-rated films that were broadcast on one of the three premium cable channels in the 1995–1996 season analyzed by Hamilton, only 12 carried a G rating, and only half of those had been made within the previous ten years. Forty-seven percent of the PG-rated films and 62 percent of those rated PG-13 contained some sexuality, and 62 percent of those in both categories contained violence.

HBO reports that only 93,000 of the 6.6 million viewers of its "Sex and the City" series were girls 12–17, though there are anecdotal reports that some girls eagerly accepted the show's stars as role models. Michael Patrick King, an executive producer of the show, explains, "We've taken the word 'sex' and put bubbles and lights and a little bit of laughter around it, because it's so completely dipped in dark shame that no one even knows how to talk about it, where to talk about it, what to say."[34] But the "dark shame" of Nathaniel Hawthorne's era has scarcely any counterparts in twenty-first-century America.

How does the mix of programs on pay cable differ from that of the broadcast networks, described earlier? Only a tiny proportion are rated as suitable for children to watch.[35] I analyzed the HBO schedule for the first week of December 2002. For Hollywood films, the original ratings were used, and for HBO-produced programs, the network's own ratings. Of a total of 128 programs of varying length, 5 percent carried no rating. One program (1 percent) was G rated by its Hollywood producers; one (1 percent) got a TV-G from HBO, and one a TV-7. Thirty percent were rated by Hollywood as PG-13, and 8 percent got a roughly equivalent HBO rating of TV-14. Five percent got a theater film rating of PG and 18 percent the HBO equivalent of TV-PG. Almost a third carried the film rating of R (17 percent) or the HBO rating of TV-MA (14 percent).

Sixty programs carried content advisories in addition to the ratings. (This, like the previous count, includes multiple repeats, both of theater films and of HBO's own productions.) Of these, 65 percent were labeled AC (adult content); 57 percent AL (adult language); 12 percent GL (graphic language); 15 percent MV (mild violence); 37 percent V (violence); 10 percent GV (graphic violence); 1 percent BN (brief nudity); and 8 percent N (nudity). In addition, some carried the standard broadcast designations: 8 percent S (for sexual content); 8 percent L (for "adult" language), and 1 percent D (for "adult" dialogue with sexual innuendos). It is evident that premium cable programming is more replete with violence and sex.

A pay-cable executive acknowledges that more restrictive labels do better in drawing the audience:

> People are paying extra for the service, and they expect more explicit sex and language. The racier the better. The broadcast networks are geared to women. We have more of a male audience. We're geared to 18–49. Our content changes a lot more than the broadcast networks'. The bulk of our content is movies. Twenty percent of our programming is original. I don't think people pay much attention to the advisories. We're unedited, unlike the broadcasters. We're not [audience] ratings-driven because we don't carry advertising. But we do have affiliates [that is, cable systems operators] to worry about.

He appears to vacillate between his programming's appeal to a segment of the public and his desire for a broad spectrum of viewers of all kinds:

> People tend to watch themselves on TV. A program with a lot of African Americans will be watched by African Americans. A show with younger adults will be watched by younger adults. The later in the evening, the younger the audience profile. The contents determine who watches. We go after the whole audience. Anyone who writes a check for the service, you want to satisfy. We try for a balance of product to satisfy the audience.

An executive of a rival pay-cable firm argues that it is not the label but the content itself that attracts the viewers:

> I don't think people tune in because of the ratings. Except for teens. Their hormones are raging. I don't think the label is a catalyst for attracting audience. Sex programming gets a higher audience rating. Not because of the code. If a show comes up with sexual content, people watch. With so many channels,

people are constantly surfing, sampling what's out there. So if they happen upon something with sex, they'll watch. They don't come in at the beginning because of the rating. Length of tuning is always less than the length of programming.

He maintains that programs reflect their makers' values and impulses rather than marketing considerations:

> We don't design movies with a rating in mind. There's a creative image that our producers have that we want to uphold. We don't add gratuitous sex or violence in order to get a different content label.
>
> We have people on staff who review the content and assign a rating and the labels. We also spell out what's in the program— if it's a rape or extreme violence. It's in very small type in the program guide.

A spot check verifies that it's in very small type indeed.

Another pay-cable executive explains how his network's made-for-TV movies differ from theater films: "We're picking up slack where the theatrical producers have been left behind. Theatrical films have been geared to producing what we call popcorn. Very rarely do you see Hollywood movies that are geared to the young adults or middle America."

He seems somewhat pressed when asked if there is content he would not use:

> Bestiality. There was a show called "Animal Passions" that we turned down. There's a matter of taste where you don't want to cross the line. We don't show X-rated products. We show softcore sexual product but not hard-core. [Who decides whether it's hard or soft core?] It's done at all levels. Scripts, pilots. It gets to a wide array of people before a show gets on the air.

Even on pay cable, the time scheduling is sensitive to children's presence in the audience. But this is now harder to predict.

> You don't put an R-rated movie on at six in the evening as kids are viewing. Anything that ends before 6 a.m. is okay. After 11 p.m. The harder [core] it is, the later it gets on the air. The trouble with TV now is that you have so many different feeds that it's hard to control when kids are watching. There's video on demand. So the technology has outpaced the rating codes. You can't control TV once it gets into mass circulation. With TiVo, kids can record shows when the parents aren't home, without their knowledge. Whose responsibility is it? While the rating code is a good idea, it's pretty impossible to put the responsibility on the TV provider.

Pay cable's use of scenes and language that would have been inconceivable only a few years ago has had perhaps its greatest impact not on the viewers but on the producers of advertising-supported television programs. We must therefore return to the relationship between marketers' search for potential consumers and the television industry's need to please and attract those consumers.

8

The business effects
of TV labeling

Have the labels influenced advertisers? Pay cable's success depends on its direct responsiveness to what its viewers are willing to pay for. But pay cable represents only a fraction of what the public actually watches. Ultimate control over the contents of "free" TV rests with the advertisers who determine what kinds of audiences they want to reach.

Television programmers are ever alert to the sensibilities of advertisers, who are well aware of the context in which their messages appear and generally shy away from offensive programming. This enters into the calculations of those who produce TV's content.

Dennis McGuire of Carat (a worldwide media-buying organization) says that "certain clients want to be on controversial shows. Other clients don't want to be associated with them. It comes from the gut feel of the client." (He also says, "I tell clients that a handful of letters of protest shouldn't counteract hundreds of thousands of viewers. Advertisers react to the loudest voice.")[1]

But fewer voices of protest are heard now. Cable's vastly increased array of choices makes it easy for viewers to avoid what they don't want to see. (As Jeff Lucas of Universal TV says, "Viewers do vote with that remote control.") NBC's Allen Wurtzel compares the present situation with that when three broadcast networks reigned supreme: "We used to get a lot of letters of complaint from viewers twenty years ago, because they basically had only three choices. Now we get none. Because people select what they want to see."

Advertisers' sensitivities are felt at many levels in program development. As a star actor-producer puts it, "Self-censorship comes from advertising." Broadcasters and producers generally believe that controversial programs lose advertiser support. (In the mid-1990s an episode of "Law and Order" dealing with the bombing of an abortion clinic reduced advertising income by $800,000.) But the definition of what is controversial has changed through time.

Advertisers' expected responses also figure in internal discussions. A leading film and television personality describes the struggle over a police series, which, he asserts, "was opposed because it dealt in ideas. A lot of the cops use five 'fucks' in every sentence. The responsibility is first to entertain. Afterwards if you want to explore ideas, so much the better." (It is revealing that this star invokes an intellectual or social motive to explain his zeal to employ the street language he favors.)

Did the labels, as some advocates hoped, steer advertisers away from programs marked unsuitable for children? A few withdrew, but lots of others stood ready to replace them. In a survey of seven hundred "advertising leaders"[2] conducted before the rating system was in place, two of three said it would influence network program content.

Complaints about a specific show may not be worth bucking, but a whole category is hard to avoid. Advertisers look first at the number of viewers they can buy for a dollar, and second at who those viewers are. As we have seen, the younger adult viewers many advertisers seek are, more than any other part of the population, attracted to programming loaded with violence and sex. Advertisers have been ready to follow those viewers wherever they go in the audience ratings race, and broadcasters have not been likely to take a chance on departing from their slam-bang formulas just because the output carried a label. The label merely provided the excuse to go farther beyond what was previously considered the permissible edge.

Advertising Information Services (AIS), owned by an agency consortium, was started in 1975. At that time TV preachers (Donald Wildmon and Jerry Falwell were the most notorious) were organizing mass mailings of protest letters to major corporate advertisers. AIS advance-screens prime-time programs on the six broadcast networks, except for the news shows, as well as cable programs for specific clients. The only program screening service for advertising, it employs thirty-five people in New York and Los Angeles.

Since the networks began to apply program ratings, AIS has passed these screening reports on to the ad agencies.[3] For a program series, advertisers generally look at each individual episode rather than the series as a whole.

In the first three months of 2003, AIS screened 1,928 programs, including repeats. Of these, fewer than 3 percent carried advisory or disclaimer information.

Originally the agencies supplied AIS with product-specific guidelines. "An insurance company wanted to pull its commercials from a program dealing with insurance fraud, a food advertiser wouldn't want to be on a program on botulism." An AIS executive comments that

> some advertisers have always been sensitive to scenes of violence as they are shown today. People's sensitivities change. The networks, to keep people interested, have pushed the envelope further every year. One year it was violence, one year sex, the next year sexual allusions. Advertisers wanted to know if it was gratuitous sex and violence. With a James Bond movie, some clients called it violence and some called it fantasy. Years ago we screened a movie that started with a pretty brutal rape for the first five minutes. The rest of the movie was about the woman's search for the guy who did it, and then the court battle. We described it. A report is a report.

AIS encounters the familiar problem of quantifying subjective judgments:

> One of the problems is how to keep a count. In a battle scene there might be five hundred people killed. Is that five hundred acts of violence? There was a time when Ricky and Lucy [of "I Love Lucy"] slept in separate beds. We tell the young people that we hire as screeners, 'We don't care if you believe in sex before marriage or how you feel about violence.' The screeners call the agency and get on the phone and give them a synopsis of the show or what happens between the [commercial] breaks. If they see someone's breast, they bring it to the attention of the advertiser. The client then makes the decision and may call the TV network and ask them to put the commercial at the end of the show, or they may withdraw from the show altogether. This is driving the networks crazy, because they sell the show up-front [in the spring, "up-front" buying season of negotiation for positions in the networks' fall schedules]. There could be

some episodes that aren't right. Some shows some clients don't want to be on. Some agencies won't go to certain shows.

How do the agencies use this information? A media director comments on labeling:

I haven't heard anything about the V-chip in some time. I haven't seen any evidence that people are paying any attention to it, or to the ratings. We're not making any decisions on that basis. Every program we put a commercial in we review the AIS report. For between 5 and 10 percent we'll reposition or reschedule the commercial. A lot of programs are vetted in the initial negotiations [on prices].

She blames what she regards as the debasement of content on the competition for viewers:

The choices become more difficult when you go into an on-going series. It's really a search for [audience] ratings. As a result, we see more programming on the air that I personally find very distasteful but that people want to watch. We have progressed as a society. We go to movies that have themes that wouldn't be shown before. TV claims that they only mirror society. When you see in the paper a thirty-two-year-old teacher with a family having sex with a fourteen-year-old, she can claim she saw something like this on TV. We keep on pushing the boundaries, and both the society and the media are guilty of pushing the edges. [Is it cyclical or a trend?] I don't see any reason why it's going to be pulled back. Everything is a race for viewership. What's going to bring it to a halt? The evangelists, when they get hold of a program that attacks the church or that deals with homosexuality? It's frustrating that there's no prospect for change.

The shift from a fully sponsored program to "scatter plan" placement of commercials has reduced advertisers' sense of responsibility for their ads' programming context, as she points out:

> The media and the advertisers used to work very closely together when advertisers were associated with particular programs. They have gone separate ways. The craving for audiences has brought this about. The number of shows that we won't go in has grown dramatically in the last few years. It's remarkable that they continue to do the reality shows. "Fear Factor" [on which contestants were given such tasks as eating the eyes of animals or picking through garbage for a meal]—putting someone in a grave—or the dating shows, they put advertisers in a very delicate position. People write to clients saying, "I can't believe I saw your ads in this kind of program." And companies listen to them.
>
> Advertisers don't want to offend any consumers. "Find some other show that's not offensive," that's the general request. It was Westerns at one time, cop shows at one time. Reality shows are cheaper to produce than "Friends"—putting six characters on at a million dollars a week each. So the networks have cut back the series from thirty-six to thirty-two to twenty-six and now to eighteen episodes. No wonder the cable networks are getting more audience. Most of the shows on cable are reruns of what was on the networks. TV is TV. Some of the cable networks like USA run programs that are more aggressive and violent. Again, to get more viewers.

Another media executive, the leading TV buyer for a large agency group, points to the power of pressure groups:

> [The evangelists] target the bigger networks first. The labels on programs are a way to appease the critics, who can be a real pain

in the ass to a corporate chairman. You can't please everybody. We in New York would watch anything, but it won't necessarily be acceptable in other parts of the country. The labels are a way to say, "We have really addressed this."

Although advertisers originally shied away from reality TV programs, these became more attractive to them as their audiences grew, especially among young viewers. Some programs, like NBC's "Fear Factor," remained off limits for some. Vicky Mayer of conservative Procter and Gamble, which advertises on some reality shows, says,

> In all our advertising we follow our guidelines very closely to make sure we don't insult our consumers, and in the shows we advertise in, we make a determination episode by episode. There are also shows that are big draws but that don't meet our criteria, and we stick to our guidelines no matter how large the viewership is.[4]

A leading agency media research executive: "P & G always considered program content. Now that they've done the program classification, I don't think that would affect them. It makes it easier for them to have an independent source. It helps them fine-tune what most of them were doing anyway. Nobody wants to upset the public opinion out there."

Yet P & G has not hesitated to go where the audience is. An episode on its long-running daytime soap opera "Guiding Light" in February 2004 showed a young woman pulling down her boy friend's pants to reveal his bare behind.

Relaxation of the old inhibitions is welcomed by some advertising decision-makers. "We really consider this on a case-by-case basis, says Coca-Cola's Julie Eisen, "looking for what's appropriate and consistent for our brands." The leading TV buyer for a large agency group asks:

> Are we leading the crowd, or are we behind it? I think we're just reflecting what's going on. Look at reality television. I think it's good. We don't live in a vacuum. The violence that they sing about in the rap music is a reality. Eminem [a white rapper] is striking a chord that other kids can relate to.

"Once a big name [advertiser] comes in, there's a domino effect," says the WB network's Jed Petrick.[5] Fox Broadcasting's Jon Nesvig says, "If you have programs that deliver the goods in terms of sizable audiences and good demographics, and there aren't content issues that make audiences uncomfortable, you've got something that works big time."

What really matters is the appraisals by advertisers and agencies of specific shows and episodes rather than the labels placed on them by the producers. A media director says his agency follows no uniform rules: "It's on a client-by-client basis. They're more guided by their own judgment rather than by the labels."

Another agency media director comments on the program labels: "I don't monitor that stuff, and I don't think the clients do. Every advertiser has a hit list. Some are more sensitive to content than others. The popularity of the reality shows has driven prices up on all of television, because they have drawn the audience from the other types of programs."

A well-known media executive:

> Sitting in client meetings talking about strategy, I have never heard anyone bring up program ratings. They're just a nonissue. The reality shows may be vulgar and tasteless, but if the audience is there the clients are not turning away from them. The people who run the networks now are bureaucrats, and their

job is to generate numbers. They're not looking at a creative vision. When someone creates a great show it's by accident. The theory is, "Clone what works." They're programming specifically for the available audience. Talk shows in the afternoon, game shows in the early evening, dating shows on late night. Television is a simple business. It's driven by one word: greed. Never by content or mission.

The principal television buyer for a very large agency group:

Those programs with excessive violent content—it's really up to the viewer or the head of household to decide what to view. I don't think [labeling, the V-chip] it's had any effect on how advertisers look at programs. Every advertiser knows that there are some risks involved, and it's up to them. I haven't heard of any over-the-top writing in from viewers. There's been only one example in five years where somebody got letters from viewers. We understand there are some risks involved, but if you don't take them you've lost out.

Another powerful media executive echoes the sentiment that the viewers don't really care:

Particularly youth marketers have to be on the cutting edge of what those kids want to watch. Unless it's excessive or at an inappropriate time. "Will and Grace" [about a gay man and his best friend, a straight woman] was on at nine and the first comments were, "It's unbelievable." That program is now in syndication and running at seven or five o'clock [when kids are watching], but you don't hear a peep about it.

Television executives reflect on their business. If the people who buy television commercial time are dubious

about the effects of program labels, the ones who generate programming appear to be almost uniformly cynical on the subject.
A veteran television executive comments:

> It's an invitation for forbidden fruit. What offends you and me
> doesn't affect the fourteen-year-olds. So I have a highly skepti-
> cal view. The more restrictive the rating, the greater the appeal.
> No one goes to G-rated movies any more. Every producer
> knows that a G is a deterrent, so they try to make it a PG by
> throwing in some language or scenes to make the movie dirty.
> In [a highly acclaimed film] the expression "What the fuck" was
> used. It was reality and I won the case, so the rating was up-
> graded. I personally hate gratuitous use of language or scenes of
> violence if they are not organic to the story line, if they're aes-
> thetically incorrect. In the film *Eight Mile*, with Eminem,
> there's no way to avoid that language because it has a profound
> message about social outcasts who use that kind of language.
> This isn't done to push it into an R.
>
> When TV was only broadcast, the broadcaster was supposed
> to operate in the public interest and reflect public values in full
> view, with no ability to restrict anything. Because of Congress
> and pressure groups, everything was homogenized. When cable
> was introduced, the standards went out. It raised the level of rel-
> ative morality. When you got into pay TV you paid explicitly to
> get "The Sopranos" and "Sex and the City." The do-gooders
> paved the way for the pornographers. Public access, which can't
> be censored, created a whole new breed of pornographers. You
> escalated from broadcast responsibility. Smoking and drinking is
> now used as a sign of a stupid person. I wonder whether "The
> Sopranos" would be successful without the language and vio-
> lence and nudity. I think they add that extra level of shock value.

He comments on the problem of putting Hollywood feature
films on television:

Almost by definition, someone who gets permission and back-ing to get a major movie made is not going to be a nihilist. The film is either going to be immensely commercial or immensely artistic. The *Dirty Harry* movies are morality plays. They're comic. QED, that's why the rating system is a good system. Vis-conti's *The Damned* had a scene of incest, so it was unrated. It was put on at 11 p.m. Then a congressman denounced the net-work for putting it on the air.

A leading film and TV executive refers to the difference be-tween the standards accepted for the movie theater and those for television. He seems to suggest that there is not enough gore in television productions:

I had the network tell me that they wouldn't show [a critically acclaimed film] because of a nude scene. [The director] wouldn't take it out. Context is so important. That's the problem of the rating system. Everything gets lumped in a body count. For thirty years I ran [a cartoon series] and every shooting scene I cut out. With [a drama series] it only took one shot, and then the perpetrator was only wounded in the leg. I wonder whether we haven't sanitized violence too much. We may have gotten some of the reality back with the forensic shows.

The impetus to be "edgy" sometimes comes spontaneously from a show's writers and may actually have to be restrained. A network executive says: "The creative side is always pushing the limit. 'I have to have that shot.' Or 'that word!' You have to have those big names on your side."[6]

A film and TV writer:

We try to get away with as much as we can. In TV, standards and practices [internal screening operations by the networks] was a joke. Nobody thought about it, except to be as free as we could in what we were doing. In my experience, the writers

220 / OVER THE EDGE

really don't care except to have as few restrictions as possible. We would sometimes overdo it so they could cut us back and we'd still have something left.

In this respect, television writers are following a tradition long practiced in the film business—introducing patently unacceptable elements as bargaining chips with the censors or rating panels.

The writer Tad Friend observes that

the rules of engagement in this routine warfare [between writers and the network standards departments] are understood by everyone involved. Standards editors often tell one another, "Give them seven notes so you can negotiate." The writers, in turn, put "asshole" in the script a few times as "censor bait," knowing they'll have to cut it but hoping to keep two "bitch"es and a "balls" in exchange.[7]

Compromise and subterfuge are used to get controversial programming on the air. A producer, discussing a program with homosexual characters: "We made it [homosexuality] into a political issue rather than a sexual issue. We had a script with a gay character having an affair with a fourteen-year-old boy. In the end we made the boy over sixteen. We put the explicit scenes in the first ten minutes, before the characters were developed. The audience didn't care."

A film and television writer-producer: "In television, I am almost completely unaware of parental guidance warnings in the creation and execution of the show."

A network executive:

It's impossible to put a show into a box. What might be S or V or L for one segment of the audience would be inappropriate for another. It might also vary with the following program [in a series]. These labels are basically meaningless. Nobody seems to care about them any more. On one program last year somebody said "shit." We didn't get a single phone call objecting to that. The Comedy Channel publicized the fact that it had 162 mentions of "shit" on one show, and this was considered a publicity coup.

One thing that does concern us is imitability. There's a program called "Jackass" on MTV where the host does all kinds of crazy things. A number of kids tried to imitate them. There was no reaction. In fact they moved the show to an earlier hour so there would be more kids watching. I was astounded.

If you go to Hollywood, nobody knows about the labels. Applying standards is totally a business decision; it has nothing to do with morality. What we react to are the advertisers, the affiliates, and the Washington regulators. Advertisers pull out of programs all the time. We'll get only an occasional viewer complaint. We don't do anything that will upset Congress.

But this executive contends that advertisers will quickly abandon their prudery to follow the viewers wherever they go:

It's all about GRPs [gross rating points, a measure of audience size]. The reason why the content of programs becomes an issue is when the CEO's wife is at the country club and someone asks her, "How can your husband's company advertise on such a program?" Then the word goes out down the line.

There are very few programs where you have to be on guard about what you show. At first a lot of advertisers shied away from reality shows. Now that their ratings are up, they clamor to get on board. There are really two kinds of reality shows, some fairly innocent. Others, like "Fear Factor," can be pretty gross. They're coming ahead because they're now mainstream television. If there's been one single day in the last year that we've talked about program ratings here, that's been a lot.

So what was "pretty gross" is now "mainstream." His network screens about twenty pilots a year.

> We read every script and we look at the rough cuts. If a show is going to have a certain kind of edginess, the pilot will reflect it. Once a show is on, in the normal course of things there's rarely an issue. Some shows are just more problematic than others. "The Sopranos" and "Sex and the City" have become the gold standard. They know exactly what they can do, and the producer-writers—because the producers *are* writers—feel that's what makes a show successful.

In contrast to comments I cited earlier from those who believe that the success of these premium cable series has come from their juicy characters and plot lines, he insists that "language and sexual attribution are not what makes a program successful."

> When there are over a hundred channels to choose from, people are not going to watch programs that offend them. Those who would be offended don't watch the offensive stuff; they're just not going to be there, as they would have been when there were only the three networks.

But as a potent figure in one of those "old" networks, he invokes the old tradition of responsibility to the public interest: "At some point you have to ask what this network stands for and judge programs on that basis."

A television pioneer, still in harness, sees the current labels as an extension of long-standing restrictions:

> At the old television networks, controls were far more important than ratings attached to a program or a film. Most advertisers had their own rating systems, depending on the attitudes of the senior executives, and occasionally governed by the prod-

ucts they sold, and sometimes by outside pressures from clergy or parent groups. All delivery systems in the home are now far more uncontrollable, no matter what rating systems are used.

He believes that content is largely defined by the people who create it. This seems to value audience size rather than any independent critical judgment of artistic excellence.

Ratings systems are not established by the people who create the programs in the first place, who write the stories, provide the concepts, or sell the programs. They may be influenced by certain rules that they're familiar with as professionals, but at the point of creation they're only conscious of making it the most successful program possible.

I've been involved with every kind of rating system in broadcasting since 1948. We had a comedy program that we wanted to broadcast Sunday morning, but the station owner insisted that everyone was in church at that time and that it should be broadcast in the afternoon. That was a rating.

The creative world has always fought any regulation or interference because it has always been ahead of the curve. The creative community has historically been at the forefront of change. The movies were always on the cutting edge. Television wouldn't deal with subjects that the movies were already doing. It began to change when we were buying movies. In the mid-sixties, we showed a scene of a boy and a girl in bed high on drugs. The producer, whose daughter had become a drug addict, was trying to prove the evil of drugs. The movement of the bedcovers indicated sexual activity. We let that go on. Today the rule is "We don't want to show actual penetration." The argument is over what is left in the mind and what is suggested. This argument takes place constantly between the producer and the acceptance department. You can see the man moving down the woman's body, but not his mouth touching her genitals. The effectiveness of the scenes skirts any number or rating that can be attached to it.

He recalls that in the early days of television, "There was acceptable programming and nonacceptable programming, just as there were acceptable and nonacceptable commercials. You couldn't advertise certain products like toilet tissue. Those were rules established not only by the broadcasters but by the advertising industry and by the clients themselves."

The changing standards in advertising also influence program producers. A different, much younger television executive says,

> What has forced the change in the way that things are rated is that advertisers have exploded the rules. The broadcasters have expanded their advertising base and accepted products like contraceptives. Today the attitude of the network commercial acceptability department is that they judge the taste of the commercial, not the product. The advertising industry has flourished basically unimpaired, except by the Food and Drug Administration. I saw a commercial that showed a guy in a swimming pool with two beautiful girls and all of a sudden he says, "I've got to go!" and runs out to the bathroom. It's a commercial for Ex-Lax or something like that. I have had producers tell me, "You want *me* to put in a disclaimer and *you're* running commercials like that!"

Another broadcaster points to the constant interplay among the various media, so that what one gets away with encourages others to do the same:

> There's far more explicit violence for violence's sake, but the mores of the American public are forcing producers to be much more permissive. That will continue as long as the movie in-

dustry continues to bring the most dramatic ways of presenting violence with the aid of new digital technology. The video games are harsh indeed. There's no end in sight unless it descends into the political arena. It's a little like nuclear war. At the present time the only ending I see is that censorship and civil liberties come to a collision.

Applying standards.   Long before program labeling was introduced, the broadcast networks had set up their own standards of acceptability for what they put on the air, with departments charged with enforcing them. Labeling has added new wrinkles to their old task. The standards supervisor for a major network says:

We felt the descriptions would make everything confusing to the viewer if there was anything different between what the viewer expected and what he saw. [A highly popular show] was originally rated a PG. My boss felt we should make it TV-14 since the story lines were pushing it more. We felt we should make it a higher [more restrictive] level. We put the advisories on it. The advisories are more specific. When they started the age-based program labels, we knew we were not going to put MA [mature] programs on the network.

TV-14 lets the viewer know that the content is a little edgier. The only time I worried about the advisories was when we put [formerly late evening] shows on prime time. We have standards guidelines that are sent to the producers, and they don't vary season to season. From my perspective, I don't think the ratings icon has allowed writers to become more edgy, but society has changed. Cable has had a big effect. You watch "The Sopranos" and its language. Our writers and producers try to follow that. They say, "Look, *they're* using those words. I saw that on Comedy Central."

A standards executive for a different network declares, "With the size of the audience the network gives you, there goes a certain sense of responsibility."

Some censorship has nothing at all to do with propriety but a lot to do with political sensitivities. A network standards executive: "We don't want to offend minorities or show the use of drugs. Smoking was out for a while, and now it's come back on the part of good guys."

A network executive:

One thing we watch for is racial stereotyping. Glitches that are in extremely poor taste where you think, "Is this reflecting on the network? Are we going down to their level, the lowest level possible?" We let [a popular comedy program] use the word "Chink" to refer to somebody because they felt it was funny.

You can't say "God damn!" or "Jesus Christ!" On [the comedy show] we had a backfire when a character referred to the Jews as "Christ killers." It was supposed to show how dumb she was. It was satirical. We got a lot of flack. And we got over two thousand e-mails to protest a skit where we portrayed a comic Turkish woman with hairy armpits, because the show had a Greek woman in it. But we've never had a strong reaction to language.

A former network director of standards: "The standards people are very subjective. In the past they all used to be lawyers. Ninety-five percent of the time we were very clear about our decisions. The networks have become especially concerned about government pressure driven by special interest groups."

Broadcasters comment on the FCC's general lack of interest in program content: "There's no government constraint any more. There's less government standards interference than there was before."

The networks are buffeted by local as well as national forces. They are constrained by the moral strictures of "middle America" rather than by those of New York and Los Angeles. A network executive observes, "Networks go through local affiliates who are in communities with different constraints. The network is a kind of middleman between the artist and the patron. It's about the money."

But the standards change. "Thirty years ago we couldn't use the words 'abortion' or 'pregnancy.'"

What makes a program succeed?   Program labels have become an element, albeit a minor one, in the multifaceted environment in which TV viewers are immersed. The words and scenes that arouse contention are also absorbed into that environment. The context of television content—bland or aggressive—is often limited by TV's time limitations. "It's difficult to take a very complex problem and present the solution in forty-two minutes [the time left in a one-hour show after commercials and promos]."

The result shows up not only in weaknesses of dramatic plots and characterizations but in a resort to crudity as a substitute device to heighten attention. Producers are also hamstrung by the unwillingness of the networks to allow a show to evolve over a number of episodes if its initial audience levels are unsatisfactory.

A writer/producer: "The networks are not giving people more time any more [to show what a show can do]. All the great shows came close to being canceled. But there was someone at the helm who said, 'We're going to give them a chance.' Every great show took six months or a year to catch on."

A cable television executive makes the same point: "A show is not given time to build an attachment with the audience; they change times all the time. They have disciplined the viewer to be undisciplined. And that's one of the reasons why cable has been winning."

Seen as part of the total, overwhelming television universe, any provocative elements must stand out strongly to produce a vocal reaction. A producer insists on the preeminent importance of a program's inherent merit: "If the show is good, you won't get letters of complaint."

A network executive agrees: "If it's done well, audiences come. The most explicit shows on the air are from one to four in the afternoon. Being violent or graphic won't make a show a hit. Every one of our shows is a creative risk."

But, as a film and television star observes:

The judgment of the sense of quality is made not by the people making the show but by other people. A sense of seriousness of purpose has some power to it. A documentary about 9/11 had a firefighter saying the word "fuck." In that context, no one would object. The FCC complained because [a network] broadcast [the film] *Saving Private Ryan* unexpurgated, with "fuck" among the expletives. At one time the networks wouldn't let the word "virgin" be used. The process of making you censor yourself makes you a participant with your oppressor. The artist is worried. Artists are trying to find their way through the web. The pornographic business is more profitable, but that's not the one we're in. The language that's hard to get on the air is quality.

A television personality wisecracks, "Familiarity breeds contempt, but it also breeds familiarity."

The vice president in charge of film acquisition for a cable network:

> When the movie ratings were first being introduced, I believed they would open the floodgates to pornography and distress. They turned out to be less a floodgate than an explosive that blew up the dam. I don't think there's anything to stop the ability of broadcasters to show or do whatever they wish. A lot of people were assigned to do the [content] classification. But we had already been doing this through our standards and practices department. I have never met one person who thanked me for what we did.

He also points to failures in communication: "The screeners don't confer with the producers. The major movie companies know exactly what the standards are. I think people are confused as to what's pay and what's cable or broadcast. They don't distinguish."

A cable television executive, formerly an agency media director, offers testimony that the labels have left producers free to introduce program elements that would once have been unthinkable, by falling back on the proposition that they are now clearly marked and can thus be avoided by viewers:

> [Ratings] are allowing producers greater flexibility in terms of content, because if the consumer is aware of the warnings to have their children avoid certain programs, the producer can do anything he wants within that program. The digital cable box gives a fifty- to sixty-word description of the programs that are coming up, and viewers can follow those. What [labeling] has done is take a lot of the onus off the programmer and the network because it provides information for the viewers to decide if they want to see the program or not. It has loosened things

up. If you warn people that there's going to be nudity, I probably won't let an eight-year-old kid watch that show. Adjusting
that creativity should lead to better—I'm not saying higher—
[audience] ratings, more targeted to the young people that producers see as the target. It's just an explanation that this show has
more attributes than another show in terms of violence or sex.
It also restricts more advertisers from coming into the show.

This is testimony to a critical point. As in the case of the
movies, labeling television shows has been counterproductive.
Not only does it attract the very youngsters it is intended to keep
away, but it allows producers free rein and even encourages them
to introduce elements of content they might not otherwise use.

9

Labeling other media

The ratings pioneered by the film industry and adapted for television have become models for two other entertainment media, with the same confusing consequences. Like movies and pay cable, the content of musical recordings and video games is devised to meet consumers' demands rather than the wishes of advertisers. As in the case of theater films, the heaviest consumers are young people. And, as with any other consumer product, the demand is linked to what is promoted, visible, and available through the channels of distribution.

The distribution of recorded music and video games is increasingly siphoned through giant retailers whose large sales volumes and diversified merchandise lines make them highly vulnerable to pressure from organized campaigns by self-appointed moralists. In enforcing industry efforts at self-regulation, it is no easy matter to get smaller retailers to participate actively. They make heavy use of seasonal and part-time help who are unlikely to screen purchases. Retail store clerks are often uninformed about the ratings system they are supposed to be enforcing, and in many cases youngsters can easily buy any title they want.[1]

The production of both recordings and games is linked to film and television as the giant entertainment companies expand their interests.

Video games. In a past, more innocent world, children played games like "cops and robbers" and "cowboys and Indians," using their hands to simulate guns and shouting "Bang! Bang! Bang!" The violence was entirely expressive and imaginary, and involved no infliction of pain. Good guys and bad guys exchanged sides after each bout. Little if any anger was generated. There was no body contact. It was all quite antiseptic.

Today the violent formulas of action films provide the basis for an important new medium of entertainment—video games and their offspring, computer games. In 2004 there were 71 million users of game consoles, 61 million users of PC games played offline, and 59 million users of online games. Between 1,200 and 2,000 games are produced each year, mostly by a few big companies who, as one industry specialist puts it, "know all the tricks." It takes a year, on average, to create a game.

In 2003 video game software companies sold more than 50 million games in the United States. Worldwide they were a $30 billion business.[2] The consoles sold for as little as $149 in 2004, but the profit was in the games. These typically cost $50, of which $10 goes to the console manufacturer as a license fee.[3] Game rentals cost up to $20 a month.

This industry has grown rapidly, from $4 billion in 1990, when Nintendo had a virtual monopoly. In 2004, domestic sales of game consoles were almost $3 billion, and of games themselves $6.5 billion.[4] Such a big business requires big investments. Development costs for a typical software title range from $5 to $8 million and go up to $10 million.[5]

For the game industry, as for television and film, young people are the chief marketing target. Between two-fifths and half the players are under eighteen, and they play far more often than adults.[6] But the median age of a game player is twenty-five. Altogether, three of five Americans play electronic games, two in five "regularly."[7] They spend more time (seventy-five hours a week) playing the games than they do with rented videos or DVDs.

Although more adults are taking up the activity, the number of children playing is not diminishing. Games are played by 90 percent of children and occupy 10 percent of their leisure time. As with other contacts on the internet, adults and children of different ages can play competitively without knowing their opponent's age.

The introduction to games begins early in life. Most boys aged six and younger have already played a console game, and a fourth of them play on a typical day. (Little girls play far less than boys.) With their mainly masculine appeal, the games feature male protagonists. Nine-tenths of them have no female roles.

Sales of video games have been spurred by tie-ins with Hollywood films such as *Spider-Man* and *Lord of the Rings*. But the connection has also gone the other way, as game manufacturers have begun to sell title rights to filmmakers. The license to adapt a movie for a video game can cost over $20 million. The film company Warner Bros. (part of Time Warner) formed an interactive gaming division. Viacom Chairman Sumner Redstone acquired a large personal holding in Midway Games, Inc., a video game maker. In 2004 a James Bond production, *Everything or Nothing*, was released as a game even before work began on the movie version.

There have also been ties to the music business. The Universal Music Group's Def Jam joined with the largest video game maker, Electronic Arts, to produce a series of games that featured the music firm's artists and was expected to replace radio as the main vehicle for promoting new numbers.

The growth of video and computer gaming has been accompanied by a steady enhancement of the games' imagery. Their early cartoonlike character has been supplanted by virtual recreations of high fidelity. As one informant says,

> When the industry first started it was all black and white. The chips gave us sound and color, and now we have the capacity to make the characters look real. In the hands of creative people you can have a tremendous interactive experience. You can now have complex story lines. You can be Sherlock Holmes or Mike Hammer.

A minority of all the games are violent, but these have had enormous success. In fact, 85 percent of the most popular video games fall under this heading.[8] Half of fourth-graders say their favorite video games are violent.[9] The industry is geared to satisfy these interests. As a leading critic of the games, David Walsh, observes, "As the audience gets older, the game makers push the envelope."

The video game "Grand Theft Auto: Vice City" offers players the mission of finding and killing the people who stole their cocaine. "You play one of the bad guys, what the company calls an 'aspirational gangster,' free to kill whomever you want. . . . You can also pick up a prostitute, use her for (offscreen) services, then kill her and get your money back. . . ."[10] Players are encouraged to club innocent victims to death with baseball bats. In the United States alone, this game sold 1.4 million copies in its first three days on the market. A sequel, "Grand Theft Auto II," retailing at $49, sold more than 3 million copies.[11]

Take-Two, a financially troubled firm that owns these games, also produces "State of Emergency," in which players attempt to start riots, and "Max Payne," in which a policeman seeks personal revenge against drug dealers who killed his family. Other games offer similarly aggressive fantasy.

In "Tom Clancy's Junior Miss," the player assumes the identity of Savannah Montgomery, an eight-year-old Mississippi girl contestant in the Little Miss Jr. Pageant. As described by David Cross, "Armed with a vast array of weapons and accessories, you ensure victory by killing off the other contestants without getting caught. It's so lifelike you'll swear you really are an eight-year-old girl in a beauty pageant!"[12]

Violence is not the only theme that critics of video games have called into question. Pornographic websites sometimes masquerade as video game home pages. The games themselves have also been increasingly infused with sexually provocative content. As Michel Marriott describes it:

> Dressed in a sleeveless jacket and tight-flared pants, the young woman draws shouts of obscenities as she weaves between an ill-tempered pimp and a group of barely dressed prostitutes. . . . It's all in the day of a nearly photo-realistic trick biker in BMX XXX, a video game from Acclaim Entertainment. . . . In an advertising campaign at the game's website, Acclaim promises to "Keep It Dirty." . . . While the sex play in these games tends to be more suggestive than explicit, what is striking, even startling, is how it has moved from the periphery to center stage.[13]

Executives at Acclaim say, "The realism, resulting from advances in hardware and design, blurs the line between video games and movies, which routinely include nudity, raw language, and adult situations." According to Vinnie Longobardo at G-4, a cable network for video games, the sex is a "cover-up for not having anything completely innovative and new on the game-play side."

Listeners to a music CD over headphones are likely to be physically engaged, bobbing heads and wriggling to the rhythm. This kind of active response differs from that of game players, who retain an impassive intensity of expression while they face mortal dangers and destroy imaginary opponents. A game may demand fifty hours of play before the end is reached. This encourages players to come back compulsively to the unfinished business at hand. Game playing has the same mindless attraction as gambling.

Video games are more addictive than other media because of their interactive character. This interactivity is greatly enhanced by haptic technology, which permits players to be immersed in an expanded sensory experience that incorporates tactile as well as visual or aural stimuli. Vibrations stimulate the illusion of participation in the dramas displayed on the monitor.

Video games use operant conditioning techniques like those used to train soldiers. As Dave Grossman observes, "We are reaching that stage of desensitization at which the inflicting of pain and suffering has become a source of entertainment; vicarious pleasure rather than revulsion. We are learning to kill, and we are learning to like it."[14]

Unbeknown to most parents, according to Jeffrey Cole,

There are special "blood codes" available that take the game to a higher and extraordinarily graphic and violent level. These codes are not in the instruction manual. . . . In video game magazines and on the Internet, . . . articles reveal special moves not described in the manual that allow players to rip off arms and watch them spurt blood. They also teach how to impale on hooks, slash an opponent's throat, cause an opponent's body to explode, or decapitate him or her. It is the most shocking and grisly violence imaginable.[15]

Violence is featured not only in the games themselves but in the ads that promote them. Sony's PlayStation proclaims, "We've got good news and bad news. The good news is these games kick serious butt. The bad news is you're the butt." Another game features a whip-snapping woman. The voiceover: "Meet Sophia. Her turn-ons are wimps and black leather!" (PlayStation and other games represent 15 percent of Sony's sales but 35 percent of its operating income.)

An executive at a television network that does not accept commercials for M-rated video games acknowledges that "On video game commercials we'll show the most benign sequences, rather than the most violent ones, but that gives parents the impression that the game is harmless because they never go inside the thing and see the sadism."

Like the producers of film and TV, the makers of violent games insist that their products have no proven harmful effects. Doug Lowenstein, president of the Interactive Digital Software Association: "A lot of literature suggests there's no causal relationship between watching video games and violent behavior. The bulk of the literature concludes that at worst the impact is benign."[16]

Going even further, a study by Daphne Bavelier, a neuroscientist, and Shawn Green, after a series of experiments, concludes that "first-person-shooter" video games like "Medal of Honor" "increase the brain's capacity to spread attention over a wide range of events," and that "frequent players are better at identifying objects in their peripheral vision, switching attention, and tracking many objects at once."[17] It was quickly pointed out that nonviolent video games can develop the same skills. Nearly twice as many parents think that video games hurt children's learning as think they help.[18]

The evidence on the effects of video games is not as voluminous as the research literature that links television violence to aggressive behavior, but those conclusions surely apply to video games as well. Video game players express more aggressive feelings and behavior than nonplayers.[19] An Indiana University Medical School study found that violent video games cause changes in the brain's frontal lobe and leave players desensitized to real violence.[20]

The appeal of video games, inseparable from that of motion pictures, is rooted in the traditional toy business, whose marketing practices were transformed by television. The cultural historian Gary Cross describes how, in the nineteenth century, children "were no longer automatically inducted into the labor force as they had been when work was done at home."[21] Eventually,

> The idea that toddlers and small children should be protected from the experiences of older children and adults, a hallmark of child-rearing since the days of Rousseau, was abandoned. . . . The very idea of age-graded play was directly attacked when Mattel offered preschool toys that merged sophistication and innocence [and] assured buyers that Barbie was suitable for children over the age of two.[22]

A toy called "Forward Command Post" is "recommended" by the manufacturer for children of five and older.[23] It shows a bombed-out doll house. Its "accessories" include a machine gun, rocket launcher, magazine belt, and explosives. "Burnout 2: Point of Impact," an auto racing game that features smashups, is described as "appropriate for children of six." An ad that shows a man's head going through a windshield says, "The last thing that goes through your mind will be your ass."[24] In 2003, after the U.S. invasion of Afghanistan and during the war with Iraq, toy departments featured Easter baskets, made in China, containing armed soldiers in camouflage suits. Electronic games took "playing soldier" to an even higher and more dangerous level of engagement.

Overseeing game content. The expanding game industry uses two channels, video and the internet. In both instances it is difficult to restrict children's access to games with objectionable elements. Internet game downloads, growing slowly, were only a small part of the business in 2004 but were considered to have great growth potential.

As with television program ratings, video game ratings came about as a response to the threat of government action and the fear that a host of different local control or censorship systems might be put into place.[25] According to a senior executive in the video game industry: "There was a lot of congressional pressure. It brought everyone in the business together. There's a large number of bills at the federal level and the state and local levels." In 2004, twenty-seven pieces of legislation relating to video games were being considered in fifteen states.

Before the game industry established its trade association, software publishers set up a Recreational Software Advisory Council (RSAC) to rate personal computer games (not Sega Saturn and Super Nintendo video games) for sex, violence, and obscenity, on a scale from 0 to 4. Each publisher filled out a questionnaire and put his own rating on the product.

In 1994 the Interactive Digital Software Association was formed, representing both video and computer game companies. It created an independently funded Entertainment Software Rating Board (ESRB) to rate game products. The Video Software Dealers Association endorsed the rating system and adopted a "Pledge to Parents" program "to promote and encourage voluntary enforcement."

The ESRB assigns games to these categories: E (for everyone), EC (early childhood, three and younger); K-A, six and older; T (teenagers, thirteen and over); M (mature, seventeen and older, the equivalent of an R in the MPAA system); AO (adults only, the most restrictive category, equivalent to the movies' NC-17).[26] ESRB has expanded to cover the internet with ESRBI.

ESRB rates the games "the best they can," according to an industry executive. "Some websites won't let kids on. They ask for IDs. Almost everything is rated except for some children's video games."

The ESRB emphasizes that its M and AO ratings are "strictly advisory and not a legal determination that particular video games are obscene or harmful to minors." Ratings depend not only on the type of violence but on its intensity, its realism, and whether or not the victim is human. An ESRB spokesman says:

> We work with the retailers to get them to enforce the ratings. It's voluntary. They know where the movie or the game is going to go. If you don't like the rating you can talk to people at the ratings board. It puts the onus on the vendor and criminalizes the sale of M or AO games to minors.

In addition to the ratings, there are no fewer than thirty-one "appropriate content descriptors," including "comic mischief," "blood," "animated blood," "blood and gore," "use of drugs," and "gambling/gaming." These appear on the back of the package; the ratings are on the front. By 2003 the ESRB had rated and provided content descriptors for 8,500 titles. About seven in ten games carried the descriptors.

According to the ESRB, 63 percent of video games are rated E, 2 percent EC, 27 percent T, 8 percent M, and virtually none AO. But sales volume differs for different rating categories. Mature-rated video games rose from 6 percent of games sold (as distinct from titles rated) in 2001 to 13 percent the following year.[27] In 2002 four of the top twenty titles were rated M, four T (for teen), and twelve for "everyone."

Each game is rated by a team of three persons selected from a pool of one hundred people aged twenty to sixty that, in the words of an industry spokesman, represents "all sexes and all races." They provide both the age-based labels and the content descriptions. Sometimes a game is changed to fit the raters' requirements. Sitting in separate cubicles, the raters view each game independently. Their judgments are consistent 80 percent of the time, but they can be appealed.

The publisher must submit a forty- to sixty-minute videotape of the game. The review process lasts at least forty minutes and may continue for the length of the game. When the review is completed, the content may be changed if the company is unhappy with the assigned descriptor labels. Two or three weeks before a game is released to the public, the publisher must provide a final product that the board's technicians check out to make sure that everything is in line with the earlier judgment. Typically, a game is ready for production only a week before it is marketed.

As with other entertainment media, a marketing focus on young adults inevitably ropes in young children as well. In a 1998 marketing memorandum prepared by GT Interactive Software for an M-rated video game, the ostensible target was males 17–34, but "the true target is males 9 to 34."[28] Of 118 electronic games with a Mature rating for violence, seven of ten targeted children under 17, according to the 2000 FTC report.[29]

Children of nine have no trouble getting violent video games.[30] A game that featured topless women did not warrant an AO rating. E ratings were given to games that showed sexually provocative women. Of the fan magazine *TakeGamePro*'s half-million monthly readers, 62 percent are seventeen or under. Nearly a fifth of the advertising is for M-rated games.

An astute industry observer:

Violence, sex, and nudity are interpreted differently in different cultures. No matter how objective you try to make the system, it's always going to be subjective. You need experts to agree on what violence means. Just as there are differences between the United States and Europe, there are regional differences within this country. In the South you can use any kind of language, but you can't say "God damn." In the West nudity doesn't bother them but violence does. In Europe they have much more of a problem with violence than with sex.

The original purpose of the labels was to protect children. But now the video game publishers have decided they're more for adults. The whole idea of a system is to offer advice so that the viewer or listener knows what to expect.

He expresses a view similar to that we heard expressed by Richard Heffner about the labeling of films:

The content descriptors are much more important than the [age designation] letter. A game may have an audio with strong lyrics. There is some parental responsibility here. Where does a kid get $60 or $80 for a console?

According to this observer, labeling has had the same effect in the game industry as in film and television. "Everybody wants forbidden fruit. When 'Mortal Kombat' came out they had a sanitized version, but it didn't sell, so they made the uncensored one, which was a huge success."

Music. A significant target for indignation over the changing character of popular culture has been the music industry, where rap lyrics strongly appealing to a largely juvenile market often celebrate violence and contempt for women and legal authority.

Like motion pictures, popular music finds its primary market among teenagers and young adults, and the recorded music industry creates and promotes its products to suit their appetites. Ownership of the major record labels is largely concentrated in the hands of the same conglomerates that control film and television program production. In many cases, recording stars are also stars of film and television. Their works achieve popularity through repeated performance on radio stations that form another part of the same corporate web of entertainment companies.

There are some ten thousand independent music labels, but five companies produce over 85 percent of musical recordings.[31] In 1995, Time Warner sold its stake in Interscope, a producer of gangsta-rap records, because of concern over political pressures on the corporation in Washington.[32] But its recording company, Warner Music (sold in 2003 to lighten the parent corporation's indebtedness), continued to produce large quantities of albums that required parental warnings.

More than in other media, the music industry depends on the appeal of individual performers. When their talents and reputations are the drawing card, their personal predilections may be decisive in shaping the lyrics as well as the musical style of what is recorded. Chris Blackwell, a music producer:

> I don't think the music business lends itself very well to being a Wall Street business. You're always working with individuals, with creative people, and the people you're trying to reach, by and large, don't view music as a commodity but as a relationship with a band. It takes time to expand that relationship, but most people who work for the corporations have three-year

contracts, some five, and most of them are expected to produce. What an artist really needs is a champion, not a numbers guy who in another year is going to leave.[33]

The increasingly aggressive character of popular music in the age of rock reflects its dependence on amplification and the ascendance of rhythm over melody. Musical styles defy generalizations. Pop music has fractionated into grunge, ambient, illbient, acid house, acid jazz, drum 'n' bass, Eurodance, hip-hop, trip-hop, lounge, techno, glam, industrial metal, lo-fi, dream pop, psyche rock, and riot grrrl.[34] Each style has its own youthful devotees, often drawn to the particular personalities of its well-publicized exponents.

Not all rap and hip-hop recordings (which in 2003 represented 14 percent of musical recording sales) use language and imagery of the kind that a lot of people dislike. The same kinds of words also occur in other genres: rhythm and blues "urban" (11 percent of sales, "urban" being a euphemism for "black") and various varieties of rock (25 percent).[35]

There is nothing new in the pleasure that youngsters take in "dirty words." In 1940, in a recording of "Ol' Man Mose," as the singer repeated the key line, "Ol' Man Mose, he kicked the bucket!" the "b" in bucket was gradually slurred into an "f," to the great delectation of teenagers who gathered around the phonograph to catch the illicit expression. Such childish prurience seems innocent when compared to the extremes of today's rap recordings, which arouse similarly subversive thrills.

Popular music, with its rhythmic invitation to participate kinetically, has long been associated with low life. Jazz originally flourished in saloons and brothels, where drink, drugs, and tobacco set the scene. Bawdy lyrics have always been an alluring presence in folk songs. Twentieth-century popular songs, however outwardly respectable, often incorporated lubricious double entendres in their lyrics. The Rolling Stones sang, "Let's spend the night together." Popular singers have constructed hit numbers around thinly disguised allusions to drugs. The Beatles' "Lucy in the Sky with Diamonds" referred to LSD, Bob Dylan's "Rainy Day Women #12 & 35" to a marijuana cigarette. When Peter, Paul and Mary sang "Puff, the Magic Dragon," there was no mystery about what was being puffed. The use of such themes in songs with tremendous circulation and popularity confirmed the idea that narcotics use was somehow mainstream, if not altogether respectable. The emerging alternative press and such national publications as *Rolling Stone* reinforced this notion.

It is the savage words rather than the barbaric sounds of contemporary popular music that have aroused the indignation of moralists and prompted demands for restraint. The demands reached a crescendo with the arrival of black ghetto-based rap and hip-hop and their growing appeal to mainstream youth. (Three-fourths [74 percent] of all rap albums are sold to whites.)

Rap style may have its origins in "the dozens," a contest developed in slavery, in which men tried to outdo each other in inventive insults phrased in colorful language. The more frequent use of obscenities in the everyday speech of blacks must have stemmed from the degrading experience of slavery as well as the more general prevalence of "bad manners" among the poor and poorly educated. The coming of racial integration reduced the barriers in the daily contacts of blacks and whites and made ghetto speech generally more familiar. The process of acculturation worked both ways.

Words and sentiments that were not out of place in the squalor of drug-ridden center-city neighborhoods provoked alarm among white suburban parents. In 1956 the North Alabama White Citizens Council declared that rock music was part of a plot to mongrelize America. A cynic observed that black music met with criticism only when it left the ghetto and began to attract white teenagers.

In the words of the musicologist-composer Oscar Brand, "The rap records are invulnerable because they're supposed to reflect another culture. In the ghetto, those words are common currency. . . . It's the whole thing they [the critics] are objecting to—the baggy pants, the body-piercing. If your kids are following this path, it's frightening. Because it's different. Just as was the case with the Germans, the Irish, the Italians, the Jews. The Tango was dangerous!"

Mass sales of CDs are stimulated by other means of dissemination and promotion. The success of the MTV cable channel became a worldwide phenomenon. There are more than a hundred music video channels around the world. Rock and pop concerts draw $2.5 billion in annual revenues. A fourth of their songs are estimated to contain obscenities.[36] In 2003 a new form of nightclub disk jockeying emerged, featuring "mix" tapes with language too lurid for any record company to release.

Some of the well-publicized personalities of the hip-hop scene have transferred their celebrity to feature films. Some (including such stars as Snoop Dogg, Lil Jon, and 50 Cent) have expanded their empires further to produce pornographic videos. According to Martin Edlund, "One common scenario is to depict the rapper as a pimp presiding over a stable of beautiful women. The pimp is a stock figure in hip-hop iconography, an attractive rebel, full of street savvy and sexual charm."[37]

Since young people are the principal buyers of popular musical recordings, they are naturally the main target of music promotion. The FTC report of 2000 found that Bertelsmann's BMG Entertainment, EMI, Sony Music, Seagram's Universal Music Group, and Warner Music Group all advertised music with "explicit" lyrics in teenage-directed programs on MTV, BET, and UPN as well as in teenage magazines.

As I illustrated in Chapter One, rock and roll and rap have featured lyrics in which the liberal use of obscenities is mingled with violent and often sadistic imagery. Objection to popular music's lyrics found expression through such organizations as the (now defunct) Parent's Music Resource Center, founded by a group of politically well-connected "Washington Wives."[38] From January 1986 through August 1989 the PMRC examined 7,500 releases and rated 121 of them as offensive. Only 49 of these carried a warning applied by the record producer. (Later, Tipper Gore, wife of the vice president at the time, wanted the text of song lyrics to be placed on the album cover and proposed a label of O for "occult.") Further strong and well-publicized protests came from conservative activists like William Bennett and Lynne Cheney.

Responding to such expressions, individual states moved to label recordings. As in the case of video games, this raised the prospect of a forced and confusing confrontation with a wide and inconsistent assortment of regulations. Fearing possible federal government restrictions, the music industry came up with a labeling system that was supposed to discourage the sale of unsuitable musical numbers to younger teenagers.

A recording producer:

Even before the Hays Office, writers developed artful ways of introducing sexual innuendos into [film] scripts. In rock music there's always been symbolism. The ratings haven't changed much. Years ago, Jack Paar [a late-night TV host] caused a stir when he used the words 'water closet' on television. You never can play the dirtiest stuff on AM radio. Now look at the hip-hop and black ghetto stuff! But the FCC won't black you out for using sexual words. Compare the stuff put out for public consumption today with what was true in the past. You can put any law you want on the books, but the laws have always been changed. The internet has furthered the possibilities. All the kids can now put out their own records.

In 1983 the Recording Industry Association of America (RIAA) agreed to put an "explicit lyrics" label on recordings. Two years later the association reached an agreement with the National Parent-Teachers Associations and the Washington Wives' Parent's Music Resource Center to institute voluntary labeling.

The labeling of video games, television programs, and films has in each case involved a menu of age designations and descriptions. By contrast the music industry, after much debate, set up a quite simple procedure that, theoretically at least, would keep certain recordings out of the hands of children, with no particular explanation for their restriction.

As the RIAA describes it,

Individual record companies, working with their artists, decide which of their releases should be labeled. In some instances, record companies ask the artist to rerecord certain songs or to revise lyrics because a creative and responsible view of the music demands such a revision. Sometimes songs are simply taken off an album. In other instances the artist and record company agree that there is musical and artistic credibility in the whole of the work even when the lyrics may be too explicit for mainstream distribution. In these instances, the RIAA's parental advisory label is applied.

The RIAA asked its members whether they wanted an advisory label on the jacket cover or preferred to have the text of the lyrics printed on the jacket. No one chose the latter option.

In 1990 the music industry introduced stickers reading "Parental Advisory—Explicit Content," and sometimes "Strong Language,"[39] with a distinctive logo. The major companies, but not the independents, all agreed to follow the same rules and signed a licensing agreement to put the label on the albums that required it. The parental advisory is no longer a sticker but forms part of the art work in the lower right-hand corner of the album cover. An M (for mature) and T (for teenagers) were later introduced to provide further restrictions on sales.

The decision to apply the warning label is currently made by a music company's product manager (who oversees all production), in consultation with the legal department. An executive of one of the giant multi-label music companies explains:

> There's not one person who makes consistent decisions on advisories for the entire company. Persons at each label [record division] make their own decisions. It's not a particularly rigid, policy-driven procedure. The people involved could be the product manager (which every major artist or group has), the A and R [artists and repertoire] people, the marketing people. They all have a say. All the urban albums get [the warning label] automatically. Certain words, references, the sound of gunfire, mandate the use of the advisory. The record companies [actually, divisions, under different labels, of the same large firms] have been devoted to different parts of the business. Each album will involve a different group of people. It's primarily the product manager who decides.

According to another account, it is the lawyers who really call the shots.

> The decision [to use the advisory] is very much a part of the creation of the album. There's no consistent view of what demands

the advisory. At the extremes there's not a lot of debate about it. Otherwise it's a very haphazard process. Personally I have listened to albums where I have wondered why no one put an advisory on them.

The labeling program remains entirely voluntary. An opponent of censorship remarks: "Self-labeling of records can't be legally enforced to prohibit a sixteen-year-old from buying a CD label marked M. State legislatures tried to prohibit sales to minors, but those proposed laws would be unconstitutional."

For recording artists, marketing considerations may be less important than the creative urge to express themselves as naturally as they can: "The producer today has a different function. The rock group decides what they want to play. They think about the lyrics of a song and not whether it's going to sell."

The FTC report of 2000 examined fifty-five music recordings with explicit content labels and found that all of them were targeted to children under seventeen. Marketing plans for over a fourth of them expressly identified children under seventeen as part of their target audience. The documents for the remainder had detailed plans targeting that age group in their promotion.[40]

In its 2001 follow-up report, the FTC said that "the music recording industry, unlike the motion picture and electronic game industries, has not visibly responded to the Commission's report; nor has it implemented the reforms its trade association announced just before the Report was issued."[41]

To what extent does the presence of the advisory affect an album's actual distribution? A music industry executive: "Different stores have different policies, depending on their communities. It's really up to the parents. It's basically information for the consumers and for the parents of consumers. It's strictly voluntary."

Mass merchandisers (including appliance chains) now represent about half of all music sales, and discount chains now account for over a third. Such big chains as Wal-Mart, J. C. Penney, and K Mart do not carry albums that require the advisory label, fearing that these might be objectionable to at least some of their customers. Husbanding their selling space, these stores concentrate on a relatively small handful of best-selling titles. With a growing share of the retail music business, they typically carry a limited selection of fewer than two thousand books, records, and videos. (An average chain store carries five hundred book titles, half of them "Christian" books.) Quite possibly the conservative managements of the chains felt personally uncomfortable with the products. But whatever the private preferences of the people who run them, the chains are revenue-driven, and in 2004 they were reconsidering their policies, with good reason. "They don't want to lose profits," says a music industry researcher.

To get around the censorship imposed by the big retailers, it became common practice for the record companies to release songs in both their original form and in a "sanitized" version produced with those important chain outlets in mind. The cleaned-up versions were also offered as an option in ordinary record stores, where they met with little success. The redone albums and videos, with new covers to pass the chains' censors, account for only 10 to 20 percent of hip-hop sales.[42]

Music albums, like movies, are given different forms for different ways of distribution. Content is not only modified to pass the retail censors; it is also modified for musical numbers that are broadcast on radio and television. As one industry executive remarks, "When they show a music video on MTV, the lyrics are very different from the version on the album."

The RIAA has continued to make light of obscene lyrics by describing them as responses to cultural change and as successors

to long-standing practices. Addressing the baby-boomer generation, its website proclaims:

> Children have access to the media in ways their parents never
> imagined. In that sense teenage rebellion is easier than ever be-
> fore. This media access scares some parents because of the sex-
> ually explicit themes, violence, and strong language so readily
> available. . . . Every generation throws a hero up the pop charts,
> every generation rebels. Your parents didn't like or understand
> The Who or Jimi Hendrix; you don't like or understand much
> of your children's music.

John Yahner, a writer working on behalf of RIAA, describes
a family scene in his youth, after Woodstock, when he played for
his parents a recording of Country Joe and the Fish, "Give me
an F, give me a U": "Parents need all the help they can get. . . .
But government must stay out of the way."

In the same spirit as liquor advertisements warning against
drinking and driving, the RIAA and MTV launched a "Fight for
Your Rights: Take a Stand Against Violence" ad campaign after
the 2002 Columbine High School shootings in Colorado. They
were hardly so naive as to believe that such a meaningless exhortation could have any effect.

Hillary Rosen, former CEO of RIAA, suggests that "Music
can also be an opportunity—an outlet for parents or other adults
to talk to kids and an opportunity for adults to tune into what
kids are thinking and feeling."

In 2004 the recorded music industry was in crisis as more and
more young consumers exchanged and downloaded single numbers and even albums through the internet, substantially reducing sales through the usual retail channels. In 2002, 681 million
CDs were sold, compared with 763 million in 2001. Technology

created the situation and would have to resolve it, since the industry's recourse to the courts seemed only somewhat to stem the demand for illicit recordings.

Since the 33-1/3 r.p.m. "long-playing" record replaced the 78 r.p.m. format, musical recordings have been sold as aggregates rather than as singles. But music is most commonly downloaded from the internet one number at a time rather than as an entire album. The concept of an album label has thus become increasingly anachronistic, since not every selection in an M-labeled album is necessarily obscene.

While the switch to downloaded content may eventually have an effect on those who buy popular music, it is not yet clear whether it will affect musical styles. As one music industry executive points out, "Popular music runs in cycles. Hip-hop and rap will pass, like Elvis, the Beatles, and the Rolling Stones. Right now there's a void." That may be, but it is still filled by the aggressive lyrics of hip-hop and rap.

There is a sound business explanation for this. Like their counterparts in films and television, music industry professionals accept the "forbidden fruit" principle. As one says, "They'll buy more with the warning label. It's human nature."

A recording producer: "Producers love the idea of having a record banned because the kids will buy more of them."

Teenagers gave the same music albums higher grades when they carried no advisory labels than when they did.[43] But as the experiment with "sanitized" versions has demonstrated, what youngsters say is not necessarily what they do. A senior music company executive asserts, perhaps disingenuously: "No one has studied whether [the warning label] drives sales or not. It's not a negative or a positive." But she goes on to say, "It's only a negative to the extent that it makes some artists mad because it obscures the art work on the cover. Albums will sell three times as many copies with the advisory as in the edited version that goes to Wal-Mart and some other stores."

An executive at another company asks, "Do you want the real answer or the official answer?" Asked for "the real answer," she replies, "For the fifteen-year-old boys who buy these albums, it definitely improves sales."

Internet.   Music and games are only small parts of the ever larger flow of internet entertainment that has troubled many parents and resulted in organized efforts at censorship.

The internet has special appeal to young people. Young adults (18–24) are 21 percent more likely than average to have accessed the internet within the past thirty days. (By contrast, the 65-plus group is online at 45 percent of the average rate.) Those 18–34, a fourth of the population, account for two-fifths of the total time spent online.[44] The internet is now as much an instrument of socializing as the telephone. (Young people use it mainly for e-mail and chat groups rather than for news or information.)[45]

The internet has also transformed the lives of adults, who have had to acquire the facility to use it. But for most children it is as mundane a presence as the television set or the family car; it is taken for granted. Most children now have access to computers and to the web. Computers have grown more important to them. As noted earlier, of those children who have both a computer and a TV set, 71 percent would choose the PC if they could keep only one, and 29 percent would keep the TV.[46]

Computers have become a commonplace household appliance and their use begins early in life. A precocious 11 percent of children under two are reported by their proud parents to have used a computer already. Nearly one in five of children aged six or less use a computer on a typical day. Seven of ten children aged four to six have used a computer at some time, and nearly two of five can turn one on by themselves.[47] Parents overwhelmingly believe that the computer helps their children's learning.

The internet offers infinite riches but also sordid temptations and dangers. From its earliest days it has been flooded with pornographic content, easily available to those under age. This has aroused parental anxiety and led to legislative inquiry and action. Schools and libraries in particular have been urged to find ways of blocking access to the sites of such messages, raising more general issues of censorship.

Inevitably the rise of a powerful new communications medium like the web has provided pornographers with new opportunities. In 1998 "adult" content accounted for 69 percent of internet revenues from consumers.[48] Various estimates indicate that there are 30,000 to 70,000 adult websites online, generating revenues of $1 billion to $2 billion.[49] These may be only the tip of the iceberg. In a 2004 hearing before the Supreme Court, Solicitor General Theodore Olson reported that 6.23 million sites were found in an internet search for "free porn."[50]

A fourth of internet users visit one or more such sites each month.[51] In 1999 a single website devoted to pedophiles received 3.2 million downloads of child images.[52] Young men are particularly drawn to pornographic websites. Among those 18–34, 71 percent visit them over the course of a month, more than any other type of site and at a rate two-fifths greater than among other internet users.[53]

There is an important difference between the kind of pornographic enterprises to be found on the web and the sexually laden words and images that infuse the other media. The audience for pornography comes to it voluntarily and for its own sake. In the general media, the titillation is usually incidental to the main attraction—the drama of film and television, the sounds and throbs of music, the competitive thrill of video games. In the case of the internet, the line begins to blur as the search for information or companionship can lead to unanticipated encounters.

A fifth of youngsters aged 10–17 who regularly log on to the internet say they have received an unwanted sexual solicitation.[54] (Solicitations are defined as requests to engage in sexual activities or sexual talk, or to give personal sexual information.)

One-quarter of the children who were solicited for sex— some of whom were subsequently approached in person or enticed on the telephone or by regular mail—report being extremely upset or afraid. Neither parental oversight of children's online activities nor filtering or blocking technology had much impact on whether children were solicited.[55]

Two-thirds of parents agree, "I am concerned about my children's access to information available on the internet."[56] Congress heard this.

A Communications Decency Act, which banned transmission of indecent material to minors over the internet, was ruled unconstitutional by the Supreme Court in 1997. In 2000 the Child Online Protection Act imposed jail time and fines for placing content "harmful to minors" on a website available to those under seventeen, and restricted a website's ability to gather personal information from children under thirteen without parental consent. That law was never enforced, and its constitutionality was called into question because it blocked *all* the sites of companies that also run pornography sites. It was struck down as unconstitutional by the U.S. Court of Appeals in March 2003 because it prevented not just children but *adults* from accessing sites dealing with sex. Later that year, however, the law's constitutionality was upheld by the Supreme Court, but in 2004 the Court blocked its enforcement.

Defining pornography and indecency would not have been easy under this law. Peggy Peterson, a spokesman for Representative Michael Oxley, the primary sponsor of the act, said the Kenneth Starr Report (which led to the impeachment of President Clinton) "did not even approach the 'harmful to minors' standard" although it carried a full description of Clinton's oral sex encounter with Monica Lewinsky.

Apart from sexual temptation, the internet carries hidden dangers. Some companies sell advertising to reach captive juvenile audiences and also sell information about children's internet use.[57] N2H2, a company that provides filtering software, offered access to the Roper/Starch research firm to collect data on the websites visited by children.[58] N2H2 also sold data on young people's internet usage to the Defense Department for use in recruiting.

Setting up roadblocks. Children's use of the internet can be limited in two different ways. Some content is labeled by its providers to alert parents to its potential dangers. And, increasingly, content is also blocked by filtering systems that (at least in theory) automatically exclude improper material. In blocking the Child Online Protection Act, the Supreme Court said that such filtering systems would better serve the law's intention, since they "impose selective restrictions on speech at the receiving end, not universal restrictions at the source."

Long before the Court gave its endorsement, a variety of commercial enterprises had entered the business of weeding out certain internet content without any need for parents to monitor specific web offerings.

Internet service providers have been caught in a bind. In 2001, after the American Family Association (another self-anointed guardian of morality) protested the presence of X-rated websites and "adult" videos with an organized campaign that sent 100,000 messages of complaint, Yahoo eliminated access to such sites as part of an "evaluation process." The company's action brought counterprotests.

The web provides no universal labeling system comparable to that in other media. But the efforts to restrict children's use of the internet well illustrate the difficulty of applying impersonal and standardized procedures to reduce exposure to whatever someone might deem offensive.

As in the case of other media, the software industry has responded in fear or governmental action. The video game industry's Recreational Software Advisory Council was a prime mover. Its successor, the Internet Content Rating Association (ICRA), describes itself as

> an international, independent organization that empowers the public, especially parents, to make informed decisions about electronic media by means of the open and objective labeling of content. ICRA's dual aims are to: protect children from potentially harmful material; and to protect free speech on the Internet.

Like other media associations, the ICRA oozes good intentions.

> The majority of operators of "adults only" sites are generally just as keen not to offend young children as the next person. Furthermore, labeling their site sends a clear signal to governments that the World Wide Web is willing and able to self-regulate, rather than have the heavy hand of government legislation decide what is or is not acceptable.

It is the threat of "the heavy hand of government," of course, that brought about the efforts to self-regulate.

Under the ICRA procedure, website authors fill in an online questionnaire describing their content. The topics covered are: chat, language, nudity and sexual content, violence, gambling, drugs, and alcohol. Within each broad category the author is asked questions about whether a specific item or feature is present or absent on the website. ICRA then generates a Content Label (a short piece of computer code), which the author adds to the site. Users, especially parents of young children, can set their internet browser to allow or disallow access to websites based on the information declared in the label and the subjective preferences of the user. In spite of its name, the Internet Content Rating Association does not itself rate internet content and makes no value judgments.

The content ratings or labels conform to an internet industry standard known as PICS—the Platform for Internet Content Selection—a standard created by the World Wide Web Consortium. Websites can rate themselves from 1 to 4 for nudity, sex, violence, and language. ICRA spot-checks the self-assessments. News, sports, and promotional programming are exempt, but the Internet Content Coalition, made up of news organizations, has studied the possibility of offering a similar monitoring service. The well-intentioned procedure has only a very limited application. Of a million websites, only forty thousand have adopted the system for labeling content.

PICS was incorporated into Netscape Navigator and Microsoft's Internet Explorer. It allows any organization or group to set up its own content rating system. A user can choose among the available options and block access to undesired information or sites.

Compuserve's WOW! eliminates undesirable content and e-commerce sites and routes e-mail to parents for review. Cyber-Patrol, used by Compuserve and Prodigy, allows parents to block websites, using key words like sex, satanic, drugs, beer, wine, and tobacco. The blocking lists are considered trade secrets.

Cybersitter, Net Nanny, and CyberPatrol list internet sites that parents may wish to block. Nvolve.com developed a Safe Playgrounds Initiative, with a "kid's browser" that allows parents to limit the persons with whom their children can exchange e-mail messages. Taking the opposite tack, Disney.com and Yahooligans list sites that parents may want their children to watch.

Children can break the code of any easy-to-use control system on the internet, communications consultant John Carey points out. If it is hard to use, adults won't be able to choose the content they want to block. Tests of digital cable TV services show that only 10 percent of parents use the controls (and these parents are probably better educated than average, with their children least in need of protection).

Controls by individual parents (doomed to failure, as the V-chip experience shows) are less salient than the effort to cut off children's indiscriminate use of the internet through computers in their schools and in libraries used by the general public. Unlike the situation where parents restrict their children's computer use, restrictions on public institutions raise serious First Amendment issues.

More than three-fourths of all libraries are now connected to the internet. Although a federal judge in 1998 forbade *public* libraries from installing software to filter content, such systems have been increasingly adopted. An "e-rate" program, administered by the FCC, reimburses schools and libraries for internet installation costs. The federal government brought clout to bear on behalf of juvenile protection by requiring any institution using such funding "to implement filtering or blocking technology" by standards to be set locally.[59]

Marjorie Heins points to the distinction between self-ratings of a website and ratings by an outside party.

> The Platform for Internet Content was going to be a platform with software that you could activate on the computer. The question was, who was going to do the rating? Self-rating [of websites] was not going to be feasible. It could not be policed. You have 125,000 organizations that claim to self-rate. . . . Many sites have thousands of pages. I don't know of any organization that's offering a third-party rating system that consumers can use. How transparent is that as filtering has taken over? The raters have made a lot of money selling to school systems mostly. Most schools are using these filtering sites. Some have fifty or sixty categories.[60]

The filtering systems have been notoriously unreliable. *Consumer Reports*[61] has found, after testing several of these programs, that the best one, America OnLine's Young Teen control, missed 14 percent of objectionable sites; the worst, Cybersnoop, missed 90 percent. X-stop, a software system that libraries use to filter out obscene materials, allowed access to nine pornographic sites and blocked fifty-seven innocent ones.[62] The program barred information on sexual topics, including breast cancer and gay rights.[63] In N2H2's blocking system, words that trigger a warning include interracial, shower, toilet, pregnant, toys, underage, puffy, latex, teen, free, lolita, and watermelon.[64]

Geoffrey Nunberg, a professor of linguistics, tested several filtering systems used by libraries. They blocked access to

> everything from teenage sex advice sites posted by Planned Parenthood and Rutgers University to a dollhouse furniture set, *Salon* magazine, and the home page of the Canadian Discovery Channel. . . . Systems designed to spot pornographic images . . .

can't distinguish a painting of St. Sebastian from a *Penthouse* centerfold, and routinely block pictures of pigs and tapioca pudding, which have the color and texture of human skin.[65]

A Kaiser Family Foundation study in 2002 found that, at best, restrictive-settings filters did not block many pornographic sites while they blocked half the safe-sex sites and a quarter of all health sites.[66]

Solicitor General Theodore Olson argued to the Supreme Court that libraries using filters "are simply declining to put on their shelves what has traditionally been kept off the shelves," ignoring the fact that, as Nunberg points out, "public libraries acquire the internet as a single package, along with the risks inherent when someone buys a collectible on e-Bay, enters a chat room, or hunts for a mate."[67]

The American Library Association has taken a strong stand against internet censorship, paralleling its continuing struggle against the censorship of printed matter. The association's Office of Intellectual Freedom reports that between 1990 and 2000, 1,607 complaints were lodged against libraries' carrying books because of sexual content and 1,427 for offensive language.[68] For would-be censors, the web offers even richer opportunities for troublemaking than print publications do.

Perils in cyberspace. The internet has opened opportunities for the spread of ideas that threaten the established political order in many parts of the world. Filtering pornography cannot be separated from attempts to cut off access to political information, opinions, and exhortations.

New technology makes it possible to identify internet users geographically. One firm, Quova, claims to identify the user's country of origin with 98 percent accuracy and city with 85 percent. This makes it possible for nations like China, Iran, or Saudi Arabia to limit access to what was once thought to be a worldwide sphere without boundaries.

Authoritarian governments have gone to extraordinary lengths to bar websites that they imagine to pose dangers to them. In certain cases and places, individual search engines have sometimes been pressured to censor their offerings.

Google, the powerful search engine, does not accept cigarette or liquor ads but permits users to access pornography.[69] Google blocks German, French, and Swiss customers from using Nazi or other racist material, to conform with national laws. It wisely resisted efforts to exclude an anti-Semitic site that had been the number one entry under "Jew." But Google altered its Chinese website to permit the Chinese government to block access to terms like Falun Gong (a spiritualist exercise movement that was considered a threat to the Communist regime). Google also succumbed to pressure from the "Church" of Scientology and severed links to a Norwegian site that carried information exposing this cult, on the grounds that its copyrighted material was being misused.

Even the U.S. government has hacked websites that foster criminal activity. The Drug Enforcement Administration has entered and transformed sites trafficking in drug paraphernalia, replacing the original content with a warning and a large American flag.

The internet's international character makes it especially resistant to restrictions placed by individual governments. When it comes to the protection of minors, the yardsticks applied in various countries will naturally be different. As in the case of every other medium we have looked at, the labeling of content through independent efforts at self-regulation has come about only because of the fear of government intervention. As in every other medium, it has met with little success.

10

Back to the edge?

The perplexing question of how society should cope with pornographers' use of the internet to attract youthful prey is a long way from my starting point—the consequences of the media's quest for young audiences. But sordid applications of new technology are merely aberrant symptoms of a pervasive transformation of our culture.

The mysteries of change in fashions of dress, adornment, and comportment have long beguiled social scientists and remain elusive to universal explanations. Some transformations have come about through political coercion, as in the wholesale substitution of Mao suits for conventional attire after the Communist takeover of China. The less dramatic changes in European male costumes after the French Revolution came about voluntarily but were no less a response to the realignment of social class structure. More recently we have seen such realignment in a number of traditional societies subjected to colonial rule, when the apparel of the Western rulers is adopted by the native members of the indigenous bureaucracy and then by an emerging middle class.

In the twentieth century, women's knees have appeared and disappeared with the cycle of commodity prices. The periodic sprouting and disappearance of beards, mustaches, and long hair may also be linked to political and social circumstances. New fashions are rapidly adopted once they are taken up by those in the vanguard—by whatever criterion this may be defined. Fashions in etiquette follow the same course.

In the past, fashions and styles have appeared first at society's upper levels and trickled down to the masses, but today a reverse process often seems to occur. French prerevolutionary aristocrats liked to dress up as shepherds and shepherdesses. Similarly, the baggy pants, exposed midriffs, and frayed blue jeans of the poor have become the chic attire of today's youthful middle class. Changes in the way people dress and behave can rarely be attributed to a single historical event; they arise from a confluence of many interacting forces and trends within a culture. They can only come about if that culture is being buffeted by external influences. As transportation and communication eliminate national barriers and as technology becomes ever more complex, the notion of an isolated, static society without fashion may be sustained nostalgically but not in reality.

This book has traced the ways in which the commercial impulsions of mass entertainment have reshaped America's old standards of propriety. The media are only one among many factors behind this development. Unlike some of the other causes, they are amenable to social control through government policy. In the American tradition of laissez-faire, that policy has generally been "no policy."

What has happened to mass media may perhaps be understood in terms of the social science concept of "cultural lag,"[1] which designates the time lapse between changes in the conditions of social life and human adaptation to them. Old habits and ways of thinking persist even when the circumstances that made them useful and valid in the past no longer apply.

I have dwelt on the fact that the orientation to youth in American life came about because of the enormous growth in the number of births after World War II and the marketing strategies that centered on these baby boomers. In the 1960s and 1970s it was perfectly rational for the film and music companies to target them and for advertising planners to keep them in mind as they wrote television schedules. The demographic and social realities of the twenty-first century are not the same as those of thirty years ago, but the old assumptions about media audiences often still prevail in practice, with results that this book has traced.

Much of today's media production is created by people who are themselves part of the baby boom and who inadvertently assume that the values they acquired when they were growing into adulthood are shared by their successors. Among those values is the abandonment of strong political commitment, with its goal of changing the world. It was replaced by a kind of apolitical nihilism, a rejection of the Establishment's symbols without questioning the system in which the Establishment was rooted.

It is good for a nation to be young in spirit, energetic, and strong, with high hopes for the future. But it is wrong to assume that all the tastes and values of youth are applicable to a complex and varied society, whose members are of all ages.

It is not at all likely that marketers can be persuaded to change their strategy, since they have often persisted in employing intellectual clichés. This is demonstrated in their very common use of advertising campaigns that alienate the people whom they want to persuade.[2] Advertising decisions are made one at a time. No supreme authority dictates policies to agencies or their clients, or warns them of the perils in what they do.

In arguing that the misguided focus of media producers on youth has led directly to an increased reliance on the sensational in media content, I have had to rely more on anecdotal reports than on statistics. Rarely do those responsible for a film, TV show, or music album say outright, "I threw this in there because I know it will attract the 18–24 set." The smoking gun is hard to find, but the circumstantial evidence is compelling.

Horrible examples of the kind I quoted in the first chapter represent a small fraction of the total output of entertainment media. This does not lessen their importance, any more than the fact that, on any given day, only a minute part of the population falls prey to criminals. Over time, few Americans can avoid exposure to scenes and dialogue that would in the past have offended their sensibilities.

Why do these words and images no longer have the same power to shock? Because what is repeated becomes familiar, and what is familiar tends to be accepted and liked. Thus the judgments of media producers refashion the tastes of those to whose tastes they pretend to respond. The media are governed by market forces, but they are also ruled by the assumptions made by the people who run them.

Media producers are correct when they say they reflect society and its culture, but they minimize the effect of what they produce upon the society and the culture. Most of what has been considered offensive in mass media content is introduced gratuitously with the intention of enhancing audience appeal, but it is not the principal attraction for most of the audience. With media content as with all consumer products, what gets manufactured and distributed, no matter how unappealing it may be, will find at least some consumers willing to try it.

I have referred repeatedly in this book to the mores, the habits and patterns of human interaction that prevail in every society. I have not introduced the concept of morality, which is at the heart of most criticism of what many or even most people find disagreeable in media content. The media are generally quite scrupulous about such injunctions as taking the name of the Lord in vain, but they have been ready to depict and even glorify defiance of the other biblical Commandments. Displays of the sex act and musical demands to kill the police are acceptable, but the expletive "God damn it!" is a no-no. It may be appropriate for the clergy to denounce media sin from the pulpit, but the public argument against violence, sex, and nasty words must be based on grounds other than heavenly edict.

And the argument has been, essentially, that violence, sex, and nasty words harm and corrupt the children to whom society looks for its future. In the case of violence, the proof is unassailable.

The attraction of violence in films, television, and video games lies in the intense activity that accompanies it and in the uncertainty of the outcome. Novels and plays rarely describe the details of such clashes. They deal with human conflicts on the level of intellect and emotion. The audiovisual media dwell on direct physical contact, in crude depictions that have become ever more graphic and intimidating, in contrast to the subtleties of written fiction or live theater.

The anticipation of danger can be far more frightening than its actual portrayal. When movies followed the Hays Office code, Alfred Hitchcock was able to generate far more suspense through visual allusions than Quentin Tarantino does with fake blood and gore. Suspense is far more vivid when it tracks what is not portrayed rather than what is.

Similarly, romance in fiction and in film is more convincing when its consummation is left to the imagination than when it is graphically depicted as the pumping of sweaty bodies. Media content has not become more compelling when it pretends to demonstrate private relationships in public entertainment.

The media environment has become increasingly polluted by messages that trivialize the complexity and dignity of human relationships and that substitute false intimacy for the real thing. Should children be sheltered from its worst manifestations? The consequences for them are manifest. But media exposure would be relatively harmless except in the total context of children's development. The social disorganization that breeds troubled children also encourages their immersion in the maximum amount of troublesome media content. This reinforces the ill effects of poverty and fatherless upbringing.

But the really wide-scale damage done by film and video violence and vulgarity is not to children but to adults. Americans are swathed in audiovisual fictional experience on a scale that would have been inconceivable to previous generations. The values, the heroes, the language, and the models of human relationships that Hollywood presents to us are a powerful formative influence on our characters, not only in childhood but throughout our lives.

The creative process works differently in mass entertainment than it does for a composer, a novelist, or a poet. Films, television programs, music albums, and even video games are collective products, requiring the collaboration of large numbers of people and substantial resources. All those people, not just the stars, have enormous stakes in the way things are now done and are understandably resistant to change, especially to change imposed by outsiders.

This resistance has taken the form, in every medium, of an unwillingness to accept the notion that society carries any responsibility for media content other than what takes form in the marketplace. The threat of government intervention has led to the various systems of self-regulation, bewildering in their lack of a common standard or common definitions. As we have seen, the labels applied to content are different in every medium. Some individual systems are so simple as to be useless. Some are so complex that they are misunderstood and ignored.

Among parents of children between the ages of two and seventeen, 84 percent say they want a simple rating system.[3] One attempt to establish this, a proposed Twenty-first Century Media Responsibility Act, went nowhere in Congress in 2001. Since each media industry has its own way of labeling content, there has always been a yearning for a single standard with which parents could become familiar and that would reduce confusion.

In 2003 an attempt was launched to establish such a standard. Common Sense Media, backed by business leaders and working with the publishers of the Zagat restaurant guides, was set to label content for all entertainment media on a website to which parents were expected to subscribe with an annual "donation" of $25.[4]

Jack Valenti announced MPAA's opposition to the Common Sense Media plan, saying it could be taken over by "zealots." He complained, "The chances are that people who get on that website every day making judgments about movies are going to be the ones who say it's vulgar, unwholesome, terrifying—and the world is going to hell in a handbasket."[5]

An educator formerly responsible for setting up a rating system offers a different but also pessimistic assessment: "The idea of having one rating system for all media is bound to fail, because they're all so different. We need to create a universal vocabulary for a system that will have some common elements but where each industry system can exist by itself."

This is a worthy but improbable solution. Industry self-regulation has been a sham. While descriptions of media content are better than the age-suitability designations originally imposed by the film industry, even these descriptions are largely ignored by the public. In every medium the labeling of content has represented the dangling of forbidden fruit before juvenile audiences and has attracted them to whatever they are told they are too young to see or hear. A more important consequence is that imposing labels has freed media producers to become ever more outrageous and ingenious, to go farther over the edge in what they produce. Their contention that they merely obey the free market's expression of public taste is as specious an abnegation of responsibility as the claim, "I was only following orders."

How can those who generate and control the content of media be awakened to a sense of obligation to serve the public interest? The best chance may be in broadcasting, simply because it is licensed and regulated. The television industry's fabulous profits are reflected in large contributions to election campaigns, and the industry's huge influence on public opinion has strengthened the intimate ties of politicians and licensees. The political influence that multimedia corporations and their lobbyists bring to bear on candidates, legislators, and government agencies has grown more and more powerful as their size and resources have expanded. These facts of life discourage a return to the notion that broadcast media should be run with a sense of obligation to the common good.

There can be no redirection of those media to serve the public interest without reappraisal of the economic structure of the industry itself and of its political underpinnings. The content of cable and satellite television remains outside federal regulation. But the audience does not readily distinguish the source of the programming it receives. Whether it comes over the air, by cable, or through a satellite dish, it is all perceived as "TV." The law says otherwise, but what real justification is there for cable and satellite transmission to be exempt from the kind of supervision that the Federal Communications Commission exercises, at least in theory?

A more vigilant FCC that meticulously monitored the content of what goes out over the air or the wires would require an enormous staff and budget, and could degenerate into a thought police. It is unlikely that Congress would appropriate the necessary resources, even if it thought this was a good idea. But a continuing examination of the many thousands of hours of television programming is not essential in order to induce a greater degree of self-consciousness and self-control among those who provide the content of what appears on the tube.

License renewals for television stations and local franchise renewals for cable system operators are now automatic; they are almost never subject to serious review and are rarely challenged. This was true even before the "public interest" requirement was abandoned during the Reagan administration, but the very existence of the mandate kept broadcasting managements alert to their social responsibilities, even if these were sometimes rationalized in ridiculous ways (for example, by claiming that slapstick cartoons were "educational"). There is no uniform rule by which stations define what constitutes public service programming, and it is virtually impossible to find out what shows are purported to fit under that heading.

The broadcast industry has always fought attempts to disturb the status quo or to hold it accountable, considering these to be assaults on its property rights, derived from its substantial capital investments. Yet the value of privately owned transmission equipment and program production facilities is small indeed compared to society's stake in the radio frequency spectrum, essential to the transmission of cable programs as well as of satellite and terrestrial broadcasting.

If only one small step at a time can be taken, the first must be to revert to the long-neglected principle that the frequency spectrum is a public good, not a preserve for private exploitation. A reassertion by Congress of broadcasting's duty to protect the public interest might go much further to solve the problems raised in this book than any of the knee-jerk punitive measures proposed to maintain "decency" in content. So would more vigorous administration of renewal procedures for station licenses and cable system franchises.

Correcting the course of television and radio will not automatically change the character of movies, video games, or music lyrics. It will not reverse the great cultural transformation in standards of propriety and civil behavior. But any measure that forces the producers of mass media content to be sensitive to the consequences of what they create is bound to make them hesitate before they step too far over the edge.

Notes

Preface

1. PriceWaterhouseCooper estimates.

1. The exceptional enters the mainstream

1. John Robinson, *Time for Life* (University Park, Pa.: Penn State Press, 1999).

2. I elaborate this point in my book *Commercial Culture* (New Brunswick, N.J.: Transaction, 1999).

3. *New York Times* (hereafter *NYT*), June 2, 2003.

4. The film, *Hollywood Homicide*, starred Harrison Ford.

5. He is quoted at length by Larissa MacFarquahar, "The Movie Lover," *New Yorker*, October 20, 2003.

6. *Dan's Papers*, October 22, 1993.

7. Alessandra Stanley, "Prime-Time Shows are Getting Sexier," *NYT*, February 5, 2003.

8. *NYT*, February 5, 2003.

9. *NYT*, July 27, 2003.

10. While cable continued to show gains in the 2003–2004 season, the broadcast networks' share of the audience fell below half the total.

11. *NYT*, February 24, 2003.

12. *NYT*, January 25, 2003.

13. Dale Kunkel, Kirstie Cope-Farrar, Erica Biely, Wendy Jo Maynard Farinola, and Edward Donnerstein, "Sex on TV" (Menlo Park, Calif.: Kaiser Family Foundation, 2003). They took a composite week for each of ten channels and added a week of prime-time programs for the four major networks. Programs that combined news and entertainment were included, but daily newscasts, children's programs, and sportscasts were not.

14. It is not only in the United States that television has changed. European TV features even more prurience than the American variety. In Britain,

ITV offers "Am I Good in Bed?" while Channel 4 has "More Sex Tips for Girls." The BBC presents a lesbian drama, "Tipping the Velvet." Dutch TV soap commercials show frontal nudity. *NYT*, January 6, 2003.

15. Stuart Elliott in the *NYT*, March 3, 2003.

16. *NYT*, February 24, 2003.

17. *NYT*, July 25, 1999.

18. It was invented by a twenty-one-year-old who called himself "Fabulous 999," and was produced by Newgrounds.com, which also produced "Kaboom." *NYT*, December 5, 2002.

19. *NYT*, January 25, 2003.

20. *NYT*, July 19, 1999.

21. *NYT*, June 19, 1998.

22. Ibid.

23. Nickelodeon doesn't use such shows.

2. The mutability of mores

1. Some had both, so that different household members could watch both local broadcast stations (not available by satellite) and cable channels, on different sets.

2. John C. Burnham, *Bad Habits: Drinking, Smoking, Taking Drugs, Gambling, Sexual Misbehavior, and Swearing in American History* (New York: New York University Press, 1993).

3. The widespread assumption that the Pill increased the frequency of premarital sex has been called into question. In an op-ed article in the *New York Times* (December 27, 2003), a British scholar, Joshua M. Zeitz, points out, "Early sex surveys revealed that about half of all women who came of age in the 1920s admitted to engaging in premarital sex (defined as coitus), a figure that held steady for women in later decades."

4. It went from 62 per 100,000 inhabitants in 1957 to 440 in 1992.

5. Between 1972 and 1998, the proportion of children living at home with their own married parents fell from 72 percent to 52 percent. Households without children at home grew from 45 percent to 62 percent. The proportion of unmarried childless persons doubled, from 16 percent to 32 percent. While the percentage of households consisting of married people with no children at home remained stable at 29 percent, the percentage consisting of unmarried adults with no children at home doubled; the percentage made up of unmarried adults with children rose from 9 percent to 11 percent. U.S. Census data analyzed by Tom Smith, "The Emerging 21st Century American Family," National Opinion Research Center, 2002.

6. Between 1970 and 2000, the proportion of men who were currently married fell from 84 percent to 66 percent, and the proportion never married rose from 8 percent to 16 percent. Among women, the proportion currently married fell from 80 percent to 66 percent, and the never married increased from 5 percent to 11 percent. The birthrate for girls 15–19 peaked at 95 per thousand in 1960 and fell to 50 by 2000. (U.S. Census.)

7. In 2000, 69 percent of black children were born to unwed mothers.

8. Norbert Elias, *The Civilizing Process, vol. 2: Power and Civility* (New York, Pantheon Books, 1982), pp. 240–241.

9. Ibid., pp. 69–70.

10. Ibid., p. 135.

11. Norbert Elias, *The Civilizing Process, vol. 1: The History of Manners* (New York, Pantheon Books, 1978), p. 56.

12. Ibid., p. 64. A later book of etiquette admonishes adults—not children: "A man who clears his throat when he eats and one who blows his nose in the tablecloth are both ill-bred, I assure you."

13. Elias, *Civilizing Process*, vol. 1, pp. 175–176.

14. Ibid., p. 82.

15. Ibid., pp. 292–293.

16. Burnham, *Bad Habits*. "Bad habits," predominantly masculine and lower class, are, in Burnham's view, a sign of "impulsiveness."

17. Ibid., p. 210.

18. Burnham also believes that the publication of the Kinsey Report (however flawed its methodology) and the widespread publicity that followed, brought a new understanding of the varieties of sexual behavior.

19. Young people have the lowest rate of identification with either major party, though they are more liberal than older people. They have a lower voting rate than in the past, while older people are voting more.

20. M. Rutter, ed., *Psychosocial Disturbances in Young People: Challenges for Prevention* (New York: Cambridge University Press, 1995).

21. In a 1999 survey.

22. An almost identical view of teenagers is held by the general public, all parents, and parents of teenagers. Steve Farkas and Gene Johnson, *Kids These Days* (New York: Public Agenda Foundation, 1997).

23. Sherry A. Benton, John M. Robertson, Wen-Chih Tseng, Fred B. Newton, and Stephen L. Benton, "Changes in Counseling Center Client Problems Across Thirteen Years," *Professional Psychology: Research and Practice*, vol. 34, no. 1 (February 2003), pp. 66–73.

24. Robert W. Blum, "The National Longitudinal Study of Adolescent Health," reported in *Monitor on Psychology*, January 2001, pp. 22–23.

25. Public Agenda survey.

26. Parents of teenagers don't regard them any differently than do parents of younger children, or for that matter the general public.

27. A third (33 percent) say it happens sometimes, and 4 percent say it happens constantly.

28. The proportion who agree is lower among blacks than among whites and Hispanics. The perception that people are now "basically treating each other with enough respect and courtesy" is stronger among women than among men. It is much higher among less-educated people than among educated ones. Blacks and Hispanics agree more than whites. Sixty-three percent of people with less than a high school education agree, compared to 38 percent of college graduates. There is no difference, however, between parents and nonparents, or among age groups. But age differences appear when a variant of the same question is posed.

29. It is lower among the college educated (36 percent) than among the least educated (61 percent). Although women report this as often as men, they are more inclined (65 percent vs. 46 percent) to say it bothers them a lot. There is virtually no difference by education, race, or parental status. Nearly half of men but only a fourth of women admit to this.

30. There is no difference by education or ethnicity.

31. David J. Harding and Christopher Jencks, "Changing Attitudes Toward Premarital Sex," *Public Opinion Quarterly,* vol. 67, no. 7 (Summer 2003), pp. 211–226.

32. A 1994 survey asked a cross section of the public whether sex for teenagers under fifteen was wrong or not. Among those 18–20, 65 percent said it was always or almost always wrong, and 15 percent said it was wrong only sometimes or not at all. Among those 21–24, the proportions were virtually the same. (By contrast, among those 70 and over, 92 percent said it was wrong and 3 percent thought it was not.) The same study inquired whether "it's a good idea for a couple who intend to get married to live together first." Among those 18–20, 70 percent agreed and 2 percent disagreed. For those 21–24, 53 percent agreed and 29 percent disagreed. Among those 70 and over, 8 percent agreed and 71 percent disagreed (National Opinion Research Center).

33. In 2004 the figure was 47 percent. Of those who had engaged in sex, three-fifths (58 percent) had used a condom on the last occasion, and a fourth (25 percent) had become infected with a sexually transmitted disease. So have a fifth of adolescents under fifteen. The proportion of high-school-age teenaged boys who have had sexual intercourse fell from 60 percent in 1990 to 48 percent in 2001; for girls the drop was from 48 percent to 43 percent (Centers for Disease Control and Prevention).

34. Kaiser Family Foundation studies, 1996, 1998.

35. J. D. Brown, K. W. Childers, and C. S. Waszak, "Television and Adolescent Sexuality," *Journal of Adolescent Health Care,* vol. 11 (1990), pp. 62–70.

36. J. D. Brown and S. F. Newcomer, "Television Viewing and Adolescents' Sexual Behavior," *Journal of Homosexuality*, vol. 21 (1991), pp. 77–91. J. L. Peterson, K. A. Moore, and F. F. Furstenberg, "Television Viewing and Early Initiation of Sexual Intercourse: Is There a Link?" *Journal of Homosexuality*, vol. 21 (1991), pp. 93–119.

37. Abbott L. Ferriss, "Studying and Measuring Civility," *Sociological Inquiry*, vol. 72, no. 3 (Summer 2002), pp. 376–392.

38. Corey L. M. Keyes, "Social Civility in the United States," *Sociological Inquiry*, vol. 72, no. 3 (Summer 2002), pp. 393–408.

39. There is also no difference between parents and nonparents. Men, whites, and the college educated are least likely to agree.

40. Among the young, 64 percent agree, compared to 77 percent among those over fifty. Agreement is lower among blacks (60 percent) compared to whites (76 percent) and Hispanics (75 percent). The college educated are less inclined (68 percent) to agree than others (75–78 percent).

41. From a 2001 Harris poll made at my suggestion in 2001. Although among people aged 18–24 only 7 percent prefer to be called by their first names, compared to 2 percent of those over sixty-five, somewhat fewer (27 percent compared to 35 percent) say, "It bothers me." Better-educated people are more bothered by intimacy; 46 percent of those with more than a bachelor's degree gave that answer, compared to 24 percent of those who had not gone beyond high school. For that reason, more self-styled liberals (39 percent) than conservatives (25 percent) prefer last names. Women (39 percent) are more bothered than men (23 percent).

3. The pursuit of youth

1. Compared to the average person, young people are 124 percent more likely to go to bars and nightclubs two or more times a week. (Those over sixty-five go at 30 percent of the average rate.) They are less likely (78 percent of the average rate) to dine out twice or more a week. They are 66 percent more likely than average to play a musical instrument at least twice a week, but far less likely (66 percent of the average) to read a book two or more times a week. Compared to an index of 100 for the entire population (1.8 percent of whom go to bars or nightclubs two or more times a week), those 18–24 have an index of 224 and those over sixty-five an index of 30, according to Mediamark.

2. 1.8 percent of the public plays a musical instrument at least two or more times a week. The 18–24 group has an index of 166, those over sixty-five an index of 67.

3. The index for those reading books (which 24 percent of adults claim to do two or more times a week) is 66 for those 18–24 and rises to 122 among those 45–64; it drops to 112 among the elderly. In 2002 the Census Bureau

found that only 42 percent of those 18–24 had read fiction for pleasure in the course of a year, down from 60 percent in 1982.

4. Young people, especially those newly eligible to vote, have always had a much lower rate of political participation than their elders. In recent years the disparity has increased. In the eight national elections between 1972 and 2000, turnout among those 18–24 fell from 50 percent to 30 percent (U.S. Census). Young people 18–24 are 18 percent less likely to be registered to vote than the average person (though even their claims may be exaggerated). They are also 14 percent above average in reporting their party identification as "independent" and correspondingly below average in identifying themselves with either major party (Scarborough Research). People under thirty-four who agreed that "most politicians are liars and crooks" were 17 percentage points less likely to vote in 2000 than those who disagreed. Among those fifty-five and over, the difference was 7 points (Robert D. Putnam, *Bowling Alone: The Collapse and Revival of American Community* [New York: Simon and Schuster, 2000], p. 85). Party identification becomes set in early adulthood (M. Kent Jennings and Gregory P. Markus, "Partisan Orientations Over the Long Haul: Results from the Three-Wave Political Socialization Panel Study," *American Political Science Review*, vol. 78, no. 4 [1984], pp. 1000–1018). See also Warren E. Miller and J. Merrill Shanks, *The New American Voter* (Cambridge, Mass.: Harvard University Press, 1996). Surveys of high school seniors over a twenty-year period (from 1976 to 1996) show that religiosity is increasingly linked to support of the Republican party (David E. Campbell, "The Young and the Realigning: A Test of the Socialization Theory of Realignment," *Public Opinion Quarterly*, vol. 66 [Summer 2002], pp. 209–234).

5. In 1996, 46 percent of 18–29s knew that the Republicans controlled Congress. Only 36 percent said they "follow the news every day," compared with 52 percent of those 30–49 and 67 percent of those 50-plus. Only 6 percent of those 18–34 watched network news.

6. Within an hour after watching a newscast, most viewers have difficulty recalling anything they saw, unless an item was of strong interest (Thomas E. Patterson, *The Vanishing Voter: Public Involvement in an Age of Uncertainty* [New York: Alfred E. Knopf, 2002]). The declining levels of exposure to newspapers and television news among young people has its counterpart in a growing political apathy.

7. The proportion of young people 18–24 who read a newspaper "yesterday" is 75 percent of the level for the public at large. But that disparity diminishes when we look at a broader time period. The percentage of 18–24-year-olds who have read at least one issue of a newspaper over the course of the last week is 91 percent of the national average. Reading frequency is the main problem that newspapers have addressed. Part of the problem arises from the challenge of distributing papers to a youthful population constantly on the move and unlikely to have a home subscription. But a large

part of the problem involves content—the editorial challenge of appealing to the special tastes of young readers without alienating the more mature ones who make up most of the audience.

8. Yet circulation of female teen-age magazines has fallen. Not surprisingly, business publications such as *Business Week, Forbes, Fortune, Barron's,* and *Kiplinger's* have comparatively few young readers. So do travel and golfing magazines that address the affluent crowd. But the levels of readership for the news weeklies (*Time, Newsweek,* and *U.S. News*) among the 18–24 group are at about nine-tenths of those for the public at large. There are strong differences among magazines that are aimed at a single sex. For example, among young women *Cosmopolitan* and *Glamour* have two and a half times the average percentages of readers, and *Vogue* twice as many. Magazines devoted to weddings and child care understandably rank high. Traditional homemaking magazines such as *Family Circle, Better Homes and Gardens,* and *Ladies' Home Journal* attract relatively few young readers with their established formulas of domesticity. *Playboy, GQ,* and *Penthouse* attract twice as many readers among young men as among all men, and *Maxim* nearly four times as many. Among sports-oriented publications, *Sports Illustrated* ranks high; boating, hunting, and fishing magazines low. Health and fitness is a highly popular subject; so are cars and computers. *Popular Science* does well among young men, *Scientific American* less so.

9. Overall, young adults' time with radio is close to the average, but teenagers (12–17) spend 70 percent as much time listening as the average adult. Their AM listening is only 15 percent of the average, and their FM hours are 83 percent. People aged 18–24 listen at 23 percent of the average level to AM but listen to FM stations 12 percent more than average. In the 25–34 group, AM is 37 percent of the norm, FM 17 percent greater (Arbitron Radar 80, March 2004).

10. My analysis of Nielsen people-meter data for September 2002 through April 2003.

11. *NYT,* January 6, 2003.

12. Coby Low, senior vice president of Honda's ad agency, Rubin Postaer & Associates.

13. Scarborough Research.

14. Young viewers are 34 percent of adult viewers of situation comedies, 30 percent of science-fiction shows, 27 percent of variety shows, and 26 percent of adventure shows.

15. Compared to an average of 100, MTV has an index of 236 for 18–24-year-olds, 17 for the elderly. VH1 has an index of 197 among the young, 13 among the old. Comedy Central has an index of 170 among the young, 33 among the 65-plus group. Surprisingly, Nickelodeon (with an 18–24 index of 138) and the Cartoon Channel (161) have substantial youth appeal, though the 25–34 group, including many parents of young children, shows even higher levels. Country Music Television has an 18–24 index of 126, and a 65-plus

index of 74. In contrast, the cable news networks, the Weather Channel, and movie channels (A&E, AMC, Bravo) have low appeal to the young and a concentration of elderly viewers.

16. Teenagers spent $172 billion on consumer products and services in 2001, reportedly an average of $69 a week per head (which seems implausible). Their aspirations are high (95 percent plan to enter college). While 57 percent get money from their parents, only 32 percent receive a regular allowance and 30 percent earn income from odd jobs. Nine of ten have a computer at home, and eight of ten have online access, three-fourths (67 percent of those 12–14 and 85 percent of those 15–17) with their own e-mail address. Forty percent live in rural areas and small towns, with the remainder divided between big cities and suburbs. In the past seven days, 60 percent say they have read a book, 70 percent have watched a rented video, 57 percent have gone to a movie theater, and 68 percent have engaged in exercise. Among those 12–14, 57 percent say they have read a newspaper for an hour or more in the past week, and among those 15–17 the figure rises to 71 percent. Of these, 25 percent of the younger teenagers and 37 percent of the older ones say they read national news; for local and community news the proportions are 24 percent and 41 percent. But half of both age groups have looked at comics and entertainment pages (Teenage Research Unlimited). Not surprisingly, teenagers' substantial buying capacity is eagerly exploited by many industries. In turn, these industries have been criticized for initiating vulnerable youth into the consumer economy. One author, Alyssa Quart, attacks the marketing practice of courting teenagers and preteens in the art of conspicuous consumption. She cites the Calvin Klein underwear ads, featuring handsome young male models reclining in vaguely suggestive poses (Alyssa Quart, *Branded: The Buying and Selling of Teenagers* [New York: Perseus, 2003]). Time Warner's *Teen People* courts "affiliates" who are indoctrinated into the world of upscale branded merchandise. In many school districts, contracts with Pepsi and Coca-Cola result in the fusion of brand logos into textbooks. Where teenagers have "bleak and atrophied familial relationships," brands become "surrogate parents." "They are part of it, but it probably started with the action films of the late 90s. . . . The boys look very different in the 1960s and 1970s." She points out that many of today's parents are baby boomers, who "defined their class identities through branded objects" (*NYT*, January 26, 2003).

17. The business is steadily more concentrated. Four media buying organizations account for 70 percent of television advertising. Twelve firms place 90 percent.

18. A vehicle can also be a particular publication or any other carrier of advertising messages.

19. "Even personal attire changed thanks to the military demand for scarce fabrics: vests, trouser cuffs, and double-breasted suits were banned for

men; for women, pleats disappeared from skirts, bathing suits grew skimpier, and hemlines rose" (D. M. Kennedy, *Freedom for Fear: The American People in Depression and War* [New York: Oxford, 1999]).

20. Lloyd H. Rogler, "Historical Generations and Psychology: The Case of the Great Depression and World War II," *American Psychologist,* vol. 57, no. 12 (December 2002), pp. 1013–1023. Rogler goes on to say that "Cyclical theories . . . hold that generations are repetitive occurrences separated by an equal number of years. According to Giuseppe Ferrari and Wilhelm Dilthey, the generation scene changed every 30 years, for Jefferson every 19 years, for José Ortega y Gasset, about 15 years, for F. Scott Fitzgerald about three times a century."

21. Theodore Roszak, *The Making of a Counter-Culture: Reflections on the Technocratic Society and Its Youthful Opposition* (New York: Doubleday, 1969).

22. Neil Howe and William Strauss, *Millennials Rising* (New York: Vintage Books, 2000).

23. In 2001, 3.97 million young people turned eighteen; in 2004 this rose to 4.04 million. Within every more inclusive population group, the mode shifted from the middle-aged to the younger members.

24. Harris survey, 2003, using a question I suggested.

25. Thomas Frank, *The Conquest of Cool: Business Culture, Counterculture, and the Rise of Hip Consumerism* (Chicago: University of Chicago Press, 1997), p. 136.

26. Ibid., p. 108.

27. Ibid., p. 25.

28. Ibid., p. 136.

29. Cited by Frank, *Conquest of Cool,* p. 270.

30. *NYT,* December 20, 2002.

31. Quoted by Burnham, *Bad Habits,* p. 77.

32. Ibid., p. 78.

33. "The older skewing programs' delivery of young adults is not much lower than the younger-skewing programs' delivery of older viewers" (David F. Poltrack, "Madison Avenue: Stuck in the '60s," unpublished paper).

34. A thirty-second spot on "Murder She Wrote," older-viewer-oriented, with a rating of 11.8, cost $100,000, while that of the youth-oriented "Simpsons," with a 5.5 rating, was $220,000. Older viewers had a per capita discretionary income of $3,857, 18–34-year-olds $1,357. A CBS survey among viewers of the two shows found that "purchase incidence was higher for 'Simpson' viewers, but not enough to justify a premium of 2.2:1." Of the "Murder She Wrote" viewers, 36 percent could be classified as "experimenters" with new products, compared to 41 percent of the "Simpson" viewers. Viewers of "Murder" correctly recalled an average of 5.2 commercials, compared to 3.7 for the (evidently less attentive) viewers of the

cartoon show. The "Simpsons" viewers, being younger, were much more likely to have visited the Disney theme parks, but for eight other brands the differences in usage were far outweighed by the greater advertising costs. Combining age with another demographic characteristic provides a better fit with actual media use. Henry Assael and David Poltrack, "Could Demographic Profiles of Heavy Users Serve as a Surrogate for Purchase Behavior in Selecting TV Programs?" *Journal of Advertising Research*, vol. 34, no. 1 (January/February 1994), pp. 11–18. Henry Assael and David F. Poltrack, "Debunking the Myth of the Consumer," *Stern Business*, Summer 2000, pp. 20–23. Henry Assael and David F. Poltrack, "Consumer Surveys vs. Electronic Measures," *Journal of Advertising Research*, vol. 42, no. 5 (September–October 2002), pp. 19–25.

35. Among the 50-plus, 4.1 percent had incomes of $100,000 and over in 1970, 12.7 percent in 2000. Those below the poverty level went from 25 percent of adults over sixty-five in 1970 to 10 percent in 2000. In 1970, 43 percent of women 55–64 were in the workforce, in 2000 52 percent. Not only are more women working, they are holding on to their jobs longer.

36. The changes have been rapid. In 1970, people aged 15–29 represented 15 percent of the total population. By 2000 those between 15 and 29 were 21 percent of the total.

37. Poltrack, "Madison Avenue."

38. *NYT*, July 16, 2003.

39. In the 1970s, Nielsen added a 25–59 breakdown in response to advertiser demand for data on household heads.

40. *NYT*, November 27, 2002.

41. *Wall Street Journal*, February 27, 2003.

42. One each said 18–49, 18–39, 18–29, 21–40, 21–30, 18–30, 29–34, and 25–40, and one waffled with "mid-twenties." A senior marketer replies, "Hmmm, 'young adults.' Off the top of my head, I think I would say 21–30."

43. *NYT*, January 26, 2003.

44. According to Maynard, Toyota's market research has found that baby boomers' primary criteria are peace of mind and luxury, while Generation X buyers—those born between 1960 and 1977—seek fun and variety. "Generation Y buyers, Toyota says, want to flaunt their personal style. . . . Todd Turner, president of Car Concepts, Inc., a consulting firm in Thousand Oaks, California, says 'If it's specifically meant for them, they're not interested.' . . . Toyota is aiming Scion (a new model) at a thin slice of Generation Y that it calls trend leaders, who it says make up less than 15 percent of the youth market . . . those who have gone to the movies more than seven times in the last six months, spend up to thirty hours a week listening to music and seven to ten hours playing sports, eat out three times a week, and visit a museum maybe once every six months."

45. Brad J. Bushman and Angela M. Bonacci, "Violence and Sex Impair Memory for Television Ads," *Journal of Applied Psychology,* vol. 87, no. 3 (June 2003), pp. 557–564. Two groups of college students were shown film clips, either from a violent film, *Karate Kid III,* or a pleasant scene from *Gorillas in the Mist,* with commercials inserted for Krazy Glue and Wisk detergent. The brand names were better recalled in the nonviolent context. Some of the eighteen shows used included "World Wrestling Federation Monday Night Nitro," "Strip Poker," and "Miracle Pets." The ads originally embedded in the program were edited out and replaced with violent, sexual, and neutral versions of ads for actual products. After viewing the forty-to-forty-five-minute TV program, participants were asked to recall the brand names of the advertised products (e.g., jeans, soft drinks, and snacks) in any order they wanted. Violent ads were 20 percent less memorable than the sexual ads and 18 percent less memorable than the neutral ads, regardless of the type of ad in the program. "These memory differences can't be attributed to brand familiarity because brand was held constant across type of ad." The type of program did not interact with type of ad to influence memory for ads. "Showing violent or sexual ads in violent or sexual programs doesn't make the ads more memorable," Bushman and Bonacci write. "The bottom line is that matching ad type to program type doesn't change the basic fact that people are less likely to remember brands advertised in violent and sexually explicit programs. Sex and violence just don't sell, in other words."

46. The actual ads in 18 cable television programs were edited out and replaced with violent, sexual, or neutral versions for the same products. Brand recall was 17 percent higher for participants who saw a neutral program than for those who saw a violent one, and 21 percent higher than for those who saw a sexual program.

4. The wisdom of wooing young consumers

1. Nielsen Media Research. The difference reflected the lower income and purchasing power of the younger group rather than their receptivity to new ideas.

2. Leo Bogart, *Finding Out* (Chicago: Ivan R. Dee, 2003), pp. 267–272.

3. Mark Dolliver, "Loyal and Disloyal Shoppers," *Brand Week,* October 14, 2002.

4. For facial tissue, loyalty to one brand rises only from 21 percent among 18-to-29-year-olds to slightly more than 30 percent for people age 60-plus.

5. People 18–24 have smoked cigarettes in the last seven days at a rate 27 percent greater than average, compared to those 65-plus, who smoke at 45 percent of the average rate. Younger people are less likely to buy off-brands of cigarettes, but their preferences for individual advertised brands show only small variations from those of people in other age groups. (They are more

likely to smoke king sizes, but Marlboro and Newport, the two leading brands, show similar patterns.)

6. For example, those 18–24 have an index of 130 for Budweiser, compared to 57 for those over 65, whereas for Miller Genuine Draft they have an index of 93, for Coors an index of 109, for Michelob an index of 94 (my analysis of Mediamark data). Soft drinks are more often purchased by younger people, though the 18–24 and 25–34 groups are similar. Scarborough (another syndicated research company) shows both Coca-Cola Classic and Pepsi with consumption almost two-fifths above average among young consumers and nearly half below average among older ones. In contrast, young consumers are far below average in their consumption of diet and caffeine-free soft drinks.

7. For Colgate's Tartar Control, the 18–24 index is 110 (with small variations among the other age groupings); it is 141 for Colgate with Baking Soda and Peroxide; for Colgate Regular the young have an index of 91, those over 65 an index of 113. Competing manufacturers show similar variations: Aquafresh has an index of 114 among the 18–24 group, Crest Tartar Control Gel an index of 93, Crest Tartar Control Paste an index of 84, Crest Regular an index of 91.

8. Mediamark's report on shampoo use indicates that Pantene and Clairol are strongly favored by young people, and Alberto VO-5 by the elderly, while other brands show less age variation. Suave shampoo has been used in the last seven days at an index level of 113 among the young, 56 among the elderly. Head and Shoulders has a level of 79 among the young, 106 among those 65-plus. In contrast, Alberto VO-5 is 109 for those 18–24, 80 for those 45–54, and 125 for the 65-plus group. Scarborough data show much the same kind of differences between young and old. The proportion who have drunk a domestic beer in the past thirty days is 15 percent above average among those 18–24, and 66 percent of the average among those 65-plus. Budweiser scores 40 percent above average for the young, 59 percent of the average for the elderly. Miller High Life has the same kind of difference, while Miller Genuine Draft and Michelob show a fairly even distribution across age groups, except for those of 65 and over. Microbrews are especially favored by young people and ignored by older ones.

Beer and cigarettes are not consumed by everyone, but other products are. Toothpaste, for instance. Major manufacturers have extended their product lines to appeal to consumers with different tastes and demands. Mediamark finds that Colgate Regular is somewhat more favored by those over 55 than by those under 34, while Colgate's Total brand is consumed at 33 percent above the average rate by those 18–24 and at only 70 percent of the average rate among those 65-plus. Colgate Tartar Control shows relatively minor variations across age groups while Colgate with Baking Soda and Peroxide is strongly favored by young people (41 percent more than average by those

18–24, and 53 percent of the average by those 65-plus). Procter and Gamble's Crest, with a Tartar Control Paste, Regular Mint Paste, and Regular Gel, has its greatest appeal to those of middle age, with relatively little variation across age groups for all three entries. In the case of household cleaners, where the "homemaker" reports on purchases, younger women (less likely to be married and concerned with domestic chores) report somewhat less consumption than those in other age groups, but there are no significant patterns in brand preferences. When it comes to cold breakfast cereals, however, middle-aged homemakers show somewhat more purchasing of Cheerios, and older ones favor Kellogg's Corn Flakes and Raisin Bran, but not Frosted Flakes. Those under 35 show no particular pattern.

9. Mediamark data on automobiles purchased or leased most recently show that Ford and Chevrolet have a strong tilt toward older consumers while Honda (especially the less expensive Civic, 81 percent above average) is strong among younger ones. Ford, most mentioned as the most recent make bought or leased, has an index of 75 among those 18–24 and 134 among those 65 and over. Similarly, Chevrolet has 79 with the two youngest age groups and 127 with the 65-plus group. In contrast, the Honda Accord registers at 146 among the young and 61 among the elderly; the Honda Civic has an even sharper age profile: 181 for the young, 28 for the old. Clearly price is an important distinguishing feature.

10. Younger women (less likely to be married and concerned with domestic chores) report somewhat less consumption of household cleaners than those in other age groups, but there are no significant patterns in brand preferences. The leading brand, Pine-Sol, is used within the past three months at an index level of 101 among homemakers 18–24, 115 among those 35–44, and 82 among those 65 and over. The next-best seller, Formula 409, has an index of 85 among the youngest group and 81 in the oldest.

11. Cheerios, the leading cold breakfast cereal, is indexed at 77 among those 18–24, 120 among those 55–64, and 96 in the 65-plus group. By contrast, Kellogg's Corn Flakes shows a clear-cut pattern, rising from a low index of 67 among the 18–24 to 160 among the oldest housewives. But this too may merely reflect the general popularity of cold cereals at different age levels.

12. According to Mediamark, the 18–24 group use Minute Maid Regular at a rate 24 percent above average, and the 65-plus group use Tropicana Regular at a rate 21 percent above average; but other brands show only minor variations across the age range. Store brands rate at 75 percent above the average among young homemakers. Minute Maid Regular orange juice has an index of 124 (with one or more glasses consumed on an average day) among the young and of 101 among the elderly. Younger homemakers report less use (with an index of 75) of store brands than older homemakers (109). Tropicana Regular has an index of 78 for the 18–24 group, 121 for older people.

5. Protecting the innocent

1. Dave Grossman, *On Killing: The Psychological Cost of Learning to Kill in War and Society* (New York: Little Brown, 1995).

2. James T. Hamilton, *Channeling Violence: The Economic Market for Violent Television Programming* (Princeton: Princeton University Press, 1998).

3. Henry J. Kaiser Family Foundation, *Kids and Media at the New Millennium*, November 1999. The average child under age twelve spends 8.8 hours a day asleep, 2.1 hours with TV, 1.3 hours on schoolwork, .99 hours reading, and .87 hours at the computer (which he prefers). Seventy-one percent of those children who have both a computer and a TV set would choose the PC if they could keep only one; and 29 percent would keep the TV.

4. Of all the time children spent with media in 1995, according to a study by Statistical Research, Inc., 56 percent was with TV, videos, and films, 22 percent with tapes, audio, or radio, 5 percent with video games, and 5 percent with computers. Only 12 percent was spent reading. On a given day, 57 percent read a book "for fun," 51 percent a magazine, and 31 percent a newspaper. Six percent watched a TV newscast. In both age groups, three-quarters of an hour was spent reading. Those 8–18 listen to CDs or tapes for over an hour and 5 minutes, to radio for 48 minutes; they play video games for 27 minutes and use the computer for 31 minutes, 13 of these on the internet.

5. *NYT*, June 4, 2003.

6. Hamilton, *Channeling Violence*. As Hamilton puts it, "Television violence generates negative externalities, which economists define as costs that are borne by individuals other than those involved in the production activity" (p. 79). "Even if broadcasters jointly would be better off reducing levels of television violence, however, each individual broadcaster has the dominant strategy of continuing to broadcast television violence" (p. 4).

7. *NYT*, April 6, 1998.

8. Hamilton, *Channeling Violence*, p. 158.

9. Dimitri A. Christakis, Frederick J. Zimmerman, David L. Di Giuseppe, and Carolyn A. McCarty, "Early Television Exposure and Subsequent Attentional Problems in Children," *Pediatrics*, vol. 1, no. 4 (April 2004), pp. 708–712. Their study tracked 1,278 infants at age one and 1,345 at age three and tested them at age seven.

10. Victoria J. Rideout, Elizabeth A. Vandewater, and Ellen A. Wartella, *Zero to Six: Electronic Media in the Lives of Infants, Toddlers and Preschoolers* (Menlo Park, Calif.: Henry J. Kaiser Family Foundation, 2003). Their survey was conducted among 1,065 parents of children between 6 months and 6 years of age. On an average day, 59 percent of babies aged between 6 months and 2 years watch television, and 42 percent a video or DVD, for a total of over 2 hours. Six percent of them actually have a remote control of their own, especially designed for children.

11. By their parents' reports (81 percent from mothers), four of five children between the ages of six months and six years on a typical day are read to by parents, and the same number play outside. About the same proportions listen to music and use "screen media" (TV, videos, DVDs, or computers). They spend on average as much time with these media as they do playing outdoors, far more than listening to music or being read to. Three of four watch television, and the same proportion watch a video or DVD. (Over half of children aged six and younger have twenty or more videos to choose among.) Among babies under two, three of five watch TV on a typical day, and two in five watch videos—in each case for nearly an hour and a half (Rideout, Vandewater and Wartella, *Zero to Six*).

12. Of the people who often switch in prime time, two-thirds (65 percent) say it's because the program ended. Other answers: they want to watch other programs, 54 percent; they dislike the program, 42 percent; a commercial came on, 32 percent; someone else wanted to switch, 18 percent; a promo came on, 11 percent. In the last few minutes: 34 percent switched from a sportscast; from talk, 26 percent; from comedy 25 percent; from children's 23 percent; from a movie 22 percent; from news, public affairs 17 percent. (Maura Clancy of Statistical Research, Inc., in a report to the Advertising Research Foundation, 1998).

13. Hamilton, *Channeling Violence*, p. 12.

14. In addition, 45 percent have a video game player and 21 percent a computer. Among the youngest children, 42 percent have a radio and 36 percent a tape player. Of time spent on the computer, 26 percent is with games, 22 percent with schoolwork, 10 percent on internet chat rooms, 15 percent web surfing, and 9 percent using e-mail (Kaiser Foundation, *Kids and Media*).

15. The proportions are seven in ten among blacks, half among whites, and three-fifths for Hispanics. This is a fairly recent development. In 1970, 6 percent of sixth-graders had a set in their bedrooms; by 1999 the figure was 77 percent. This is true for three of five children 13–17, half of those 10–12, and two-fifths of those 5–9, 43 percent for those 4–6, and 30 percent for those 3 and younger.

16. A. C. Nielsen.

17. Rideout, Vandewater, and Wartella, *Zero to Six*.

18. George A. Comstock and Erica Scharrer, *Television: What's On, Who's Watching and What it Means* (San Diego: Academic Press, 1999). Between 1987 and 1997, both people-meter and diary data from Nielsen indicated that Saturday morning viewing by children 2–11 fell by nearly one-third. Total viewing throughout the week also fell, but only by about one-sixth.

19. Rideout, Vandewater, and Wartella, *Zero to Six*.

20. Twenty-eight percent had two, 28 percent three, 20 percent four, and 12 percent five or more sets. There are three or more sets in half the households

where there is a child of six or younger. (Only a third of the households have a newspaper subscription.)

21. *NYT*, September 8, 1998.

22. Steve Farkas, Jean Johnson, and Ann Duffett, *A Lot Easier Said Than Done: Parents Talk About Raising Children in Today's America* (New York: Public Agenda, 2002).

23. A Pew Research Center survey (released January 1997) of 552 parents asked how often they watched television with their children. Nine percent of parents said they always watched television with their children, 35 percent usually, 31 percent half the time, 16 percent sometimes, and 8 percent hardly ever or never. When they were not viewing with their children, 55 percent said they usually knew what the children were watching, 18 percent said they always knew, 13 percent knew half the time, 9 percent sometimes, 4 percent hardly ever or never. Among parents of 5–9-year-olds, three in four say there is an adult always present when the child is watching; for those 10–12, the proportion is half, and it is under a third for the 13–17 year-olds.

24. A 1995 "children's lifestyle" study by Statistical Research, Inc.

25. A third of the parents say they are with the child all the time when viewing takes place, and 37 percent say they are there most of the time.

26. Reported by Emily Yoffe in the *NYT*, July 13, 2003.

27. The terrorist attacks of September 11, 2001, evoked considerable anxiety among the millions of children who joined their parents in fascinated horror at the drama that filled their TV screens. On September 11 children watched an average of three hours of the coverage; while 73 percent of children aged 5–8 watched an hour or less, 51 percent of those aged 17–18 watched five hours or more. The stress was greatest among those who watched the coverage most. A third of the parents (even more among those of young children and those who reported that their children were stressed) limited or prevented their children from viewing. Among those who did not limit access to the news, stress was greater among those watching most. Virtually all parents discussed the attack with their children, one in seven for nine hours or more. Among adults, stress was greatest among those who watched the most television coverage. Seventy percent of parents of 2–4-year-olds say their child watched the same video more than one time. This is true of 61 percent for children 5–7, 49 percent for those 8–10, and 34 percent of those 11–14.

28. *USA Today*, April 10, 2003.

29. Pew Center survey.

30. In another survey conducted three to five days after the attacks of September 11, 35 percent of parents said their children showed stress symptoms; 18 percent said the child had been "avoiding talking or hearing about what happened," and 47 percent said the child had been "worrying about his

or her safety or the safety of loved ones" (Mark A. Schuster, Bradley D. Stein, Lisa H. Jaycox, Rebecca L. Collins, Grant N. Marshall, Mark N. Elliott, Annie J. Zhou, David E. Kanouse, Janina L. Morrison, and Sandra H. Berry, "A National Survey of Stress Reactions After the September 11, 2001, Terrorist Attacks," *New England Journal of Medicine*, vol. 345, no. 20 (November 15, 2001), pp. 1507–1512).

31. Philippe Ariès, *Centuries of Childhood: A Social History of Family Life* (New York: Vintage Books, 1962).

32. Lawrence Joseph Stone, *The Family, Sex and Marriage in England, 1500–1800* (London: Weidenfeld and Nicolson, 1977).

33. Nicholas Orme, *Medieval Children* (New Haven: Yale University Press, 2001).

34. Linda A. Pollock, "Parent-Child Relations," in David I. Kertzer and Marzio Barbagli, eds., *The History of the European Family: vol. 1, Family Life in Early Modern Times, 1500–1789* (New Haven: Yale University Press, 2001), p. 219.

35. On the web, for instance, there are Mattel's Barbie.com and similar sites. Advertisers are increasingly offering financial and other incentives, such as "free" computers, in order to gain access to in-school sites. Mathematics textbooks are laced with references to such products as Barbie dolls, Oreo cookies, Nike footwear, Cocoa Frosted Flakes, and McDonald's hamburgers. McGraw-Hill offered the books incorporating these hidden ads free to the state of California.

36. Joel B. Cohen, "Playing to Win: Marketing and Public Policy at Odds Over Joe Camel," *Journal of Public Policy and Marketing*, vol. 19, no. 2 (Fall 2000), pp. 155–167. John E. Calfee, "The Historical Significance of Joe Camel," *Journal of Public Policy and Marketing*, vol. 19, no. 2 (Fall 2000), pp. 168–182.

37. It went from 4 percent to 12 percent, but eventually fell back to 9 percent.

38. Centers for Disease Control and Prevention.

39. In 2001, young people of 12–20 saw 45 percent more beer ads in magazines than adults did. Ten magazines with more than a fourth of their readers under twenty-one accounted for almost a third of all alcoholic beverage advertising in magazines.

40. Radio listeners 12–20 heard 8 percent more beer commercials per capita, 12 percent more for malt alcoholic beverages, and 15 percent more commercials for distilled spirits than older listeners—though 75 percent fewer for wine (a 2001 survey of nineteen markets by the Center on Alcohol Marketing and Youth at Georgetown University).

41. A 1974 study by Thomas Robertson and John Rossiter found "all commercials" trusted by 65 percent of first-graders but by only 7 percent of fifth-graders (*APA Monitor*, November 2002, p. 37).

42. A. C. Huston, E. Donnerstein, H. Fairchild, N. D. Feshbach, P. A. Katz, J. P. Murray, E. Rubinstein, and D. Zuckerman, *Big World, Small Screen: The Role of Television in American Life* (Lincoln, Nebr.: University of Nebraska Press, 1992).

43. James Potter, Daniel Linz, Barbara J. Wilson, Dale Kunkel, Edward Donnerstein, Stacy L. Smith, Eva Blumenthal, and Tim Gray, "Content Analysis of Entertainment Television: New Methodological Developments," in James T. Hamilton, ed., *Television Violence and Public Policy* (Ann Arbor: University of Michigan Press, 1998), pp. 55–103.

44. Studied by a research group at the University of Texas, Austin.

45. National Coalition on Television Violence. Evidence of this was gathered as part of a three-year National Television Violence Study funded by the National Cable Television Association and conducted by researchers at four universities. A team from the University of California, Santa Barbara, analyzed the content of 2,757 programs for the 1995–1996 season. Over seven days (6 a.m. to 11 p.m.) measured on twenty-three channels, 58 percent of the programs contained violence. This from the second volume of the NCTA-sponsored National Television Violence Study, directed by Jeffrey Cole, Center for Communications Policy, UCLA. The most violent programming was on cable networks. His team watched six thousand hours of television a year.

46. Dominic Lasorsa, Wayne Danielson, Ellen Wartella, D. Charles Whitney, Marlies Klijn, Rafael Lopez, and Adriana Olivarez, "Television Violence in Reality Programs: Differences Across Genres," in Hamilton, ed., *Television Violence and Public Policy*, pp. 163–177.

47. According to the National Coalition on Television Violence.

48. *NYT*, February 2, 1998.

49. According to Children Now.

50. Julie Salamon, a *New York Times* reporter, observes that "today's prime-time television families tend to exist as mechanisms for adult characters to wrestle with their personal distress" (*NYT*, July 30, 2001).

51. Fredric Wertham, *The Seduction of the Innocent* (New York: Rinehart, 1954).

52. Henry James Forman, *Our Movie-Made Children* (New York: MacMillan, 1933).

53. It is hard to connect anti-social behavior directly to the influence of the media. Although Japan has less crime than any other highly developed nation, its media abound with extreme violence. *Manga* comic books are filled with scenes of rape. In one film directed by Kinju Fukasaku, a group of students are taken to an island, given weapons, and told to kill each other. "There was a debate about the bill in Parliament, and it was barred to anyone under 15, an unusual act of censorship in Japan" (*Economist,* February 1, 2003).

54. James T. Hamilton, "Media Violence and Public Policy," in Hamilton, ed., *Television Violence and Public Policy,* p. xv.

55. Hamilton, *Channeling Violence,* p. 3.

56. Ibid., p. 4.

57. Barbara J. Wilson, Edward Donnerstein, Daniel Linz, Dale Kunkel, James Potter, Stacy L. Smith, Eva Blumenthal, and Tim Gray, "Content Analysis of Entertainment Television: The Importance of Context," in Hamilton, ed., *Television Violence and Public Policy,* pp. 13–53.

58. Craig A. Anderson, Leonard Berkowitz, Edward Donnerstein, L. Rowell Huesmann, James D. Johnson, Daniel Linz, Neil M. Malamuth, and Ellen Wartella, "The Influence of Media Violence on Youth," *Psychological Science in the Public Interest,* vol. 4, no. 3 (December 2003), pp. 81–110.

59. Ibid., pp. 105–147.

60. Ibid., pp. 149–152.

61. Hamilton, *Channeling Violence.*

62. Jeffrey Johnson, et al., *Science,* March 29, 2002. Six percent of those who had watched an hour or less a day exhibited signs of aggressive behavior in later years, compared to 25 percent of those who watched three or more hours.

63. Brad J. Bushman, "Moderating Role of Trait Aggressiveness in the Effects of Violent Media on Aggression," *Journal of Personality and Social Psychology,* vol. 69 (1995), pp. 950–960.

64. L. Rowell Huesmann, "Longitudinal Relations Between Children's Exposure to Television Violence and Aggressive Violent Behavior in Young Adulthood," *Developmental Psychology,* vol. 39, no. 2 (March 2003).

65. Edward Donnerstein, Daniel Linz, and Steven Penrod, *The Question of Pornography: Research Findings and Policy Implications* (New York: Free Press, 1987).

66. Brad J. Bushman and Craig A. Anderson, "Media Violence and the American Public: Scientific Facts Versus Media Misinformation," *American Psychologist,* vol. 56, no. 6/7 (June/July 2001), pp. 477–489.

67. Bushman and Anderson attribute this to "the vested interests of the news, a misapplied fairness doctrine in news reporting, and the failure of the research community to effectively argue the scientific case."

68. Christopher J. Ferguson, "Media Violence: Miscast Causality," *American Psychologist,* June/July 2002, pp. 446–447.

69. Craig A. Anderson and Brad J. Bushman, "Media Violence and the American Public Revisited," *American Psychologist,* June/July 2002, pp. 448–450.

70. Marjorie Heins, "Blaming the Media," *Media Studies Journal,* Fall 2000, pp. 14–23. She also says, "Despite the exaggerated claims by pro-censorship forces, a meticulous review of the research shows weak to nonexistent evidence of any widespread causative effect."

71. Wilson, et al., "Importance of Context," in Hamilton, ed., *Television Violence and Public Policy,* pp. 13–53.

72. *NYT*, January 28, 2001.

73. A 2003 survey of one thousand parents, conducted by Common Sense Media.

74. Thirty-nine percent worry "a lot" and 34 percent "some." Steve Farkas and Gene Johnson, *Kids These Days* (New York: Public Agenda, 1997). Steve Farkas, Jean Johnson, and Ann Duffett, *A Lot Easier Said Than Done: Parents Talk About Raising Children in Today's America* (New York: Public Agenda, 2002).

75. Seventy-four percent, compared to 56 percent who "hardly ever supervise."

76. Ibid.

77. This is true not only in the United States. Britain's Independent Television Commission asks people if they have seen anything offensive in the past year. In 1988, 57 percent said they had been offended—30 percent by violence, 29 percent by bad language, 15 percent by sexual scenes, 11 percent by mentions of sex, 10 percent by crude jokes. Items they would not like to see on TV were violence (27 percent), sex scenes (18 percent), bad language (9 percent), and scenes of people killed or dying (7 percent). When asked what if anything should never be shown, 16 percent named violence, 14 percent sex scenes, 5 percent scenes of dying, 5 percent child abuse, and 4 percent bad language. When shown a list of items they would not want to see, 55 percent chose rape, 31 percent explicit sex scenes, 29 percent the killing of an innocent victim, 28 percent animals killing or attacking each other, 26 percent bad language, 16 percent frontal male nudity, 14 percent the killing of a criminal, and 13 percent frontal female nudity.

78. A 1997 poll of 1,607 parents for *U.S. News and World Report*.

79. A 1997 survey commissioned by the Pew Center for Democracy.

80. Between 1997–1998 and 1999–2000, the percentage of comedies with sexual content grew from 56 percent to 84 percent, and the number of scenes an hour from 5.8 to 7.3. Dale Kunkel, Kirstie Cope-Farrar, Erica Biely, Wendy Jo Maynard Farinola, and Edward Donnerstein, "Sex on TV" (Menlo Park, Calif.: Kaiser Family Foundation, 2003). Kunkel and his associates content-analyzed 1,114 television programs for the 1999–2000 broadcast season, taking a composite week for each of ten channels and adding a week of prime-time programs for the four major networks. Daily newscasts, children's programs, and sportscasts were not included, though programs that combined news and entertainment were covered.

81. Survey by the Kaiser Family Foundation.

82. Only 5 percent of the scenes and 10 percent of the programs contained any reference to the risks and responsibilities of sex, and only 1 percent of the talk about sex involved getting expert advice on the possibilities of disease or pregnancy.

83. Quoted by Tad Friend, "You Can't Say That," *New Yorker*, November 11, 2001.

84. Charles Winick, "Pornography," in Edgar F. Borgatta and Rhonda J. V. Montgomery, eds., *Encyclopedia of Sociology*, 2nd ed. (New York: MacMillan, 2000), vol. 3, pp. 2184–2185.

85. Ibid., p. 2186.

86. Ibid., p. 2187.

87. Over two-fifths (42 percent) of visitors to "adult" websites are female, especially in the 18–24 age group, according to Comscore Media Metrix. Adam and Eve, a mail-order pornography firm, says women account for 30 percent of its catalog sales but 40 percent of sales made on the internet. (*NYT*, February 20, 2004).

88. Allan Sherman, quoted by Burnham, *Bad Habits*, p. 201.

89. Two of five hotel rooms provide adult movies; half of all guests occupying those rooms watch them.

90. *NYT*, October 23, 2000.

91. Charles Winick, "Pornography," in Derek Jones, ed., *Censorship: A World Encyclopedia* (London: Fitzroy Dearborn, 2001), vol. 3, pp. 1907–1912.

92. *NYT Magazine*, May 20, 2001. Five to ten billion dollars is spent on adult video rentals, $150 million on adult pay-per-view in hotels and homes. *Adult Video News* has its own Oscar-type awards.

93. Federal Trade Commission, "Marketing Violent Entertainment to Children: A Review of Self-Regulation and Industry Practices in the Motion Picture, Music Recording and Electronic Game Industries," 2000.

94. Hamilton, *Channeling Violence*, p. 112.

95. Newton L. Minow and Craig L. La May, *Abandoned in the Wasteland: Children, Television and the First Amendment* (New York: Hill and Wang, 1995), p. 22.

96. *NYT*, September 11, 1997.

97. Cf. Diane Ravitch, *The Language Police: How Pressure Groups Restrict What Students Learn* (New York: Knopf, 2003).

98. Cited by K. Anthony Appiah, "Into the Woods," *New York Review of Books*, December 18, 2003, pp. 46–51.

99. Justice William Brennan declared that the test for obscenity was "whether to the average person, applying contemporary community standards, the dominant theme of the material taken as a whole appeals to the prurient interest."

6. Labeling films

1. Harris Interactive YouthPulse survey, 2003.

2. *NYT*, June 23, 2003.

3. The DVD took off rapidly after its introduction in 1997; by 2004 it was selling almost five times as many movies as VHS videocassettes. The studio's profit on a DVD was 66 percent, on a cassette 45 percent. Total spending on recorded movies reached $24 billion in 2004, far eclipsing theater box office receipts.

4. Video Software Dealers Association, 2002.

5. Ibid.

6. National Association of Theater Owners.

7. Ibid.

8. Mediamark does both a large national sampling each year and a survey of teenagers 12–17. The 2002 surveys provide an excellent basis for calculating the proportion of monthly movie theater admissions represented by young people. I calculated attendance both for the adult sample (18-plus) and for the combined sample of all persons 12 and over. (Seventy-three percent of the population is over 17, 80 percent over 14, and 7 percent 12–14.)

9. David Shaw, "Inhale. Lie. Exhale. Lie," *Los Angeles Times*, February 13, 2001.

10. Leo Bogart, "The Return of Hollywood's Mass Audience," in Hubert J. O'Connor, ed., *Surveying Social Life* (Middletown, Conn.: Wesleyan University Press, 1988), pp. 487–501.

11. *Variety*, March 8–14, 2004.

12. Shaw, "Inhale . . .".

13. David Shaw, "A Boffo Newspaper War Gets Hotter in Movieland," *Los Angeles Times*, February 14, 2001.

14. Quoted by David Shaw, "Tinseltown Spins Yarns, Media Take Bait," *Los Angeles Times*, February 12, 2001.

15. Diana Altman, *Hollywood East: Louis B. Mayer and the Origins of the Studio System* (New York: Birch Lane Press, 1992), p. 264.

16. Burnham, *Bad Habits*, p. 37.

17. "In movies, the moral earnestness of reformers became consistently a subject of satire" (Burnham, *Bad Habits*, p. 247).

18. After the MPAA adopted the NC-17 rating in 1990, another serious film, *Henry and June*, was the first to be given this designation.

19. On the MPAA website. Valenti retired from the MPAA presidency in 2004.

20. According to Valenti, "No one in the movie industry has the authority or the power to push the Board in any direction or otherwise influence it. One of the highest accolades to be conferred on the rating system is that from its birth in 1968 to this hour, there has never been even the slightest jot of evidence that the rating system has ever deliberately fudged a decision or bowed to pressure. The Rating Board has always conducted itself at the highest level of integrity. That is a large, honorable, and valuable asset."

21. At the outset there were also representatives of the film importers, but their organization had long since disappeared.

22. January 18, 1985, letter from Richard Del Belzo of Warner Brothers to Robert Franklin, cited in Heffner archive, Columbia University.

23. In *Swope vs. Lubbers* (1983) a federal appellate court ruled that an X rating did not establish that a film was pornographic. The National Society of Film Critics wanted a new Adults-only category to replace the X.

24. *NYT*, August 17, 2003.

25. Quoted by Bernard Weinraub in the *NYT*, August 17, 2003.

26. Quoted by Tad Friend, "Credit Grab," *New Yorker,* October 20, 2003, p. 168.

27. Survey by Penn, Schoen, and Berland for Common Sense Media.

28. B. A. Austin, "The Influence of the MPAA's Film-Rating System on Motion Picture Attendance: A Pilot Study," *Journal of Psychology*, vol. 106 (1980), pp. 91–99.

29. *NYT*, September 27, 2000.

30. *NYT*, October 1, 2000.

31. After release of the FTC report, the Fox Network announced that it would no longer accept ads for R-rated films on programs in which 35 percent or more of the audience is seventeen or younger. Both Fox Film and Warner Brothers announced that they would not show commercials for their own R-rated films on such programs on any network. (Few programs other than those directed at young children would meet this criterion.) ABC announced that it would not show commercials for R-rated films between 6 and 9 p.m.

7. Labeling television

1. CBS also removed a scene from a late night show that briefly showed the naked behind of a criminal running from a bathtub. *NYT*, March 15, 2004.

2. Clear Channel, which controls twelve hundred radio stations, dropped Howard Stern from six of them in 2004, in the wake of a wave of congressional concerns about broadcast smut. According to Stern, the chain's owners were really moved to act because of his fulminations against George W. Bush. Stern switched to satellite radio, exempt from FCC rules.

3. Reed E. Hundt, *You Say You Want a Revolution: A Story of Information Age Politics* (New Haven: Yale University Press, 2000), p. 123.

4. *Los Angeles Times*, December 15, 1996.

5. This estimate, by Valenti, apparently does not allow for the repetition of programs.

6. In December 1996.

7. *NYT*, December 13, 1996.

8. The technical origin of the V-chip is disputed among three inventors: Tim Collings, a Canadian engineering professor; Carl M. Elam, a former air force engineer; and John Olivo, owner of a company called Parental Guide. Acacia Research, with a controlling interest in Soundview Technologies, holds the patent on the V-chip.

9. *NYT*, April 11, 1996.

10. *NYT*, December 20, 1996.

11. For those squeamish souls who are willing to incur extra expense and effort, a simple solution has been found. A software program, Moviemask, censors films and TV programs, providing the actors with "virtual" clothes to mask their nudity. Breck Rice, head of the manufacturer, Trilogy Studios, says, "We provide choice to consumers." There are, of course, simpler ways to exercise such choice.

12. *Time*, February 18, 1996, cited by James T. Hamilton, "Does Viewer Discretion Prompt Advertiser Discretion? The Impact of Violence Warnings on the Television Advertising Market," in Hamilton, ed., *Television Violence and Public Policy*, pp. 213–266.

13. Senator John McCain threatened NBC with review of its own stations' license renewals if it failed to conform to the new labeling process, which the network considered coercive. In a threatening letter addressed to NBC's president, Robert Wright, Senator McCain pointed to the findings of a *Los Angeles Times* survey which showed that four of five parents approved of the new ratings system. McCain said NBC was "the only company in the industry that puts its own interests ahead of its viewers."

14. *NYT*, September 27, 2000.

15. *NYT*, September 30, 1997.

16. *NYT*, October 9, 1997.

17. Survey commissioned by the Pew Center for Democracy.

18. Stephen B. Withey and Ronald P. Abeles, eds., *Television and Social Behavior: Beyond Violence and Children* (Hillsdale, NJ: Lawrence Erlbaum Associates, 1980).

19. Forty-two percent thought the labels would be somewhat helpful, 18 percent not too helpful, and 9 percent not at all helpful (Roper study for the Media Studies Center).

20. Annenberg School conference, February 28, 2003.

21. Thirty-seven percent said the day and time of the program were influential, and 26 percent chose the channel or network.

22. Survey by the Aragon Group.

23. Of programs directed at the general audience, 32 percent were rated TV-G, 41 percent TV-PG, and 15 percent TV-14. (None were rated TV-MA.) Content descriptors were shown for a third of the TV-PG programs and nearly two-thirds of those rated TV-14. Of the children's programs analyzed,

70 percent were rated TV-Y and 21 percent TVY-7. (Of these, 56 percent were described as having fantasy violence. D. Kunkel, W. J. Farinola, K. M. Cope, E. Donnerstein, E. Biely, and L. Zwarum, *Rating the TV Ratings—One Year Out: An Analysis of the Television Industry's Use of V-chip Ratings* (Menlo Park, Calif.: Henry J. Kaiser Family Foundation, 1998).

24. This was based on the proportion who had acquired a TV set since the chips were made mandatory at the start of 2000.

25. Of those who knew they had the chip, 36 percent had used it. Of the remaining two-thirds, half say an adult is usually around when their children watch TV, and a fourth trust their children to make their own decisions. (We have already seen that parents overstate their level of involvement.)

26. Half (51 percent) say the ratings accurately reflect program content, but 40 percent say they do not. Age-based ratings are understood better than content-based ratings. Eighteen percent prefer to use the age ratings, while 55 percent say the content ratings provide the most useful information.

27. Seven of ten adults (71 percent) are aware of the Parental Guidelines, but only 55 percent know where to find them, and 19 percent report using them to make decisions about watching shows. Over half (55 percent) can name a place where a show's rating can be found, but only 35 percent say it can be found on the TV screen. Of the minority who claim to use content ratings, 61 percent know that V stands for violence, and 51 percent say S stands for sex; 43 percent know that L is for coarse language; only 14 percent know that FV means fantasy violence and 4 percent that D stands for suggestive dialogue. Two-thirds of these users say they referred both to age and content labels, 8 percent to age ratings only, and 22 percent to content ratings only. Compared to the 19 percent of parents who use TV ratings, 54 percent say they use movie ratings, 33 percent movie advisories, 31 percent video game ratings, and 26 percent internet ratings. Naturally, better-educated parents and parents of younger children are more apt to use the ratings.

28. In a special analysis made for this book, Nielsen Media Research looked at ten prime-time programs: two comedies, two news magazines, two dramas, two reality shows, and two movies. Forty-five percent of the total viewers were there for the first minute, but the proportion was much lower (28 percent) for movies and higher for comedies (56 percent) and dramas (57 percent).

29. In a message to me from his chief of staff.

30. Hamilton, *Channeling Violence*, p. 131.

31. Ibid. The remaining 32 percent were older films produced before the MPAA labels were introduced.

32. Joanne Kantor, Kristen Harrison, and Marina Krcmar, "Ratings and Advisories: Implications for the New Ratings System for Television," in Hamilton, *Television Violence*, pp. 179–211.

33. *NYT*, March 27, 1997.

34. Quoted by Sarah Heppola, *NYT*, June 22, 2003.

35. The UCLA studies report that only 3 percent of the films shown on pay cable are rated G, about the same proportion as those shown in theaters.

8. The business effects of TV labeling

1. Remarks to the Radio and Television Research Council, March 15, 2004.

2. By Myers Report publisher and TV consultant Jack Myers.

3. On average, AIS screens shows three days before they go on the air, though the time can range between two days and three weeks. Few programs require special attention.

4. Stuart Elliott, "Advertisers Decide It's Time for 'Reality'—At Least on Television," *NYT*, February 14, 2003.

5. Ibid.

6. Remarks to the Radio and Television Research Council, March 15, 2004.

7. Tad Friend, "You Can't Say That," *New Yorker*, November 19, 2001.

9. Labeling other media

1. *NYT*, October 2, 2001.

2. Sony's PlayStation 2 has sold sixty million units worldwide. Jonathan Dee, "Playing Mogul," *NYT Magazine*, December 21, 2003.

3. *Economist*, December 8, 2003.

4. PriceWaterhouseCooper's estimates. In January 2002 sales of Nintendo's GameCube were up 31 percent over the preceding year, Microsoft Xbox was up by 29 percent and Sony's PlayStation 2 by 24 percent.

5. *Economist,* March 27, 2004. Both Microsoft and Sony introduced devices that linked consoles with the internet, using broadband connections. Microsoft was spending $2 billion over a five-year period to build Xbox Live, a subscription network. (The Xbox was the only game console that could be programmed for parental controls.) Microsoft had already sold five million consoles by the end of 2003; Sony's well-established PlayStation 2 had sold forty million. Mobile phones already have some simple games built in, and the latest ones, with color screens, can download software. Wireless phones like Nokia's N-Gage could be used in competitive gaming (*Economist,* December 14, 2002).

6. Different surveys show somewhat different percentages.

7. Interactive Digital Software Association.

8. E. F. Provenzo, *Video Kids: Making Sense of Nintendo* (Cambridge, Mass.: Harvard University Press, 1991).

9. D. D. Buchman and J. B. Funk, "Video and Computer Games in the '90s: Children's Time Commitment and Game Preferences," *Children Today*, vol. 24 (1996), pp. 12–16.

10. *NYT*, October 27, 2002.

11. *NYT*, May 23, 2002.

12. David Cross, "Games Gone Wild," *Wired,* November 2003.

13. *NYT*, November 11, 2002.

14. Dave Grossman, *On Killing: The Psychological Cost of Learning to Kill in War and Society* (New York: Little Brown, 1995).

15. *The UCLA Television Violence Monitoring Report*, 1995.

16. David Barboza, *NYT*, December 26, 1997.

17. Summarized from *Nature*, June 2003, by Sandra Blakeslee, "Video-Game Killing Builds Visual Skills, Researchers Report," *NYT*, May 29, 2003.

18. Victoria J. Rideout, Elizabeth A. Vandewater, and Ellen A. Wartella, *Zero to Six: Electronic Media in the Lives of Infants, Toddlers and Preschoolers* (Menlo Park, Calif.: Henry J. Kaiser Family Foundation, 2003). Their telephone survey sampled more than one thousand parents of children aged two months through six years.

19. Studies by Jeanne Funk, a psychologist at the University of Toledo, reported in the *NYT*, June 5, 2003.

20. Edward Miller, letter to the *NYT*, December 19, 2002.

21. Gary Cross: *Kids' Stuff: Toys and the Changing World of American Childhood* (Cambridge, Mass.: Harvard University Press, 1997), p. 33.

22. Ibid., pp. 218–219.

23. The Lion and Lamb Project of Bethesda prepares an annual list of "toys to avoid."

24. Cited by Bob Herbert, *NYT,* November 28, 2002.

25. Representative Betty McCollum has pointed to restrictions of alcohol, tobacco, firearms, and driving, and asks why there are none on games.

26. A call to the Interactive Digital Software Association number is answered by the Entertainment Software Rating Board.

27. NPD survey, based on a national sampling of purchases, recorded in diaries.

28. *NYT*, September 27, 2000.

29. The marketing plans for sixty of these, or 51 percent, expressly included children under seventeen in the target audience. Documents for the remaining twenty-three games showed plans to advertise in magazines or on television shows with a majority or substantial under-seventeen audience.

30. A 2003 video games report by David Walsh, president of the National Institute on Media and the Family.

31. In 2003, two of the giants, Sony and Bertelsmann, merged their operations.

32. David Walsh report.

33. Quoted by John Seabrook, "The Money Note," *New Yorker*, July 7, 2003, p. 46.

34. *Economist*, October 31, 1998.

35. Website of RIAA.com.

36. Few groups use explicit themes in almost every song.

37. *NYT*, March 7, 2004.

38. These included the wives of Vice President Al Gore, Senator Ernest Hollings, and former Secretary of State James Baker. Claude Chastagner, a professor at Université Paul Valéry, Montpelier, has reviewed the history of this organization on his website.

39. It has also been proposed that rock concerts be given obscenity warning ratings, with R for concerts barred to unaccompanied minors.

40. Of twenty-nine music recordings advertised on programs aimed at teenagers, twenty-one were hip-hop or "r&b" (rhythm and blues). Twenty of these were advertised on programs and in magazines with large audiences under seventeen.

41. "Movies: The study found virtually no advertisements for R-rated movies in the popular teen magazines reviewed. A spot-check of movie trailer placement revealed general compliance with the industry's commitment not to run trailers for R movies in connection with G- and PG-rated feature films. The motion picture studios now routinely include reasons for ratings in their print and television advertisements. Further, at least three-quarters of the official movie websites reviewed included the film's rating, the reasons for the rating, and links to sites where information on the rating system may be obtained. However, the Commission found more remains to be done, as ads for R-rated movies continue to appear on television programs most popular with teens, and the rating reasons in ads were usually small, fleeting, or inconspicuously placed."

"Music: The Commission found advertising for explicit-content labeled music recordings routinely appeared on popular teen advertising programming. All five major recording companies placed advertising for explicit content music on television programs and magazines with substantial under-17 audiences (in some cases more than 50 percent under 17). Furthermore, ads for explicit-content labeled music usually did not indicate that the recording was stickered with a parental advisory label: only 25 percent of the print ads, 22 percent of the television ads, and about half of the 40 official recording company or artist websites reviewed showed the explicit content label or otherwise gave notice that the recording contained explicit content. Even when the parental advisory label was present, it frequently was so small that the words were illegible, and the ads never indicated why the album received the label. None of the recording company/

artist websites reviewed linked to an educational website for information on the labeling system. The single positive note was that almost 40 percent of the websites included the music's lyrics."

"Games: The Commission found no ads for M-rated games on the popular teen television programs reviewed. The game company print ads nearly always included the game's rating icon (or the rating pending icon) and, in a large majority of instances, content descriptors. Television ads gave both audio and video disclosures of the game's rating, and more than 80 percent of the official game publisher websites displayed the game's rating. However, the electronic game industry continues to place ads for M-rated games at the same rate as before in gaming magazines with a substantial under-17 audience."

42. *NYT*, February 18, 2003.

43. P. Christenson, "The Effects of Parental Advisory Labels on Adolescent Music," *Journal of Communication*, vol. 42, no. 1 (1992), pp. 106–113.

44. 2004 study by the Online Publishers Association.

45. The young are 21 percent more likely than average to have accessed the internet within the past thirty days. (The 65-plus group has 45 percent of the average rate.)

46. 1997 study for the National Radio Network.

47. Rideout, Vandewater, and Wartella, *Zero to Six*.

48. According to Datamonitor.

49. Frederick S. Lane III, *Obscene Profits: The Entrepreneurs of Pornography in the Cyber Age* (New York: Routledge, 2000).

50. *NYT*, March 3, 2004.

51. Media Metrix.

52. *Economist*, April 21, 2001.

53. Comscore Media Metrix, reported in the *NYT*, March 29, 2004.

54. From a national survey of fifteen hundred children, conducted by Kimberly Mitchell of the Crimes Against Children Research Center at the University of New Hampshire, and reported by Reuters, June 19, 2001. The finding was distorted in post office posters which said that "one in five children" has been sexually solicited on the internet. But this ratio applied only to regular users within a specific age group. The risk was higher for troubled youth and for the most frequent users of internet chat rooms.

55. "Add Internet solicitation to the list of childhood perils about which (authorities) should be knowledgeable and able to provide counsel to families. . . . At the same time, the concerns are not so alarming that they should by themselves encourage parents to bar children from accessing the internet," said the report (*Journal of the American Medical Association*, June 2001).

56. "The American Dream," Roper/Starch survey for Hearst magazines.

57. *NYT*, March 19, 2001. N2H2, a company that provides filtering software, decided to drop advertising from its pages but offered access to the

Roper/Starch research firm to collect data on the websites visited by children (*NYT*, December 21, 2000). Double-Click maintains a database of users' movements on the web, to allow its advertisers to personalize the messages it delivers (*NYT*, February 7, 2000). Websites were collecting names, addresses, and phone numbers from children under thirteen (Center for Media Education).

58. *NYT*, December 21, 2000.

59. Donna Ladd, "Machine Age: Congress Versus Porn," *Village Voice*, March 13, 2001, p. 27.

60. Marjorie Heins, *Sex, Sin and Blasphemy: A Guide to America's Censorship Wars* (New York: New Press, 1993).

61. March 2002.

62. A test by the Loudon County (Va.) Library Board, reported in the *NYT*, February 7, 1999.

63. Larry Gruenemeier, "Filters Fail to Keep Kids Safe," *Consumer Reports*, March 19, 2001.

64. Cited by John Schwartz in the *NYT*, July 5, 2003.

65. *NYT*, March 9, 2003.

66. University of Michigan researchers checked filters used by twenty school districts and library systems. Only one set its filter at the least restrictive setting, merely barring pornography. Others were set at an intermediate level, barring nudity and drugs, or at the most restrictive level, which in half the cases blocked web pages like the Journal of the AMA's site for women's health and the FDA's report on clinical trials.

67. *NYT*, March 9, 2003.

68. There were 317 complaints about nudism and 224 about sex education. Homosexuality aroused 515 objections. In 1,256 cases, books were described as "unsuited to the age group." There were 842 accusations of Satanism or manifestations of the occult. Only 737 were complaints about violence. In addition, 419 objected to the promotion of religion, 267 about racism; 202 were called "anti-family."

69. Josh McHugh, "Google Sells Its Soul," *Wired*, January 2003, pp. 130–135.

10. Back to the edge?

1. It was introduced by the sociologist William Fielding Ogburn in his book *Social Change: With Respect to Culture and Original Nature* (New York: B. W. Huebsch, 1938).

2. One illustration is the commercials for a less familiar brand of laundry detergent that compare its performance with that of a leading familiar brand. It is the familiar brand rather than the advertised one that viewers typ-

ically remember. A quickly discontinued series of ads sought to position Kentucky Fried Chicken as a low-fat health food, turning off its devoted grease addicts. Similarly, a brand of Scotch proclaimed, "There's nothing better you can put in water!"—though the big drinkers prefer their whiskey with minimal dilution. A vacuum cleaner brand was described as powerful and effective because of the amount of noise it made, repelling the users who valued quiet and smooth operation. (An impressive review of the evidence on counterproductive advertising may be found in Eric Marder, *The Laws of Choice: Predicting Customer Behavior* [New York: Free Press, 1997]).

3. A 2003 survey of one thousand parents, conducted by Common Sense Media.

4. Common Sense Media, founded by James P. Steyer, author of *The Other Parent*, attracted two former FCC chairmen, William Kennard and Newton Minow, as members of its board of directors. "The existing rating systems are either sponsored by the industry or don't work," says Kennard. "This is not about telling them what they can put on the air, it is empowering adults to make responsible choices."

5. *NYT*, May 20, 2003.

Index

A NOTE ON THE AUTHOR

Leo Bogart has been a student, a practitioner, and an analyst of mass media and communication for more than fifty years. After receiving a Ph.D. in sociology from the University of Chicago, he directed public opinion research for the Standard Oil Company (New Jersey), marketing research for Revlon, and account research service for McCann-Erickson advertising, and was for many years executive vice president of the Newspaper Advertising Bureau. He has also taught at New York University, Columbia University, and the Illinois Institute of Technology, and has been a senior fellow at the Center for Media Studies at Columbia and a Fulbright research fellow. He has received distinguished achievement awards and citations from the American Marketing Association, the American Association for Public Opinion Research, and the American Society of Newspaper Editors. He and George Gallup were the first persons elected to the Market Research Council's Hall of Fame. He now writes a column for *Presstime* and is a director of the Innovation International Media consulting group. He lives in New York City.